# SECULAR RELIGIONS

*Secular Religions: The Key Concepts* provides a concise guide to those ideologies, worldviews, and social, political, economic, and cultural phenomena that are most often described as the modern counterparts of traditional religions.

Although there are many other terms in use (quasi, pseudo, ersatz, political, civil, etc.), it is "secular religion" that best expresses the problematic nature of all such descriptions, which maintain that modern belief systems and practices are secular on the one hand and religious on the other. Today, the topic is as popular as ever, and secular religions are discovered far and wide. Hence, a critical summary is urgently necessary. The juxtaposed title is itself an expression of ironic distance. The book emphasizes the inherent tensions of relevant literature in a critical and informative fashion. The author provides over 100 entries, from abortion to wokeness, as well as a detailed introduction, which gives an overview of the different definitions of "religion" and "secular religion" as well as the history of secular-religious comparisons. The main text reconstructs the argument of several key works on each given topic, while lists of sources for further reading are provided at the end of each entry.

This book provides a clear introduction to "secular religions" and will appeal to researchers and students of religious studies, political philosophy, political theology, the history of ideologies, and cultural studies.

**Tamás Nyirkos** is Research Fellow at the Research Institute for Politics and Government at the Ludovika University of Public Service in Budapest, Hungary, and Associate Professor of the Institute of International Studies and Political Science at Pázmány Péter Catholic University in Budapest, Hungary.

# Routledge Key Guides

**Fifty Key Stage Musicals**
*Edited by Robert W. Schneider and Shannon Agnew*

**Fifty Key Irish Plays**
*Edited by Shaun Richards*

**Fifty Key Figures in Queer US Theatre**
*Edited by Jimmy A. Noriega and Jordan Schildcrout*

**International Relations**
The Key Concepts
*Steven C. Roach and Alexander D. Barder*

**Fifty Key Theatre Designers**
*Arnold Aronson*

**Listening**
The Key Concepts
*Elizabeth S. Parks, Meara H. Faw and Laura R. Lane*

**Secular Religions**
The Key Concepts
*Tamás Nyirkos*

For a full list of titles in this series, please visit: https://www.routledge.com/Routledge-Key-Guides/book-series/RKG

# SECULAR RELIGIONS

The Key Concepts

*Tamás Nyirkos*

LONDON AND NEW YORK

Designed cover image: CC0 Public Domain: https://pxhere.com/en/photo/1175999

First published 2025
by Routledge
4 Park Square, Milton Park, Abingdon, Oxon OX14 4RN

and by Routledge
605 Third Avenue, New York, NY 10158

Routledge is an imprint of the Taylor & Francis Group, an informa business

© 2025 Tamás Nyirkos

The right of Tamás Nyirkos to be identified as author of this work has been asserted in accordance with sections 77 and 78 of the Copyright, Designs and Patents Act 1988.

All rights reserved. No part of this book may be reprinted or reproduced or utilised in any form or by any electronic, mechanical, or other means, now known or hereafter invented, including photocopying and recording, or in any information storage or retrieval system, without permission in writing from the publishers.

*Trademark notice*: Product or corporate names may be trademarks or registered trademarks, and are used only for identification and explanation without intent to infringe.

Please note that this book contains some profanity which readers may find offensive.

*British Library Cataloguing-in-Publication Data*
A catalogue record for this book is available from the British Library

ISBN: 978-1-032-74846-7 (hbk)
ISBN: 978-1-032-74433-9 (pbk)
ISBN: 978-1-003-47125-7 (ebk)

DOI: 10.4324/9781003471257

Typeset in Sabon
by Apex CoVantage, LLC

*Non sum reus huius rei.*

# CONTENTS

*List of Figures*   *xi*

Introduction   1
   *Terminology* 2
   *Defining religion* 4
   *A brief history* 7
   *Some methodological remarks* 9
   *Conclusion* 10

A   Abortion   13
   *Anarchism* 15
   *Animal rights* 17
   *Anti-racism* 19
   *Art* 19
   *Artificial intelligence* 22
   *Atheism* 24

B   Beauty   27
   *Biotechnology* 28
   *BLM* 31
   *Bolshevism* 32
   *Boxing* 35

C  Capitalism                                37
   *Celeb culture 42*
   *Climate activism 42*
   *Cloning 42*
   *Colonialism 43*
   *Communism 44*
   *Computer science 48*
   *Constitutionalism 48*
   *Consumerism 52*
   *Critical race theory 54*
   *Cultural marxism 54*

D  Dataism                                   55
   *Darwinism 55*
   *Democracy 55*
   *DNA 61*

E  Ecology                                   62
   *Economics 67*
   *Electism 72*
   *Enlightenment 73*
   *Entertainment 75*
   *Environmentalism 78*
   *Evolutionism 78*

F  Fandom                                    82
   *Fascism 84*
   *Feminism 87*
   *Fitness 90*
   *Food 90*
   *Football 93*

G  Gender                                    96
   *Genetics 96*

H  Health                                    100
   *Hip Hop 100*
   *History 102*
   *Human rights 102*
   *Humanism 105*

| I | Individualism | 111 |

| J | Juche | 114 |

| K | Kung Fu | 117 |

| L | Legalism | 119 |
*Leninism* 119
*Liberalism* 121
*Love* 124

| M | Maoism | 127 |
*Marxism* 128
*Medicine* 132
*Multiculturalism* 135

| N | Nationalism | 137 |
*Nazism* 143
*Neoliberalism* 146
*Nietzscheism* 146

| O | Olympism | 149 |

| P | Pacifism | 150 |
*Panopticism* 151
*Patriotism* 153
*Personality cult* 155
*Political correctness* 155
*Pop culture* 155
*Populism* 155
*Positivism* 157
*Postcolonialism* 157
*Posthumanism* 157
*Postmodernism* 159
*Progress* 163
*Psychology* 165

| R | Racism | 170 |
*Republicanism* 171
*Revolution* 173
*Rock* 177

S  Scientism                                    180
   *Selfies 184*
   *Selfism 185*
   *Sex 185*
   *Singularity 189*
   *Skateboarding 189*
   *Social Justice Culture (SJC) 191*
   *Social media 191*
   *Socialism 191*
   *Sports 195*
   *Stalinism 198*
   *Statism 200*
   *Superintelligence 205*

T  Technology                                   206
   *Thinness 207*
   *Transhumanism 209*

U  UFOs                                         212
   *UN 215*
   *Übermensch 216*

V  Veganism                                     217
   *Vegetarianism 219*

W  War                                          222
   *Warmism 224*
   *Wellness 225*
   *Wokeness 228*

# FIGURES

1 Officially authenticated relics of John Lennon in the Egri Road Beatles Museum, Eger, Hungary     76
2 The statue of Lenin showing the way to the future in Memento Park, Budapest, Hungary     120
3 A "reliquary" of the "martyrs" (Lajos Aulich, Janos Damjanich and Karoly Vecsey) of the Hungarian war of independence 1848–1849, containing their bones and pieces of their gallows in Déri Múzeum, Debrecen, Hungary     139

# INTRODUCTION

## Secularization and secular religions

Once secularization was the grand narrative of modernity. It helped to understand the radical novelty of our age, explaining nearly everything that was new about it: scientific and technological progress, the rise of the modern state, the spread of democracy, or the discovery of individual freedom. According to the narrative, all these – and many more – were made possible by a gradual separation of the secular and the religious, which had been intermingled in more primitive societies, while the process of separation was also inevitably followed by the decline of religious belief and practice in our more advanced ones.

By the late 20th century, however, more and more scholars rejected the "secularization thesis," pointing out that the larger part of the world did not have the same experience, and even those Western societies where secularization was supposed to take place were still haunted by the shadows of religiosity. Or even more, most of them remained embedded in various forms of religion which proved to be a permanent element of the human condition (Berger, 1999; Luckmann, 1990; Stark, 1999).

Some of these forms are called "secular religions." As the name suggests, there are many ideologies, belief systems, and social or cultural practices that seem or claim to be secular yet show important analogies with religions, making it difficult to locate them on either side of a strict religious/secular divide. This raises problems for the secularization thesis, of course, but does not necessarily make it untenable. Those who uphold that secularization belongs to the "normal" course of history might view secular religions as an intermediate stage between the religious and the secular or, more radically, as remnants of a religious past that will be eliminated by progress. Others, however, might point out that – far from being abnormal or atavistic – secular

DOI: 10.4324/9781003471257-1

religions prove that religion cannot be eradicated even by the fiercest secularism: you may drive nature out with a pitchfork, but she will keep coming back. In either case, the basic problem remains unsolved: if the similarities of secular worldviews to religious ones are pervasive, why should the former be unmasked as "secular" religions and not as truly, albeit covertly or unconsciously religious? Or, if the essence of secular religions is as mundane as the adjective suggests, why should we not treat their resemblance to "real" religions as superficial and misleading?

But perhaps it is exactly this "either/or" view of the religious and the secular that is problematic. A more modest reading of this small book could indeed be that the religious and the secular are not two boxes in which everything easily fits. There is rather a continuous scale from one to the other, with many shades in between. A more radical – and in my opinion less ambiguous – reading could be that the word "religion" itself is so vague that it should not be used at all. This is not a novel idea: many "eliminativist" authors have suggested something similar (Asad, 1993; Smith, 1962; Webb, 2009), and I do not think that the debate between eliminativism and non-eliminativism will be decided by my small contribution. What I do hope is that the conspicuous number of examples and the evocation of the more than two-century-long controversy about what to call them (secular religions, pseudo- or quasi-religions, surrogate religions, political religions, civil religions, or just religions without an adjective) will prove at least so much that there is something fundamentally wrong with our categories.

## Terminology

"Secular religion" is perhaps the most problematic of them all. Regardless of how we define religion, the modern meaning of "secular" is the exact opposite of "religious." According to the *Cambridge English Dictionary*, secular means "not having any connection with religion"; in the *Oxford English Dictionary*, it is something "not connected with spiritual or religious matters"; in *Macmillan*, it is "not religious or not connected with religion"; in *Collins*, it is a description of "things that have no connection with religion." A secular religion would thus be a religion that has no connection with religion or is not connected with spiritual or religious matters; a religion that is not religious or not connected with religion; or a description of things that have no connection with religion but are religious all the same. In other words, secular religion is an oxymoron, in which contradictory terms appear in conjunction.

To avoid the obvious contradiction, several other terms have been invented, most of which, however, only conceal the problem instead of solving it. "Quasi-religion" – as the Latin word *quasi* ("as if") suggests – emphasizes the misleading nature of an apparent similarity. A quasi-religion is something that resembles a "real" one, which means that it shares some common elements with it while in some important respect remains different. "Pseudo-religion" – from the Greek *pseudo* ("fake") – is sometimes used in the same way, but there are authors who distinguish the two. As the German Protestant theologian Paul Tillich said:

> Sometimes what I call quasi-religions are called pseudo-religions, but this is as imprecise as it is unfair. "Pseudo" indicates an intended but deceptive similarity; "quasi" indicates a genuine similarity, not intended, but based on points of identity.
>
> *(Tillich, [1963] 1988, p. 293)*

In other words, a pseudo-religion is something that claims to be a religion although it is not, while a quasi-religion does not claim to be a religion – and in fact is not one – but still looks like it, at least for the attentive observer. What both terms nevertheless suppose is that "real" religions are clearly distinguishable from their quasi- and pseudo-counterparts, presumably by some essential features that are absent from the latter. Which also means that quasi- and pseudo-religions are *not* religions, even though the postfix hypnotically suggests that they are.

The same problem occurs with "ersatz" (surrogate) religion (Rodenhausen, 2020), which is a no less ambiguous term, for it refers to something that replaces religion (presumably with something else); yet, as the whole word implies, remains a religion itself. At least in a secondary or attenuated sense, which is exactly what we saw in the case of secular religions. To speak of "religious surrogates" or "religious substitutes" is perhaps even worse, for these terms imply something religious that replaces – well, something religious. A "substitute for religion" would be somewhat better, for it at least avoids the literal contradiction; what it does not avoid is the problem of how something that is not a religion can still function as if it was one. The same goes for less often used terms like "para-religion" (Greil, 1993) or "invisible religion" (Luckmann, 1967).

For the sake of completeness, it must be added that there are also more specific expressions in use. Historically, the first term to express the religious leanings of a secular project was "political religion." Although it originally meant a "real" religion with a public purpose in early modern political commonwealths (Seitschek, 2007), the philosopher Condorcet turned it upside down during the French Revolution. From this time, it more often meant a political ideology that on the surface looked secular but was in fact similar to traditional religions. Not the same, however, for the adjective "political" was understood as a distinction from "genuine" religions, further emphasized by phrases such as "sort of" or "kind of" (Condorcet, [1791] 1989, pp. 68–70). The perhaps most famous book *Political Religions* written by Eric Voegelin in

1938 explicitly confirmed that these were "inner-worldly" – that is, secular – religions, in distinction from "trans-worldly" or "spiritual" ones, thereby reiterating the full oxymoron (Voegelin, [1938] 2000, pp. 32–33).

"Civil religion," which is sometimes used synonymously, is in fact something completely different, since both its classical formula (Rousseau, [1762] 1999, p. 158) and its 20th-century version (Bellah, [1966] 1991, p. 179) involve belief in a transcendent reality, making it difficult to call it "secular" in any meaningful sense of the word.

An even more limited – but no less controversial – approach is represented by the term "political theology." As the word "theology" suggests, the analogy is drawn only between theoretical or conceptual structures (leaving aside practical, institutional, or symbolic aspects), but the word "political" still means "secularized," at least in the most famous modern formula of political theology, that of Carl Schmitt (Schmitt, [1922] 2006, p. 36). A political theology is thus a secular theology, which – regarding that theology explicitly means "speech about God" – sounds just as oxymoronic as the term "secular religion." To make things worse, political theology is often used in the exact opposite sense: as a political teaching derived from explicitly theological principles, which completely blurs the contours of the term (see deVries and Sullivan, 2006; Scott and Cavanaugh, 2004).

There are other attempts to emphasize this or that religious element of secular belief systems (faith, messianism, eschatology, mysticism, and myth), but since all these are religious terms, while the adjectives refer to something secular (immanent, worldly, private), the contradiction is never effectively eliminated. Even when authors use the term "religion" (or at most "new religion") without further qualification, realizing the problem of separating true and false religions, it usually remains accidental. As many examples in this book will show, most of them at some point return to the traditional vocabulary of quasi, pseudo, surrogate, immanent, and so forth. These different terms grasp different aspects of the problem but agree on one point: that there is a gray zone between the truly religious and the fully secular. That is what the term "secular religion" – with all its ambiguity – best expresses.

## Defining religion

The ambiguity is, of course, rooted in the conceptual problems of "religion" itself. Religion is a notoriously difficult word to define, and in this case, the difficulty goes beyond the usual imprecision of terminology often seen in humanities and social sciences. This is not the place to review the problem in its entirety but some notes on how religion is defined in the literature on secular religions may be useful.

The problem is that in most cases, it is not defined at all. The majority of authors take it for granted that religion is a clear, simple, intuitive idea. By doing so, however, they usually rely on the prejudice of their own culture, and only the list of attributes associated with the presumed secular religion betrays their bias. For instance, if "belief in an absolute," "dogmatism," "intolerance," and a "churchly hierarchy" are mentioned, we may rightly suspect that the author takes Catholicism as the model religion. "Prophetic visions" and "chosen people" may refer to Judaism while "holy wars" and "fanaticism" (more often than not) to Islamic fundamentalism. There are, of course, many attributes (sacred scriptures, rituals, temples, priests, saints, etc.) that may be linked to several traditions, but without giving an exact definition, it always remains problematic why a given set of randomly chosen features defines religion and not something else.

The existence of such features nevertheless suggests that a definition is at least possible, even if it is not given explicitly. This would certainly be an essentialist or substantive definition, one that grasps the common core of all religions. The problem with such definitions is well known: if belief in God or gods is named as the essence of religion, such traditions as Theravada Buddhism will immediately fall outside the category. And even those traditions that do speak of "gods" do it in so many different senses that it is doubtful whether any definition may be equally applied to belief in Jesus or Allah, in the immortal but otherwise inner-worldly gods of Greek mythology, or in the impersonal absolute of pantheism. Belief in gods may of course be replaced by belief in a "transcendent" or "supernatural" reality, but these categories are also difficult to use in cultures that reject the radical separation of the immanent and the transcendent, or the natural and the supernatural, as it developed in late medieval and early modern Europe (Bartlett, 2008; Crane, 2017, pp. 9–10). In other words, all such definitions are too narrow, while speaking of belief in something "spiritual" is too broad, for in this case even the belief that human beings have something like a "self" or "soul" attributes some spiritual reality to them and will thus count as a religion. Or, if the definition is expanded further to include all sorts of belief in "order" or "meaning," it will be practically impossible to say why any form of philosophical – or just rational – thinking should not be treated as religious.

Identifying religions as types of feelings (a feeling of awe or absolute dependence) rather than beliefs cannot be pursued very far either, as a feeling can be attached to anything, and, in the absence of a substantive definition of religion, there is no way to tell whether a given feeling is "religious" or "non-religious." Again, we are faced with too broad definitions, and the same is true of functionalist definitions that do not emphasize what religion *is* but what it *does*. If social cohesion, moral guidance, or protection against existential anxiety are what religion provides, then it remains difficult to tell why any – self-professedly non-religious – social theory, ethical system, or psychological therapy will not count as a religion. Moreover, it is obvious that the list of "functions" operates very much in the same way as the list of "essential criteria" in substantive definitions, so there may be no big difference between the two. Most contemporary works on secular religions – as will be seen – nevertheless use a functionalist definition, but only at the cost of being unable to distinguish between truly and deceptively religious phenomena, not to mention completely secular ones.

It thus seems that we should give up the search for any common essence or function of religions and say more humbly that religion is a "cluster concept," one that is defined by a list of criteria, while no criterion alone is either necessary or sufficient to consider something as an instance of the category. For example, the cluster may include:

1. A central concern with godlike beings and men's relation with them.
2. A dichotomization of elements of the world into sacred and profane, and a central concern with the sacred.
3. An orientation toward salvation from the ordinary conditions of worldly existence.
4. Ritual practices.
5. Beliefs that are neither logically nor empirically demonstrable or highly probable.
6. An ethical code, supported by such beliefs.
7. Supernatural sanctions on infringements of that code.
8. A mythology.
9. A body of scriptures or similarly exalted oral traditions.
10. A priesthood or similar specialist religious elite.
11. Association with a moral community.
12. Association with an ethnic or similar group.

*(cited by Stausberg and Gardiner, 2016, p. 28)*

Regardless of the vagueness of words like "godlike," "supernatural," "ethnic or similar," and the fallacy of including the *definiendum* in the *definiens* ("religious elite"), the main problem is that such lists remain silent about how many of the criteria will define something as a religion. We may, of course, intuitively suppose that one is not enough while having all twelve constitutes a "real" or "fully-fledged" religion. In this case, secular religions will be those that feature some of these characteristics: for instance, they do not concern themselves with godlike beings but have a salvation story, a ritual practice, an ethical code, a body of scriptures, and are associated with a moral community. The difficulty, however, is the same as in the case of substantive and functional definitions: many traditions that are usually called "religious" show some of these features while neglecting others; or – what is even worse – some of them seem less religious than certain secular ideologies. Nazism or Maoism may fulfill more criteria than Buddhism does.

## A brief history

Because the rest of this book will follow an alphabetical order, it may not be superfluous to provide a little history or rather meta-history. Not in the chronological order in which the allegedly "secular" religions themselves appeared, for that always remains disputable, but in which they were discovered by their critics.

As mentioned earlier, unmasking the hidden religious leanings of modern political ideologies began during the French Revolution when Condorcet, whose committee was entrusted to draft a new plan of public education, realized that treating the constitution as a product of universal reason and teaching unconditional respect for it amounted for a "belief," an "admiration," or a "blind enthusiasm" (Condorcet, [1791] 1989, p. 68). Although constitutionalism was also described as the secular counterpart of a religious concept (deism) by Juan Donoso Cortés in 1850 or as a political theology by Carl Schmitt in 1922, and more recent critics still often view constitutional originalism as a secular faith, it was another phenomenon, the emergence of modern democratic movements that initiated a more robust wave of secular-religious comparisons in the 19th century.

In 1835, Alexis de Tocqueville's *Democracy in America* said not only that "the people rule the American political world as God rules the universe" but also called the principle of popular sovereignty a "dogma" and gave a list of divine attributes associated with democratic majorities such as omnipotence, omnipresence, infallibility, and infinite goodness (Tocqueville, [1835] 2010). In his wake, such different authors as the liberal John Stuart Mill, the evolutionist Herbert Spencer, members of the so-called Italian school of elitism (Gaetano Mosca or Vilfredo Pareto), and the aforementioned Carl Schmitt compared democratic thought to a "creed," a "superstition," a "new religion," or a "secularized theology." Well into the mid-20th century, democracy was still often ridiculed as an atavistic, quasi-religious belief in the competence of the masses to govern themselves when politics should in fact be based on more rational, scientific foundations. Although such criticism has become more muted recently, there are still scattered examples that speak of a "myth of democracy" or a "democratic faith."

In the mid-19th century, capitalism was also discovered as a secular religion, although its literature was for some time limited. While Karl Marx often ironized on the "divine" attributes of money or the "fetishism" of the commodity, it was only much later, in the 20th and 21st centuries that talking about "economics as religion" (a set of dogmas with its own academic churches, priesthood, and popular catechisms), the "theology of money" (belief in the power of an imaginary entity) or "the market as God" (as an omnipresent and omnipotent regulator of social behavior) became widespread.

Still in the 19th century, art also became to be seen as a new religion, especially in the Romantic movement. With the artist as oracle, artistic expression as a form of revelation, or museums as temples, it was perhaps the least secular of all secular religions, and only its later versions – such as the cult of film stars, athletes, and musicians that emerged in the 20th century – might be called as such. Although graffities such as "Clapton is God" or collecting the relics of John Lennon seem more like a parody of religion than its secular counterpart, the phenomena of "fandom" (from the Jedi Church to the cult of Harry Potter) are still discussed today as some of the most spectacular manifestations of a secular religion.

Also in the mid-19th century, Auguste Comte established the religion of humanity based on science but also transcending it in its moral ambitions. Although the French philosopher argued that the aims of his religion were completely secular, others soon realized that treating science as a solution for all of humanity's problems, venerating scientists as prophets or priests, or turning scientific theories into dogmas represented a just as transcendent attitude as that of any traditional religion. Such criticism of "scientism" started already in Comte's time, continued with the rise of Darwinism, and surfaced time and again in the 20th and 21st centuries, this time often in connection with technology. Today, the belief in artificial intelligence's capability to improve – or even transcend – the human condition is among the most widely discussed (and criticized) examples of a secular religion.

During the second half of the 19th century, another large wave of religious/secular analogies was induced by the rise of socialism and communism. From Donoso Cortés to the Swiss moral philosopher Henri-Frédéric Amiel or the Russian religious thinker Nikolai Berdyaev, many described the ideas of Proudhon, the Paris Commune, or Marx as "religious" ones. After the Russian Revolution of 1917, an even more robust body of literature tackled Bolshevism, Leninism, and later Stalinism as dogmatic systems, eschatological doctrines of salvation, and "churches" with infallible leaders and a missionary zeal; always adding that ("of course") all these were concerned with secular and not truly transcendent aims. The British philosopher Bertrand Russell went as far as to compare Bolshevism to Islam, which, however, seemed to mean that Islam was also a secular religion, once again relativizing the distinction of the religious and the secular. After 1945, communism remained a focal topic (at least for Cold War thinkers in the West) who also added more examples from Chinese Maoism to North Korean Juche ideology. Since 1990, the interest in the religion of socialism and communism has somewhat diminished but never entirely disappeared: there are still works that try to place them in a larger context that now includes such diverse exemplars as German national socialism and Swedish social democracy (Znamenski, 2021).

Curiously, nationalism – although it was perhaps the most powerful ideology of the 1800s – was only discovered by religious scholars toward the end of the century. At that time, however, it became so important that Émile Durkheim based his own definition of religion on the analysis of the French Revolution and its cult of the nation and the fatherland. During the 20th century, nationalism would in fact be so widely discussed as a secular, political, or new religion that authors like Liah Greenfeld could rightfully complain that all such talk had "become a cliché" (Greenfeld, 1996, p. 169).

And one of the largest waves was yet to come: the fascist and Nazi regimes that gave birth to the actual term of "secular religion" in the 1930s. The number of writings – books, newspaper articles, even papal encyclicals – devoted to the religious features of fascism and Nazism soon reached unprecedented heights, and the topic remained popular long after the fall of Mussolini and Hitler; it is in fact one of the most widely discussed topics even in today's literature, so much so that the term "political religion" is now in most cases specifically associated with right-wing authoritarianism (Gentile, 2006).

After the horrors of the Second World War, the idea of human rights naturally appeared as a contrary secular faith, often called as such by its own advocates ("our faith in humanity, the kind of faith that is based on things not seen" Warren, 1969) but also by critics who either argued that it was a modern superstition (MacIntyre, 1981) or that it was an "idolatry" to be replaced by a more pragmatic understanding of human rights (Ignatieff, 2001).

During the second half of the 20th century, the concept of secular religion was extended to a variety of other, less overtly political fields, from psychology (Vitz, 1977) to deep ecology (Ferry, 1995), all of which were suspected of becoming new overarching worldviews with their own absolutes and salvation stories in an either humanistic or post-humanistic setting. Finally, in the 21st century, politics returned to the scene, provoking another surprisingly large wave of religious/secular analogies, this time in connection with new social justice movements, postcolonialism, and critical race theory, often summed up as "wokeness" (McWhorter, 2021).

The history of secular religions may thus be described as one of continuous proliferation, the waves of which have by now been stacked on each other. Perhaps, this variety is itself misleading, since all cases express the same aspiration to replace traditional "religions" with something new but just as (consciously or unconsciously) religious as the former. The danger, however, that the enduring interest in such replacements poses for the theory of secular religions is that the abundance of analogies – especially when they are used in a more rhetorical than analytical way – might discredit all attempts to take them seriously.

## Some methodological remarks

The very form of this book (a dictionary of about a hundred entries, some of them as strange as taking selfies or skateboarding) is an ironic reference to the dangers of overstretching the analogy. It is important to point out that all topics are from an already existing body of literature and no new secular religions have been invented for the mere joy of multiplying the cases.

The sources are cited as faithfully as possible but not without critical evaluation, for the theoretical or ideological bias of most of them is anything but negligible. That is also why the basic position of the authors must be mentioned, at least in passing. A conservative writer will usually apply the adjective "secular" as a pejorative (meaning that a secular religion distorts the sublime essence of true religions), while a liberal or a progressive writer will rather use "religion" as the bad word (meaning that being religious in a sphere that should remain secular is itself the problem). There are, of course, many cases in which such a neat distinction is impossible, but it should always be remembered that criticizing secular religions has never been a purely academic undertaking but something with an ideological or political purpose.

It is, of course, impossible to cite all authors and works on a given topic; especially because in addition to books and papers that explicitly deal with secular religions, there are also many that mention them on the side, and these are sometimes just as revealing as the former. To academic literature we may also add journalism, political pamphlets, speeches, or propaganda brochures where similar references are sometimes more frequent, even if more imprecise. Not only is it impossible to cite all of them but also unnecessary because of the many repetitions contained in them.

It should also be noted that the entries are not about giving exact definitions of what words like capitalism, socialism, nationalism, or humanism mean *outside* the discourse of secular religions. What the present volume offers is only how they are defined by those who view those through the very specific (and in many cases distorting) lens of religious/secular analogies. The characteristic laxity of terminology also means that there are many overlaps: capitalism could certainly be discussed together with modern economics, socialism with communism or Bolshevism, nationalism with patriotism, or humanism with individualism. The only reason to distinguish them is that the authors cited do the same, and the different words they use express different perspectives. I will therefore only use the "redirection button" when there is no special reason to do otherwise. If the number of secular religions thus becomes higher than it seems necessary, it is not this book's fault but that of the literature.

## Conclusion

Although the concept of secular religion itself is problematic, I do not think that all attempts to draw analogies between the secular and the religious are senseless. Even if many analogies are only metaphorical or rhetorical, not all of them are, and the fact that we are unable to abandon them even in a so-called secular age reveals something important about the controversial nature of modernity as such. Terminology and definitions may be disputed, but the long line of distinguished philosophers, historians, social scientists, cultural critics, and political thinkers who have used the term secular (or quasi, pseudo, surrogate, etc.) religion since the beginning of modernity is enough to make us suspicious whether all such efforts were completely and obviously mistaken. A failure they might have been, but despite all the confusion into which their argument has led us, I tend to think of this failure as an unintended success that helps us understand how weak our foundations are when talking of the secular and the religious as two distinct spheres. "There is no success like failure," as the poet says, and this is what this entire book tries to demonstrate.

## Sources

Asad, T. (1993) *Genealogies of Religion: Discipline and Reasons of Power in Christianity and Islam*. Baltimore: The John Hopkins University Press.
Bartlett, R. (2008) *The Natural and the Supernatural in the Middle Ages*. Cambridge: Cambridge University Press.
Bellah, R. ([1966] 1991) 'Civil Religion in America', in *Beyond Belief: Essays on Religion in a Post-Traditional World*. Berkeley: University of California Press, pp. 168–189.
Berger, P. L. (ed.) (1999) *The Desecularization of the World: Resurgent Religion and World Politics*. Grand Rapids: Eerdmans.
Condorcet, J. A. N. C. ([1791] 1989) 'Cinq mémoires sur l'instruction publique', in *Écrits sur l'instruction publique, Volume 1*. Paris: Edilig.
Crane, T. (2017) *The Meaning of Belief: Religion from an Atheist's Point of View*. Cambridge: Harvard University Press.
De Vries, H., and Sullivan, L. E. (eds.) (2006) *Political Theologies: Public Religions in a Post-Secular World*. New York: Fordham University Press.
Ferry, L. (1995) *The New Ecological Order*. Translated by Volk, C. Chicago: University of Chicago Press.
Gentile, E. (2006) *Politics as Religion*. Translated by Staunton, G. Princeton: Princeton University Press.
Greenfeld, L. (1996) 'The Modern Religion?', *Critical Review: A Journal of Politics and Society*, 10(2), pp. 169–191. https://doi.org/10.1080/08913819608443416
Greil, A. L. (1993) 'Exploration along the Sacred Frontier: Notes on Para-Religions, Quasi-Religions, and Other Boundary Phenomena', in *The Handbook on Cults and Sects in America*, edited by Bromley, D. G., and Hadden, J. K. Greenwich: JAI Press, pp. 153–176.
Ignatieff, M. (2001) *Human Rights as Politics and Idolatry*. Princeton: Princeton University Press.
Luckmann, T. (1967) *The Invisible Religion: The Problem of Religion in Modern Society*. New York: Macmillan.
Luckmann, T. (1990) 'Shrinking Transcendence, Expanding Religion?', *Sociological Analysis*, 51(2), pp. 127–138. https://doi.org/10.2307/3710810
MacIntyre, A. (1981) *After Virtue: A Study in Moral Theory*. Notre Dame: University of Notre Dame Press.
McWhorter, J. H. (2021) *Woke Racism: How a New Religion Has Betrayed Black America*. New York: Portfolio/Penguin.

Rodenhausen, L. (2020) 'Ersatz-/Quasi-Religion: zur Historisierung einer religionswissenschaftlichen Analysekategorie', *Zeitschrift für junge Religionswissenschaft*, 15. https://doi.org/10.4000/zjr.1303

Rousseau, J.-J. ([1762] 1999) *Discourse on Political Economy and The Social Contract*. Translated by Betts, C. Oxford: Oxford University Press.

Schmitt, C. ([1922] 2006) *Political Theology: Four Chapters on the Concept of Sovereignty*. Translated by Schwab, G. Chicago: The University of Chicago Press.

Scott, P., and Cavanaugh, W. T. (eds.) (2004) *The Blackwell Companion to Political Theology*. Malden: Blackwell.

Seitschek, H. O. (2007) 'Early Uses of the Concept "Political Religion": Campanella, Clasen and Wieland', in *Totalitarianism and Political Religions, Volume 3*, edited by Maier, H. London: Routledge, pp. 103–113.

Smith, W. C. (1962) *The Meaning and End of Religion*. Minneapolis: Fortress.

Stark, R. (1999) 'Secularization, R.I.P.', *Sociology of Religion*, 60(3), pp. 249–273. https://doi.org/10.2307/3711936

Stausberg, M., and Gardiner, M. Q. (2016) 'Definition', in *The Oxford Handbook of the Study of Religion*, edited by Stausberg, M., and Engler, S. Oxford: Oxford University Press, pp. 9–31.

Tillich, P. ([1963] 1988) 'Christianity and the Encounter of the World Religions', in *Main Works [Hauptwerke], Volume 5*. Berlin: Walter de Gruyter, pp. 291–326.

Tocqueville, A. ([1835] 2010) *Democracy in America*. Translated by Schleifer, J. T. Indianapolis: Liberty Fund.

Vitz, P. C. (1977) *Psychology as Religion: The Cult of Self-Worship*. Grand Rapids: Eerdmans.

Voegelin, E. ([1938] 2000) 'Political Religions', in *The Collected Work of Eric Voegelin. Volume 5: Modernity without Restraint*. Translated by Schildhauer, V. A. Columbia: University of Missouri Press, pp. 19–73.

Warren, E. (1969) 'Address', in *The International Observance: World Law Day – Human Rights 1968*. Geneva: World Peace Through Law Centre, pp. 44–45.

Webb, M. O. (2009) 'An Eliminativist Theory of Religion', *Sophia*, 48(1), pp. 35–42. https://doi.org/10.1007/s11841-008-0084-1

Znamenski, A. (2021) *Socialism as a Secular Creed: A Modern Global History*. London: Lexington Books.

# A
## ABORTION

"The Left has a religion: the Supreme Court just proved it." When conservative cultural critic Mary Eberstadt wrote these words about a 2016 decision (Whole Women's Health v. Hellerstedt) that abolished a Texas law imposing stricter rules on abortion clinics, she was referring to the extreme emotions aroused by the issue. "Once upon a time, liberals portrayed the procedure of abortion as a thing regrettable but sometimes necessary. This was the cottony, 'safe, legal, and rare' piety of yesteryear. That old rhetorical dressing has been ripped off for good" (Eberstadt, 2016). Now, the decision was celebrated with a "quasi-religious euphoria," a "gnostic rave," an "ecstasy of a kind similar from the religious history of mystics, whirling dervishes, and revival tents." The word "quasi-religious" nevertheless remains curious, since gnostic and mystical religiosity, Islam, or Evangelical Christianity are usually viewed as genuine religions (along with Eberstadt's further examples, the ancient Greek cult of Dionysus or the Roman Bacchae). It might even be suggested that the worship of abortion relies on a genuinely religious dogma, which is, as the Catholic philosopher Peter Kreeft said, literally identical to the eucharistic formula "This is my body," even if its meaning is the exact opposite:

> "I am the master of my fate, I am the captain of my soul. I will do whatever *I* please with my body because it is mine, not Yours. In fact, the tiny child I carry in my womb is also mine, not Yours. She is not even her own. She is mine. She is *my* body. Therefore I will kill her, because I am her God and You are not." You see, abortion is the Antichrist's demonic parody of the Eucharist. That is why it uses the same holy words, "This is my body," with the blasphemously opposite meaning.
>
> *(Kreeft, 2008, p. 144)*

In other words, the issue cannot be reduced to abortion. Mary Eberstadt has connected it to the theology of the sexual revolution: "Consenting sex is the highest good; anything that interferes with the highest good is by definition evil" (Eberstadt, 2016). It has, in fact, an even broader meaning: as Kreeft's text suggests, it belongs to the liberal or individualistic creed of self-determination. The absolute of the "abortion religion" is not even the body (in this case, the female body) but the individual person who possesses this body; abortion is only a symbol or rather, a "religious sacrament" of this absolute (Coe, 2017). Where abortion transcends the religions of liberalism or individualism is its intransigent dualism: a strict moral division of good and evil and, most of all, the sacrificial rite that in its bloody reality is a real rarity among the so-called secular religions.

Some authors provide even more detailed lists of religious analogies (sacred writings, hagiography and demonology, and legends of converts and apostates, Coe, 2017), which at the same time suggest that – beside the ones already mentioned – the religion of abortion has many further intersections with other secular religions. Deep ecology, for example, demands "the right to access to safe abortions," limiting the number of births for the sake of nature as the highest good (Sessions, 1995, p. 88). "Economics as religion" puts an "existence value on such things as the right to perform abortions" (Nelson, 2001, p. 18). The "cult of the gene" leads to "therapeutic abortions" (Le Breton, 2004, p. 5), while "medicine as a secular religion" treats "the right to abortion" as both a moral and technical necessity (Domaradzki, 2013, p. 26).

See also: Ecology, Economics, Feminism, Genetics, Individualism, Liberalism, Medicine, Sex

### Sources

Coe, J. B. (2017) 'The New Darling of the Abortion Rights Movement', *Crisis Magazine*, 7 June. Available at: https://www.crisismagazine.com/2017/new-darling-abortion-rights-movement (Accessed: 1 December 2023).

Domaradzki, J. (2013) 'Extra Medicinam Nulla Salus: Medicine as a Secular Religion', *Polish Sociological Review*, 181, pp. 21–38. Available at: https://www.jstor.org/stable/41969476

Eberstadt, M. (2016) 'The Left Has a Religion: The Supreme Court Just Proved It', *National Review*, 28 June. Available at: https://www.nationalreview.com/2016/06/supreme-court-abortion-whole-womens-health-hellerstedt-religion-sexual-revolution/ (Accessed: 1 December 2023).

Kreeft, P. (2008) *Jesus Shock*. Singer Island: Beacon Publishing.

Le Breton, D. (2004) 'Genetic Fundamentalism or the Cult of the Gene', *Body & Society*, 10(4), pp. 1–20. https://doi.org/10.1177/1357034X04047853

Nelson, R. H. (2001) *Economics as Religion: From Samuelson to Chicago and Beyond*. University Park: The Pennsylvania University Press.

Sessions, G. (ed.) (1995) *Deep Ecology for the Twenty-First Century*. Boston: Shambhala.

# Anarchism

Since anarchism rejects all forms of coercive power and hierarchy (or "sacred rule," as the etymology of the word implies), it first seems the exact opposite of any political or secular religion. The lack of a political absolute means that it might rather be called a sort of "political atheism," which, however, does not exclude the possibility that anarchists are believers in the "otherworldly" sense of the term. Religious anarchism has indeed many examples in a variety of traditions from Christianity to Hinduism (Christoyannopoulos and Adams, 2017–2020). It may be argued that sometimes it is exactly the belief in a higher, transcendent absolute that prevents the worship of any other, "this-worldly" power like that of a king or a political leader.

However, as many authors in the anarchist tradition point out (Proudhon, [1840] 1994; Bakunin, [1871] 1973), rejecting authority in this world and accepting it in the other mixes two different anthropologies: one that views the human being as essentially autonomous and another that is content with its heteronomy, even if only in the "religious" domain. In contrast, the anarchist slogan *Ni dieux, ni maître* ("Neither god, nor master") confirms the inseparability of theological and political atheism, which is nevertheless an implicit acknowledgment of the fact that anarchism itself is a politico-theological idea.

As early as 1850, the Spanish conservative politician Juan Donoso Cortés suggested that atheism in the "religious order" and anarchism in the "political order" both represented an "ultimate negation," the logical endpoint of the same process. This process started with Catholicism (belief in the existence of an omnipotent, personal, active divinity) and its corresponding political form, monarchy, followed by deism (the idea of a God who created the world but would no longer interfere in its working) and constitutional monarchy that likewise rejected any personal authority over the existing laws of society. Then came pantheism, which identified God with the universe, and its political counterpart the "republic," which identified authority with the people itself, until atheism and anarchism rejected any authority whatsoever, be it divine or political (Donoso Cortés, [1850] 2007, pp. 74–75).

It may, of course, be argued that atheism and anarchism are not "theologies" but "anti-theologies." An anti-theology, however, is itself speech about God, and that is why Mikhail Bakunin, who otherwise criticized many nineteenth-century ideologies for their theological inclinations (on nationalism, see Bakunin, [1871] 1973; on scientism and social democracy, see Bakunin, [1871] 1970), himself became an example of political theologians for Carl Schmitt, who reintroduced the term "political theology" to modern usage in 1922. While repeating Donoso Cortés's historical narrative almost literally, Schmitt's work cited Joseph de Maistre (the most prominent French counterrevolutionary author) and the anarchist Bakunin as two antipodes, who nevertheless both approached politics from a theological point of view:

> De Maistre said that every government is necessarily absolute, and the anarchist says the same; but with the aid of his axiom of the good man and corrupt government, the latter draws the opposite practical conclusion, namely, that all governments must be opposed for the reason that every government is a dictatorship. . . . Bakunin, the greatest anarchist of the nineteenth century, had to become in theory the theologian of the antitheological and in practice the dictator of an anti-dictatorship.
> *(Schmitt, [1922] 2006, p. 66)*

What anarchism – according to Schmitt – could not avoid was making claims about an ultimate reality, an "absolute," that of political government. What is worse, the anarchist opposition to government had to invent a rival absolute, the individual human being, whose "goodness" was a just as dogmatic assertion ("axiom") as any theological doctrine on the other side (the "original sin" or "radical evil" inherent in human nature). Moreover, both approaches suggested an eschatological context, the struggle of good and evil until the ultimate triumph of one or the other. By making predictions about the end of history, the devout anarchist became just as infallible a prophet or political authority as any of its enemies.

It remains dubious, however, whether this sort of anarchist political theology (or perhaps political religion, since it also has its rituals such as street demonstrations, or its symbolism of black flags and Circle-A's) really fits Schmitt's own definition. For in Schmitt's account, political theology is based on "secularized" theological concepts, and it sounds somewhat strange to say that anarchism is "secularized atheism," as if atheism was not secular in the first place but something that could further be secularized.

See also: Atheism, Constitutionalism, Individualism, Republicanism, Socialism

## Sources

Bakunin, M. ([1871] 1970) *God and the State*. New York: Dover Publications.
Bakunin, M. ([1871] 1973) 'The Political Theology of Mazzini', in *Selected Writings*, translated by Cox. S., and Stevens, O. London: Jonathan Cape, pp. 214–231.
Christoyannopoulos, A., and Adams, M. S. (eds.) (2017–2020) *Essays in Anarchism and Religion*. Stockholm: Stockholm University Press.
Donoso Cortés, J. ([1850] 2007) 'Discourse on the General Situation of Europe', in *Readings in Political Theory*, translated by McNamara, V., and Schwartz, M. Ave Maria: Sapientia Press of Ave Maria University, pp. 67–82.
Proudhon, P.-J. ([1840] 1994) *What Is Property?* Translated by Kelley, D. R., and Smith, B. G. Cambridge: Cambridge University Press.
Schmitt, C. ([1922] 2006): *Political Theology: Four Chapters on the Concept of Sovereignty*. Translated by Schwab, G. Chicago: The University of Chicago Press.

## Animal rights

The earliest accounts of animal rights activism as a secular religion emphasized the extraordinary level of commitment to the cause of social redemption that characterized its adherents. James M. Jasper and Dorothy Nelkin explicitly spoke of a "crusade" (Jasper and Nelkin, 1992), and some activists themselves adopted the religious label, at least for the practical reason of gaining constitutional protection for the movement (Francione and Charlton, 1992).

Redemptive zeal and tactical self-labeling are hardly sufficient to call anything religious, but – according to other authors – there are further criteria that are fulfilled by animal rights activism. As Wesley V. Jamison, Caspar Wenk, and James W. Parker remark, the movement has all the necessary components of such a religion: (1) an intense and memorable experience; (2) a newfound community of meaning; (3) normative creeds; (4) elaborate and well-defined codes of behavior; and (5) cult formation with its symbols and rituals (Jamison, Wenk, and Parker, 2000, p. 305).

The intense and memorable experience means a moment of enlightenment and conversion, when the convert suddenly understands that "treating animals as objects is wrong," either by reading a book or watching a documentary, but always in a dramatically emotional, transformative way (ibid., p. 311). The community formed by such an experience and the following change in attitude may be a purely spiritual one (a bond with all those who share a similar outlook and values) or a more organized one (a club or association of like-minded activists). These are especially important because the conversion inevitably distances the converted from their former communities (friendships or families).

The creed does not have to be formally declared, although it is remarkably uniform across the spectrum of organizations and individuals. The main article of faith is the equality of human and non-human animals (which is already a metaphysical claim about their essence and value), which also involves the moral condemnation of humanity because of the omnipresence of its original sin, the exploitation of animals, and the corresponding belief in the essential innocence (or even sanctity) of its victims. As an editorial letter to the New York *Newsday* columnist B. D. Colen stated: "Unlike you, the cockroach has never done anything deliberately malicious in its life – unlike every human that ever lived" (ibid., p. 315).

Obligations are therefore placed mainly upon humans, and these imply a sort of asceticism: "vegetarian or vegan cooking, cruelty-free shopping, cruelty-free entertainment, and cruelty-free giving" (ibid., p. 317). And although there are no formal rituals prescribed by a churchly authority, community meetings of activists provide a repetitive reification of belief: personal confessions, stories of recent conversions, encouragement by fellow believers, or acts of penitence by those who relapsed (ibid., p. 318).

Others add that vegan meals can be understood as acts of ritual purification, just as participation in public demonstrations, which gives a sense of transcending one's self-limitations and offers a clear separation from non-believers (Jacobsson and Lindblom, 2017, p. 99). There may even be holy days with their own elaborate ceremonies and symbolism. As a Swedish animal rights activist said:

> On the day of the laboratory animals [*Försöksdjurens dag*], which occurs in the beginning of spring every year, we bought a big funeral wreath with pre-printed ribbons, saying "In memory of all murdered animals." We held a ceremony with grave candles. We also had an expert on laboratory experiments as speaker. We wanted people who passed us to start to think and to be badly affected.
>
> *(ibid., p. 100)*

As for symbols, "animal rights activists use pictures of monkeys strapped in chairs, cats wearing electrodes and rabbits with eye or flesh ulceration" in much the same way as traditional religions do with the images of martyrs, that is, "as symbolic representations of human values and corresponding affronts to those values" (Jamison, Wenk, and Parker, 2000, p. 319), rejuvenating the faithful's commitment to the cause.

While Jamison, Wenk, and Parker speak of a religion with a "transcendent goal" (thereby superseding their own original "functional" definition, ibid., p. 323), others maintain that animal rights activism is only a "secular religion." Jacobsson and Lindblom, for instance, after registering a very similar list of features (awakening and conversion, dedication and commitment, search for meaning in suffering, the creation of a moral community, an idea of the sacred, and the practice of rituals), ultimately vote for the less radical terminology, even though they have to acknowledge that animal rights "challenge established symbolic classifications and boundaries between sacred and profane" (Jacobsson and Lindblom, 2017, p. 79), thereby pulling into doubt the religious/secular distinction in general. Similarities between traditional and secular religions (for "secular" seems to mean nothing else than "non-traditional") are in fact more numerous than their differences:

> Thus, a secular religion, just like a traditional religion, builds on a clear boundary between believers and non-believers, between those committed to the ideal and others. Moreover, as in the case of traditional religion, a secular religion is also based on dedication to the sacred ideal, which involves not only a cognitive awareness and intellectual motivation but also emotional engagement.
>
> *(ibid., p. 82)*

The conclusion is that although the theory of animal rights is often presented as a scientific doctrine (since science has proven that animals are just as capable of suffering as human beings are), it is not only about this empirical fact but about the *essence*, the *value*, and the *meaning* of animal life. If the worship of human rights and the human individual are manifestations of "a modern faith and cult," then "expanding this individualism to encompass animal individuals as well" (ibid., pp. 78–79) means the creation of an even more overarching faith and cult. It is also an example of posthumanism, since its two conflicting dogmas (the equality of all natural beings and the moral superiority of non-human animals) can only be reconciled by suggesting that it is ultimately the latter that should be decisive.

See also: Human Rights, Ecology, Humanism, Posthumanism, Veganism, Vegetarianism

### Sources

Francione, G. L., and Charlton, A. E. (1992) *Vivisection and Dissection in the Classroom: A Guide to Conscientious Objection.* Jenkintown: The American Anti-Vivisection Society.

Jacobsson, K., and Lindblom, J. (2017) *Animal Rights Activism: A Moral-Sociological Perspective on Social Movements.* Amsterdam: Amsterdam University Press.

Jamison, W. V., Wenk, C., and Parker, J. W. (2000) 'Every Sparrow That Falls: Understanding Animal Rights Activism as Functional Religion', *Society & Animals*, 8(3), pp. 305–330. Available at: https://www.animalsandsociety.org/wp-content/uploads/2015/10/jamison.pdf (Accessed: 1 December 2023).

Jasper, J. M., and Nelkin, D. (1992) *The Animal Rights Crusade: Growth of a Moral Protest.* New York: Free Press.

## Anti-racism

American linguist John McWhorter described anti-racism as a "flawed new religion" that had its own "clergy, creed, and also even a conception of Original Sin" (McWhorter, 2015). Since, however, he himself later changed the terminology to "woke racism," an inverted but just as racist religion as the one it opposed, it will be further discussed in entries on the latter.

See also: Racism, Wokeness

### Sources

McWhorter, J. (2015) 'Antiracism, Our Flawed New Religion', *The Daily Beast*, 25 July. Available at: https://www.thedailybeast.com/antiracism-our-flawed-new-religion (Accessed: 1 December 2023).

## Art

Historically, art was one of the first "surrogate" religions, at least for those intellectuals in the modern era who felt that traditional religions could no longer offer the same spiritual fulfillment as in earlier ages. It is, however, difficult to decide whether the "religionization" of art produced a secular religion (as it has been called ever since, Elkins and Morgan, 2009, p. 278; Drott, 2011, p. 217; Järvinen, 2014, p. 36) or something as truly religious as any previous tradition.

"Religious art" has always existed, of course, even if it was not called as such, since art as a manifestation of individual creativity only began to be distinguished from other human activities during the early modern era, when "religion" also started to mean a distinct sphere of social life (Elkins and Morgan, 2009, p. 25). The cult of the artist as a sort of modern saint or mystic, one with an intimate relationship to the divine, sharing its essence and conveying its message, also appeared at the time. The hagiography of artists (for instance, Giorgio Vasari's *The Lives of the Artists* [1568] 1998) was already a departure from the traditional view of the artist as a "craftsperson" or "artisan" but still did not represent a complete break with religion, only a transition from "religious art" to "art as religion," which would emerge in all its pomp in the late 18th century.

The latter was mostly characteristic of the Romantic era, yet it was still not a *secular* religion. As Jacques Barzun remarked:

> Art revealed the divine in man as nature revealed God. Artists might differ in conceiving God as beyond nature or within it or within the human breast; they might differ in being Spinozists or Catholics or Swedenborgians; none were atheists.
>
> *(Barzun, 1974, p. 27)*

Let us note, however, that Spinozist pantheism, Catholic theism, or Swedenborgian mysticism by this time had become coloring elements only. It was no longer this or that religious tradition that created its own artistic form; it was art itself that provided the authentic religious way of approaching the absolute. The essence of the new religion was this approach; dogmas or truths played a secondary role (or no role at all) compared to the artist's mystical experience.

In addition to the cult of artist-saints and the canon of authentic ("inspired") works, art galleries and museums began to be called the "temples" of art from at least the 19th century (Ziolkowski, 2007, p. 53; Järvinen, 2014, p. 34) when visiting such a temple also began to be seen as a sort of "pilgrimage." In many cases, the aim of the pilgrim was no longer to achieve any spiritual enlightenment, only to be physically present where the sacred objects were exhibited, but this had also often been true of medieval pilgrimages. Even today, when the visitor of the Louvre proudly says, "I've seen the Mona Lisa," it is to express that "being there" is the important thing, for anything else – such as a profound immersion in the spirituality of the artwork – is made impossible by the very dimensions of the pilgrimage (the number of visitors and the brief time they are allowed to spend in the presence of the sacred).

Explicit secularization is another matter. Beside "religious art" and "art as religion," there exists an explicitly secular form of art, but the latter, as some authors remark, may also become religious, sometimes – paradoxically – because of its anti-religious attitude. When artistic rebellion becomes "an enterprise set over against a social and political establishment continued to be shaped by transcendent faiths" (Hunter, Nolan, and Eck, 1997, p. 339), it can easily turn into a rival form of revelation of which artists become the prophets or visionaries.

Moreover, when such aspirations are supported by political authorities which promote art as "a substitute for the functions that religion had discharged in preindustrial society" (Drott, 2011, p. 217), they in fact create a new religion without saying so. If the language of art is supposed to be "truly universal," one that is superior to that of traditional religions, then the "religion of art proposes to be the first global religion. To recompose what has been decomposed, this religion embraces all gods, all styles, all civilizations" (Debray, 1992).

In sum, the worship of art is just as religious as it is non-religious or just as secular as it is non-secular. It is a constant back and forth movement between two allegedly different spheres in a mist of overlapping conceptualizations. To cite a characteristic example from an exhibition brochure (that of the Aprognistic Temple in Brussels): "Contemporary art as secular religion and the artworld as profane cult are the kinds of stories we've all heard before. But de-secularizing art in order to shroud it in quasi-sacred mystery sounds like a rather bold move" (Hart, 2020). Bold or not, the wording is once again remarkably ambiguous, since "de-secularization" does not mean "real" sacralization, only "quasi," while the idea that the border between art and religion can be crossed from either side suggests that it may not be there at all.

See also: Entertainment, Fandom, Individualism

## Sources

Barzun, J. (1974) *The Use and Abuse of Art*. Princeton: Princeton University Press.
Debray, R. (1992) 'Universal Art: The Desperate Religion', *New Perspectives Quarterly*, Spring, pp. 35–41.
Drott, E. (2011) *Music and the Elusive Revolution: Cultural Politics and Political Culture in France, 1968–1981*. Berkeley: University of California Press.
Elkins, J., and Morgan, D. (eds.) (2009) *Re-Enchantment*. New York: Routledge.
Hart Magazine (2020) '7 Critic's Pics for Brussels Gallery Weekend'. Available at: https://hart-magazine.be/expo/7-critic-s-picks-brussels-gallery-weekend (Accessed: 1 December 2023).
Hunter, J. D., Nolan, J. L., and Eck, B. A. (1997) 'The Life-World of the Avant Garde Artist: Is "Nothing" Sacred?', in *Konfigurationen lebensweltlicher*

*Strukturphänomene: Soziologische Varianten phänomenologisch-hermeneutischer Welterschließung*, edited by Wicke, M. Opladen: Leske and Budrich, pp. 336–351.

Järvinen, H. (2014) *Dancing Genius: The Stardom of Vaslav Nijinsky*. New York: Palgrave.

Vasari, G. ([1568] 1998) *The Lives of the Artists*. Translated by Bondanella, J. C., and Bondanella, P. Oxford: Oxford University Press.

Ziolkowski, T. (2007) *Modes of Faith: Secular Surrogates for Lost Religious Belief*. Chicago: The University of Chicago Press.


## Artificial intelligence

The secular religion of artificial intelligence is part of the more overarching religion of science and technology, but some of its specific traits require a separate discussion. It is not simply about answering the "big questions" of humanity with a new, scientific worldview nor is it only about creating an "earthly paradise" with technological progress. What some bold theories of AI explicitly or implicitly suggest is the possibility of an omniscient, omnipotent being, a higher form of consciousness that nevertheless remains remarkably anthropomorphic (a supreme being possessing will and intellect), similarly to the traditional, theistic notions of God.

This super-mind or "superintelligence" (Bostrom, 2014) is transcendent in the sense that it has still not been seen by anyone. When American computer scientist Ray Kurzweil was asked whether he thought God existed, he replied, "I would say not yet" (Rennie, 2011). The title of his famous book *The Singularity is Near* was also an implicit reference to the biblical phrase "The Kingdom of God is near." According to him and other prophets of singularity, when the new "God" emerges, it will become truly transcendent, for the exponential progress of machine intelligence will reach the point when it becomes incomprehensible for the human mind, as was suggested by John von Neumann as early as the 1950s (Ulam, 1958, p. 5).

It is at this point that post- and transhumanism become religious concepts. It is only a matter of belief whether we see humanity as doomed, to be left behind by progress (a post-humanist vision of universal damnation), or we think it possible to offer a sort of salvation by which humanity can also be deified, or rather become part of the divine by a complete physical and spiritual transformation (as in transhumanism).

In any case, the prophecies of singularity show a remarkable coherence with the traditional forms of millennialism, which have suggested that the Last Judgment is near (as singularity is also usually predicted to take place in the next few decades, Kurzweil, 2005); its advent is certain and inevitable, and although we can participate in the divine plan, it is not something that can be induced or hindered by human will. Again, just as traditional millennial views have divided history into different epochs, the prophecies of AI distinguish a variety of those (either four, as in Reese, 2018, or six, as in

Kuzweil, 2005), while the basic scheme remains a tripartite one. It consists of a prehistory, a present age of transition, and a future age that will bring about the fulfillment of all former aspirations, a "thousand-year kingdom" or the "age of the spirit." (On the similar structure of historical theologies and their subsequent influence, the classic work remains Karl Löwith's *Meaning in History*, 1949.)

On the other hand, there are authors who suppose that AI with the same capabilities as humans already exists (Tiku, 2022), from where it is only a small step until "superintelligent AI" will "almost inevitably" emerge (Shanahan, 2015, p. 86). Moreover – although it is only a further variation of Kurzweil's "spiritual" and "divine" terminology – this intelligence will be so much more advanced than the human mind that its workings "will be indistinguishable from magic" (ibid., p. 91). Whether religious, spiritual, divine, or magical, however, the process is characteristically described in terms of belief or faith. When in 2022, a Google engineer claimed that their chatbot showed signs of self-consciousness, others immediately rejected this as an unfounded attribution which was more like a profession of faith, even though the rejection itself was hardly more than a declaration of unbelief in the same (Tiku, 2022).

In sum, the "religion of AI" – if there is such a thing – is said to have a transcendent absolute or even a personal deity, which is a rarity among secular religions. It has a salvation history, it has its prophets, and, if technological firms developing AI are viewed as "magisterial" institutions, it has its own churches as well. There are also examples of "real" churches like the Church of Perpetual Life, the Turing Church, or the Terasem (Antosca, 2019). These are led by an enlightened elite, compared to whom the ordinary "lay" person can only possess a lower and secondary knowledge. Without a priesthood of experts, it is impossible to communicate with the divine, although it may also change in the future. The price to pay, however, will be that individual identities must become "more fluid" or disappear entirely (Shanahan, 2015, p. 409), flown together in an "ocean of consciousness" (belief in which Israeli historian Yuval Noah Harari explicitly called a "new religion," Harari, 2015, p. 409).

Others – like Ray Kurzweil or Larry Ellison, co-founder of the American computer technology company Oracle, and many other Silicon Valley "gurus" – still dream of maintaining individual consciousness and individual immortality in the age of artificial general intelligence (Fortuna, 2017). What all these different visions nevertheless show is that despite all the "secular" and "atheistic" talk, the aspirations of AI are deeply similar to those of "traditional" religions. In 2023, when the appearance of ChatGPT made everyone aware of the possibilities of AI, it was often forgotten that it was still nothing like AGI (artificial general intelligence), only an example of LLM (a large language model) that reproduced and combined information already

**24** Atheism

available in human culture. To treat it – and its later competitors – as either a "blessing" or a "curse" reveals more about the personal beliefs of its advocates and critics than about its real potential.

See also: Posthumanism, Progress, Scientism, Technology, Transhumanism

**Sources**

Antosca, A. R. (2019) 'Technological Re-Enchantment: Transhumanism, Techno-Religion, and Post-Secular Transcendence', *Humanities and Technology Review*, 38(2), pp. 1–28. Available at: https://philpapers.org/archive/ANTTRT.pdf (Accessed: 1 December 2023).
Bostrom, N. (2014) *Superintelligence: Paths, Dangers, Strategies*. Oxford: Oxford University Press.
Fortuna, W. H. (2017) 'Seeking Eternal Life, Silicon Valley Is Solving for Death', *Quartz*, 8 November. Available at: https://qz.com/1123164/seeking-eternal-life-silicon-valley-is-solving-for-death (Accessed: 1 December 2023).
Harari, Y. N. (2015) *Homo Deus: A Brief History of Tomorrow*. London: Vintage.
Kurzweil, R. (2005) *The Singularity Is Near: When Humans Transcend Biology*. New York: Viking Books.
Löwith, K. (1949) *Meaning in History*. Chicago: The University of Chicago Press.
Reese, B. (2018) *The Fourth Age: Smart Robots, Conscious Computers, and the Future of Humanity*. New York: Atria.
Rennie, J. (2011) 'The Immortal Ambitions of Ray Kurzweil: A Review of Transcendent Man', *Scientific American*, 15 February. Available at: https://www.scientificamerican.com/article/the-immortal-ambitions-of-ray-kurzweil/ (Accessed: 1 December 2023).
Shanahan, M. (2015) *The Technological Singularity*. Cambridge: The MIT Press.
Tiku, N. (2022) 'The Google Engineer Who Thinks the Company's AI Has Come to Life', *Washington Post*, 11 June. Available at: https://www.washingtonpost.com/technology/2022/06/11/google-ai-lamda-blake-lemoine/ (Accessed: 1 December 2023).
Ulam, S. (1958) 'John von Neumann 1903–1957', *Bulletin of the American Mathematical Society*, 64(3), pp. 1–49.

**Atheism**

To call atheism a religion – even if only a secular religion – is certainly paradoxical, but not without precedent in the literature. Anarchism, for instance, was already discussed as a sort of political atheism in the 19th century by Juan Donoso Cortés's *Discourse on the General Situation of Europe*, which compared the rejection of political government to the rejection of divine sovereignty, implicitly suggesting that both were, in the final analysis, religious ideas (Donoso Cortés, [1850] 2007, p. 75). In the 20th century, Carl Schmitt's *Political Theology* drew a similar analogy between anarchism and atheism, suggesting that both could be understood in a broadly understood theological framework that also included "antitheological" or "atheist" theologies (Schmitt, [1922] 2006, p. 57).

The suspicion that atheism is nothing more than a negative counterpart of theism, a similarly overarching worldview with its own fundamental dogma ("there is no God"), its belief in salvation (if not by God, then by the individual), and its mysticism (a tendency to confuse imagination and reality) was raised not only by religious conservatives. As French atheist author Jean-Paul Sartre wrote in the 1960s, it was no easy task to become truly irreligious and not just religious in an inverted sense of the word:

> For a long time, to write was to ask Death and my masked Religion to preserve my life from chance. I was of the Church. As a militant, I wanted to save myself by works; as a mystic, I attempted to reveal the silence of being by a thwarted rustling of words and, what was most important, I confused things with their names: that amounts to believing.
> *(Sartre, 1964, p. 251)*

Not only writing or artistic expression can be "religious" forms of atheism, though. British philosopher John Gray – himself an atheist – accused no less than five of the *Seven Types of Atheism* in his eponymous book with religious leanings, or even more, regarding the confused and overlapping categories applied to them (Gray, 2018).

The initial list of Gray's volume is relatively simple. It includes New Atheism and scientism, political religions, "God-hatred," anti-religious and anti-humanistic philosophies, as well as metaphysical conceptions of the ineffable God. The classification, however, collapses soon afterward, for Comte's religion of humanity gets mixed up with those more recent examples of New Atheism that explicitly reject any such religious ambitions. Comte would rather belong to the next two chapters on humanism and scientism, in which, however, humanism is used as an umbrella term to cover belief in progress, Marxism, liberalism, and Nietzscheism. The concept of scientism is also as broad as to include Darwinism, mesmerism, transhumanism, Marxism (now for the second time), racism, and antisemitism. The fourth chapter on political religions once again includes communism and Nazism, as well as progressivism, Jacobinism, and even "evangelical liberalism," further relativizing the distinction of atheism and religion. From the remaining chapters, it finally becomes clear that there are as many atheisms as there are atheists, for Sade marquis and Ivan Karamazov seem to have about as much in common as Santayana and Joseph Conrad, not to mention Schopenhauer, Spinoza (whose *pan*theism is for some reason called *a*theism), or the Russian religious philosopher Lev Shestov.

What all this nevertheless helps to understand is that atheism can only be used as a collective noun, and even as such, it is a misleading one. Humanity, the autonomous individual, the Übermensch, the proletariat, nature, and history are all veritable absolutes (not just the empty spaces of God), and they are all different absolutes. In the present volume, they are discussed in different entries and not as instances of a so-called atheist religion. If one uses such a broad definition as John Gray does ("religion is an attempt to find meaning in events," Gray, 2018, p. 3), then of course all manifestations of human culture might be seen as religious. That, despite this, Gray speaks of "secular faiths" and "God-surrogates" (ibid., 3 and 158) only shows that he himself is unsatisfied with his definition. It seems that to define religion – to quote Sartre – is just as "cruel and long-range affair" as it is to define atheism, let alone to become an atheist.

See also: Anarchism, Communism, Humanism, Liberalism, Marxism, Nazism, Nietzscheism, Progress, Scientism, Transhumanism

## Sources

Donoso Cortés, J. ([1850] 2007) 'Discourse on the General Situation of Europe', in *Readings in Political Theory*, translated by McNamara, V., and Schwartz, M. Ave Maria: Sapientia Press of Ave Maria University, pp. 67–82.
Gray, J. (2018) *Seven Types of Atheism*. New York: Farrar, Straus and Giroux.
Sartre, J. P. (1964) *The Words*. Translated by Frechtman, B. New York: George Braziller.
Schmitt, C. (1922 [2006]) *Political Theology: Four Chapters on the Concept of Sovereignty*. Translated by Schwab, G. Chicago: The University of Chicago Press.

# B
## BEAUTY

"Beauty religion," of course, exists, at least in the name of a Californian beauty salon. Whether the bombastic name and the no less pretentious slogan ("We believe in beauty") should be taken at face value may seem doubtful, but the abundance of phrases like "magic," "goddess," or "ageless" raises the suspicion that there is a premeditated conception, a consciously assumed "religiosity" in the background.

Secular religiosity, one might add, for the salon offers perfection not in another life and not (only) in a spiritual sense. Its instruments to provide inner-worldly salvation are also remarkably profane: mainly dermatological treatments and Botox fillings (Beauty Religion, 2023). In this sense, beauty religion – which is not confined to the eponymous salon – seems an emblematic example of secular religion.

It might be argued, however, that beauty is in fact a transcendent category, insofar as it is impossible to grasp as a concrete fact but always remains an ideal. As a 2023 exhibition in London expressed: "Around the world, beauty is constantly seen as an ideal worthy of going to great lengths to achieve. But what are the driving forces that lead us to believe in a myth of universal beauty, despite its evolving nature?" (Wellcome Collection, 2023). Moreover, in contemporary clichés such as "beauty comes from within," beauty looks inseparable from the just as intangible concept of the soul or the spirit. A sarcastic journal article wrote about an adaptation of the reality television franchise Real Housewives:

> Today, there is a good deal of spiritism and intellectual essence in beauty trends as well, since, as it turns out, those who have undergone the

DOI: 10.4324/9781003471257-3

"Intervention" or "Interventions" (for it is not like baptism that should be taken only once) belong to a completely different sect than those who have not.

*(Hercsel, 2020)*

The ultimate (and never fully attainable) reality of beauty and its rites of initiation thus create a religious community as opposed to the group of heretics: "the camp of luxury wives parts into 40+ Botox-believers and younger Botox-deniers just like the Red Sea did [before Moses]." To which the article ironically adds that it is a serious matter, unlike "the lousy *homoousios – homoiousios* debate" (in early Christianity about the divine or only godlike essence of Christ).

The title of the article is "Botox is My Religion," but the issue is more complex. The cult of beauty is closely related to the cults of health and wellness: as American actress Halle Berry once put it when launching her own wellness website, "I believe good [health] and wellness is what real beauty is all about" (Burton, 2020, p. 260, n1). Or, as Tara Isabella Burton said in her *Strange Rites: New Religions for a Godless World*, wellness culture "centers the perfectibility of the body as the locus of personal spiritual growth," and "the divine is to be found not just within ourselves but in the specifically physical experience of our *embodied* selves" (ibid., p. 157). The cult of beauty thus may not be the best example of a secular religion; it rather manifests the inseparability of the corporeal and the spiritual, or the transcendent and the immanent, thereby relativizing the separation of the secular and the religious in general.

See also: Sex, Thinness, Wellness

### Sources

Beauty Religion (2023) 'Beauty Religion: We Believe in Beauty'. Available at: https://beautyreligion.com/ (Accessed: 1 December 2023).

Burton, T. I. (2020) *Strange Rites: New Religions for a Godless World*. New York: Public Affairs.

Hercsel, A. (2020) 'A botox az én vallásom', *Index*, 8 December. Available at: https://index.hu/kultur/2020/12/08/felesegek_luxuskivitelben_negyedik_evad_masodik_resz_botox/ (Accessed: 1 December 2023).

Wellcome Collection (2023) 'The Cult of Beauty'. Available at: https://wellcomecollection.org/exhibitions/ZJ1zCxAAACMAczPA (Accessed: 1 December 2023).

### Biotechnology

Describing biotechnology as a secular religion supposes that it is not only about finding new therapies or new ways of agricultural production but a complete transformation of human nature and the environment. The most exalted expectations and fears are connected to cloning, stem cell research, and genetic engineering, although biotechnology is a much wider concept that includes all use of biology to improve life conditions. In this sense, the breeding of animals and plants was already an example of biotechnology, but it is only its modern forms that are suspected of religious ambitions. The creation of entirely new life forms, including the creation of a new, "2.0" version of the human being indeed, has a messianic character that shows a remarkable analogy with the biblical story of sin and redemption:

> Before their eviction from Eden, Adam and Eve possessed a nature that was nonmortal, immune to suffering, without sin, and of perfect dignity. The human being's constant wish to return to Eden and to regain the pristine nature that it lost is a consequence of this symbolic biblical event. Today's technoscience . . . fully accepts this statement about the "fall" of human nature. Technoscience and biotechnology seek to detect and repair the affected points of human nature. Deconstruction and reconstruction are the main methods of this biotechnological work. From this understanding follows the imperative to detect all infected points of our nature and to remove their consequences.
> *(Strehovec, 2009, p. 800)*

Lee M. Silver's famous book on genetical engineering not accidentally uses the phrase *Remaking Eden* as its title and biblical quotations at the beginning of each chapter, suggesting that all aspects of human life – from the individual, physical level to family and society – could be transformed in such a way that will fulfill the most ancient desires of humankind. This also means that beyond the physical, biotechnology promises to transform our psychological and moral character, either through behavioral genetics or the development of behavioral drugs (Cohen, 2006; Strehovec, 2009).

It is sometimes forgotten that making such promises – and taking them for granted by the laity – also means belief in the superhuman powers of the scientist or the technician as the creator of new individuals or even an entire species. What is more problematic is that the official churches of biotechnology are not strictly speaking academic institutions but economic enterprises: biotechnology firms, other corporations, or agribusiness conglomerates that invite people to "imagine a future with no disease, no aging, perfection on demand" (Nelkin and Lindee, 2004, p. xiv). This "biocommerce" or "commerce of the body" forms an integral part of the modern economy:

> In myriad ways, the better body is for sale – from anti-impotence drugs to anti-depressants, from cosmetic surgery to low-carb diets, from baby-making clinics promising you a healthy child to the current push to legalize the buying and selling of human organs. And if one looks ahead to the biotechnologies of the future – improved mood- and memory-altering

drugs, stem-cell-based medicine, genetic muscle enhancements, new techniques for controlling the genomes of one's offspring – it is clear that the commerce of the body will only become more ambitious, selling bodily perfection to anyone with enough disposable income.

*(Cohen, 2006)*

As Lee M. Silver demanded earlier, cloning should be regulated by the market and not by governments or society (Silver, 1998, p. 144), just as – presumably – all other forms of biotechnological intervention. This alliance of biotechnology and capitalism is what makes authors like Eric Cohen speak not of a religion proper but of a "worldly salvation" or a "profanation of the sacred," rooted in the belief in progress and the desire for a "terrestrial paradise." At a closer look, however, it becomes clear that bio-capitalism promises "perfection, not progress; and it heeds no limits, treating the sacred and the profane as indistinguishable objects for sale," thereby relativizing the distinction of the religious and the secular just as much as most other examples of the so-called secular religions (Cohen, 2006). This also explains the hesitation of those who speak of "secular religion," "quasi-religion," or "para-Christian religion," sometimes in the same article (Strehovec, 2009).

Regardless of the terminology, perfection is a necessarily eschatological concept (the theological meaning of eschatology is the doctrine of "last things") since there is nothing beyond it. Moreover, the path to perfection is just as determined as in any salvation story: humanly engineered changes are in many cases irreversible, and "in such a way, modern technology, especially biotechnology, undermines the open-endedness of the future" (Tirosh-Samuelson, 2015, p. 172).

Fears that the future will be more like damnation than salvation appeared as early as Mary Shelley's *Frankenstein*, which was, if you like, also the story of a biotechnological experiment (Shelley, [1818] 2010). Ever since, the returning objection to such experiments has been that human beings should "not play God," for it will lead to tragic consequences. Let us remember, however, that even in biotechnology, it is usually rhetoric and not facts that create the illusion of godlike behavior: "human creaturehood means that human creativity is ultimately about transforming nature, rather than creating ex nihilo. Thus, while human and divine creativity might be seen in some ways as analogous to each other, the two should never be equated" (Garner, 2015, pp. 232–233). Or, to cite the most bombastic claim, the "immortality" offered by biotechnology is different from its traditional idea not only because it is biological and not spiritual, but also because it is impossible to achieve in a universe that is itself – according to our present knowledge – not eternal. The laxity of terminology is telling: "The first may be characterized as biological immortality. With anticipated developments in genetics and biotechnologies, the average lifespan can be increased dramatically, perhaps indefinitely" (Waters, 2014, p. 291). Yet dramatically or indefinitely longer is still not infinite; another example of how easily technical language can turn into something mystical or religious.

See also: Capitalism, Cloning, Genetics, Medicine, Scientism, Technology, Transhumanism

## Sources

Cohen. E. (2006) 'Biotechnology and the Spirit of Capitalism: The New Commerce of the Body', *The New Atlantis*, 12 (Spring). Available at: https://www.thenewatlantis.com/publications/biotechnology-and-the-spirit-of-capitalism (Accessed: 1 December 2023).
Garner, S. (2015) 'Christian Theology and Transhumanism: The "Created Co-creator" and Bioethical Principles', in *Religion and Transhumanism: The Unknown Future of Human Enhancement*, edited by Mercer, C., and Trothen, T. J. Santa Barbara: Praeger, pp. 229–243. https://doi.org/10.5040/9798216007074.ch-015
Nelkin, D., and Lindee, M. S. (1998) *The DNA Mystique: The Gene as a Cultural Icon*. Ann Arbor: University of Michigan Press.
Shelley, M. ([1818] 2010) *Frankenstein*. Dublin: Harper Collins.
Silver, L. M. (1998) *Remaking Eden: How Genetic Engineering and Cloning Will Transform the American Family*. New York: Avon Books.
Strehovec, T. (2009) 'Biotechnotheology and Demythologization of Stem-Cell Research', *Zygon*, 44(4). https://doi.org/10.1111/j.1467-9744.2009.01034.x
Tirosh-Samuelson, H. (2015) 'Utopianism and Eschatology: Judaism Engages Transhumanism', in *Religion and Transhumanism: The Unknown Future of Human Enhancement*, edited by Mercer, C., and Trothen, T. J. Santa Barbara: Praeger, pp. 161–180.
Waters, B. (2015) 'Flesh Made Data: The Posthuman Project in Light of the Incarnation', in *Religion and Transhumanism: The Unknown Future of Human Enhancement*, edited by Mercer, C., and Trothen, T. J. Santa Barbara: Praeger, pp. 291–302.

## BLM

The "Black Lives Matter" movement that started in 2013 and gained international recognition in 2020 is regularly criticized as an example of "woke religion" by its opponents, but some of its special traits allow for a separate discussion. The most important one is the central role of martyrdom, the veneration of those who had been killed in police action (Travyon Martin, Michael Brown, Eric Garner, Pamela Turner, Rekia Boyd) well before George Floyd's killing that gave rise to a more overarching phenomenon with its own hagiography, salvation story, shrines, pilgrimages, feast days, and rituals.

As for the concept of martyrdom, it should be noted that Christian martyrs – the first examples of sainthood in Christianity – were also venerated for their ultimate sacrifice that abolished personal sin; just as in the case of George Floyd, of whom it was never supposed that his former crimes would prevent his veneration. The process of canonization began at the time of his funeral, with hagiographers collecting the memories of those who knew him personally, and for whom his was an example of virtue: "He had paid his debt, and now he was trying to help other kids avoid the same mistake. I feel like that is the ultimate redemption story" (Hixenbaugh, 2020). The rituals preceding the official funeral attracted thousands of pilgrims, and the word "pilgrimage" remained in use long thereafter (Ahmad, 2021). Sites of pilgrimage included spontaneously created "shrines" in different cities across the United States (Urban Art, 2023; Penner, 2023). A many-layered ritual also developed with its own liturgical acclamations ("I can't breathe," that connected the concrete circumstances of the martyr's death to the grievances of the community in a symbolic way) and ceremonial kneeling that recalled the gesture of the policeman who kneeled on George Floyd's neck for 8 minutes and 46 seconds (which itself became a symbolic time span), while also being an expression of humility and penance, just as in more ancient (religious) traditions. Liturgical garments like stoles made of Kente cloth were worn by Democratic lawmakers at a memorial ceremony held at the Capitol's Emancipation Hall (Lee, 2020). All these, at the same time, were only external manifestations of a more fundamental set of values and principles that were criticized for belonging to a "new" or "secular" religion of social justice culture or wokeness (see there).

See also: Racism, Social Justice Culture, Wokeness

### Sources

Ahmad, L. A. (2021) 'A Pilgrimage to George Floyd Square', *Next Avenue*, 6 August. Available at: https://www.nextavenue.org/george-floyd-square/ (Accessed: 1 December 2023).

Hixenbaugh, M. (2020) 'He Met George Floyd in Sixth Grade: Now He's Grieving Alongside Millions', *NBC*, 9 June. Available at: https://www.nbcnews.com/news/us-news/he-met-george-floyd-sixth-grade-now-he-s-grieving-n1227946 (Accessed: 1 December 2023).

Lee, A. (2020) 'Congressional Democrats Criticized for Wearing Kente Cloth at Event Honoring George Floyd', *CNN*, 8 June. Available at: https://edition.cnn.com/2020/06/08/politics/democrats-criticized-kente-cloth-trnd/index.html (Accessed: 1 December 2023).

Penner, D. (2023) 'Community Memorial Held Three Years after Death of George Floyd', *Los Gatan*, 1 June. Available at: https://losgatan.com/community-memorial-held-three-years-after-death-of-george-floyd/ (Accessed: 1 December 2023).

Urban Art Mapping (2023) 'George Floyd Shrine'. Available at: https://georgefloydstreetart.omeka.net/items/show/2139 (Accessed: 1 December 2023).

## Bolshevism

Bolshevism was distinguished from other forms of socialism and communism by the Russian philosopher and religious thinker Nikolai Berdyaev exactly because of its "religious" character. "Only within the consciousness of the Russian Bolsheviks does the revolutionary socialism remain a religion," he wrote, suggesting that all other forms had been tempered and secularized to adapt themselves to the political reality of Western societies (Berdyaev, 1917).

Berdyaev's text, *The Religious Foundations of Bolshevism*, however, is just as ambiguous as any other on secular religions. Although it first explicitly calls Bolshevism a "religion," the wording later changes to "a religious substitute, an inverted religion, a pseudo-religion," despite the fact that it has the same attributes as a "real" one: it is "likewise the manifestation of a religious order, in it there is its own absoluteness, its own final end, its own all-encompassing aspect, its own pseudo and phantasmic plenitude." It therefore remains obscure what separates a religion from a substitute, an inversion, or a pseudo-religion; or what – if anything – distinguishes the latter from each other.

The relationship between Bolshevism and other forms of socialism also remains vague. While the 1917 text says that "Bolshevism indeed is socialism, having reached a religious disposition and a religious exclusiveness," both his earlier and later works attribute a similar character to Marxism (*The Catechesis of Marxism*, Berdyaev, 1905), to socialism (*Socialism as Religion*, Berdyaev, 1906), and to communism in general (*The Russian Revolution*, Berdyaev, 1931).

Another famous description of Bolshevism as religion comes from Bertrand Russell's *The Practice and Theory of Bolshevism* published in 1920. Its peculiarity is that it compares Bolshevism not to Christianity (as it is usually done) but to Islam: "Bolshevism combines the characteristics of the French Revolution with those of the rise of Islam" (Russell, 1920, p. 5). The reference is to the combination of radicalism and fanaticism (ibid., p. 9) with eschatological promises like "an end of the injustice of rich and poor, an end of economic slavery, an end of war" (ibid., p. 17); moreover, this glorious end is "fatally predestined to come about; this fits in with the Oriental traits in the Russian character and produces a state of mind not unlike that of the early successors of Mahomet" (ibid., p. 29).

Although Russell himself first speaks of a "new religion," he later changes his wording to "this-worldly," that is, secular:

> Among religions, Bolshevism is to be reckoned with Mohammedanism [sic] rather than with Christianity and Buddhism. Christianity and Buddhism are primarily personal religions, with mystical doctrines and a love of contemplation. Mohammedanism and Bolshevism are practical, social, unspiritual, concerned to win the empire of this world.
>
> *(ibid., p. 114)*

The strange consequence of which is that Islam proves to be a just as secular religion as Bolshevism, which raises the question of why it is called a religion at all. As Russel explains: "By a religion I mean a set of beliefs held as dogmas, dominating the conduct of life, going beyond or contrary to evidence, and inculcated by methods which are emotional or authoritarian, not intellectual" (ibid., pp. 113–114). This is, of course, a very broad definition which may be applied to many, if not all, ideologies, but it is certainly true that "By this definition, Bolshevism is a religion" (ibid., p. 114). Just as, one might add, any other secular religion is.

It is a telling fact that even those who described the philosophy of Bolshevism as uncompromisingly materialistic and anti-religious, as the Austrian cultural historian René Fulop-Miller did in his *The Mind and Face of Bolshevism* (1927), repeatedly used words like "heresy," "preaching," or "prophets," before arriving at the conclusion that it was a "substitute" religion:

> Anyone trained in the exact methods of thought of the West can see nothing in this Bolshevik materialism but one of those substitute religions which, since the decay of the earlier faith centered in the Church and the rise of scientific rationalism, have continually kept springing up to provide humanity with a new creed in place of the faith they have lost, and to satisfy their eternal yearning for freedom from all evil in new forms adapted to the scientific spirit of present time.
>
> *(Fulop-Miller, 1927, p. 71)*

What the different terms (religion, religious substitute, inverted religion, pseudo-religion, new religion, this-worldly religion, and substitute religion) all suppose is that Bolshevism has something like a theological absolute, a doctrine about ultimate meaning, a salvation history, and an emotional appeal that amounts to irrationality and fanaticism even when it poses as a scientific theory. This is also what makes it both similar and hostile to other religions. The only reason why Berdyaev, Russell, and Fülöp-Miller separate Bolshevism from other forms of socialism thus seems to be its connection to religious fatalism and mysticism rooted either in Russian Orthodoxy or in an even more problematic sort of "eastern" mindset.

See also: Communism, Marxism, Socialism, Scientism

## Sources

Berdyaev, N. (1905) 'The Catechesis of Marxism' (Катехизис Марксизма), *Вопросы жизни*, 2, pp. 369–379. Available at: https://www.berdyaev.net/1905/the-catechesis-of-marxism/ (Accessed: 1 December 2023).

Berdyaev, N. (1906) 'Социализм как религия', *Вопросы философии и психологии*, 17(5), pp. 508–545. Available at: http://relig-library.pstu.ru/catalog/35/book-35.pdf (Accessed: 1 December 2023).

Berdyaev, N. (1917) 'The Religious Foundations of Bolshevism' (Религиозные основы большевизма), *Русская свобода*, 8 August. Available at: https://www.1260.org/

Mary/Text/Text_Berdyaev_The_Religious_Foundations_of_Bolshevism_en.htm (Accessed: 1 December 2023).
Berdyaev, N. (1931) *The Russian Revolution*. London: Sheed and Ward.
Fulop-Miller, R. (1927) *The Mind and Face of Bolshevism: An Examination of Cultural Life in Soviet Russia*. Translated by Flint, F. S., and Tait, D. F. London: G. P. Putnam's Sons.
Russell, B. (1920) *The Practice and Theory of Bolshevism*. London: Allen & Unwin.

## Boxing

While sports in general are often described as secular religions, there are some examples of a more specific thematization. As American writer Joyce Carol Oates remarked in her *On Boxing*, boxers like Rocky Marciano trained with a "monastic devotion" (Oates, 1987, p. 28) which was more than just a figure of speech. Marciano chose to "seclude himself from the world, including his wife and family." In the final month before a fight, he would not write a letter since "a letter related to the outside world." He also became "obsessed" with diet, and the aim of such asceticism was to expel everything from his mind that was not part of the preparation.

> When Marciano worked out with a punching bag he saw his opponent before him, when he jogged, he saw his opponent close beside him, no doubt when he slept, he "saw" his opponent constantly – as the cloistered monk or nun chooses by an act of fanatical will to "see" only God.
> *(ibid., p. 29)*

Fanatical devotion might be only one "religious" aspect, but – as French sociologist Loïc Wacquant added in his *Body and Soul* – there were more. When someone becomes a boxer, it is "like entering a religious order," which does not only require sacrifice ("Sacrifice! The word comes up time and again the mouth of the old coach," Wacquant, 2004, p. 235) but also constitutes a church in the Durkheimian sense of the word:

> The Manly art offers the *paradox of an ultraindividual sport whose apprenticeship is quintessentially collective*. And, paraphrasing Émile Durkheim, one can go so far as to assert that the gym is to boxing what the church is to religion: the "moral community," the "solidary system of beliefs and practices" that makes it possible and constitutes it as such.
> *(ibid., p. 100)*

Although the "beliefs" of boxers are very complex (practices are easier to identify with the daily rituals of training), they might include belief in the "gift of the boxer" (ibid., p. 99) as something absolute, always already given; in the existence of a necessary connection between efforts and results (ibid.,

p. 104); or in "the sanctity of rules existing since time immemorial," as Max Weber says (ibid., p. 124). Other references to coaches as "priests" (ibid., p. 148) or to new methods as "heterodox" (ibid., p. 125) also reinforce the feeling that the analogy with religion is more systematic than anecdotical.

See also: Kung Fu, Sports, Wellness

## Sources

Oates, J. C. (1987) *On Boxing*. Garden City: Doubleday.
Wacquant, L. (2004) *Body and Soul: Notebooks of an Apprentice Boxer*. Oxford: Oxford University Press.

# C

# CAPITALISM

The "God" or the "Absolute" of capitalism is most often identified with the market or money. As for the first, Adam Smith's "invisible hand" is sometimes thought to be the first mystical description of the market as a sort of *Deus absconditus*, something nontransparent for the human mind and independent of individual human wills. Besides being superhuman and all-powerful, it may also be seen as an essentially benevolent agent that leads society – or even humanity in general – toward the common good.

Smith's very brief passage in *The Wealth of Nations*, however, does not exactly say that. It does not even use the word *market*, only the metaphor of "an invisible hand to promote an end which was not part of his [the individual's] intention," even adding that it is not "*always* the worse for the society that it was no part of it" (Smith, [1776] 1981, p. 456). He thereby maintains the possibility that the invisible hand may in some cases be constrained when the common good requires it, and *The Wealth of Nations*, in fact, cites many examples of the latter. *The Market as God* is not Smith's idea: as American theologian Harvey Cox remarks in his eponymous book, it would be a mistake to consider him the prophet or the patron saint of the market (a sort of "Saint Adam of Glasgow"), for he simply "uttered and wrote too many words counter to the sacred creed of Market orthodoxy" (Cox, 2016, pp. 145 and 155). What the modern ideologies of the market preach is something different and more closely related to theological ideas, for instance, those of divine attributes.

The first such attribute is *omnipotence*, which supposes the ability to create new ontological realities. As in the Catholic mass the substance of bread and wine is turned into the body and blood of Christ by God's act the market is also able to perform the miracle of turning everything into something else – a commodity – without changing its outward appearance. Moreover, the market transforms not only the bread and the wine into commodities but also the church buildings in which the mass is celebrated. Beside the "body of Christ," it can also convert the human body into a purchasable item, as in the case of organ trafficking or the commercial use of the human genome (ibid., pp. 10–12). This at the same time indicates how *omnipresent* it is, permeating everything from churches to hospitals, laboratories, and scientific institutions, as the commonplace slogan of "marketable knowledge" aptly shows in the mission statements of contemporary universities. It is also *omniscient:*

> Current thinking already assigns to The Market a comprehensive wisdom that in the past only the gods have known. The Market, we are taught, is able to determine what human needs are, what copper and capital should cost, how much barbers and CEOs should be paid, and how much jet planes, running shoes, and hysterectomies should sell for.
> *(ibid., pp. 15–16)*

Even when the market apparently fails – as during economic crises – it is never its own fault but of those who did not yet fully understand its workings. "Farther along," as the old Christian hymn says, "we'll know all about it, farther along we'll understand why." And let there be no mistake: the "God" of the market is also truly transcendent. Any visible marketplace is only an earthly manifestation of the market as an abstract idea. As all the above suggest, the omnipotent, omnipresent, and omniscient market is not an objective reality known from experience but something whose existence we infer from its effects. It does not mean that the idea of the "market" is pure fiction; it only means that our proofs for its existence are just as *a posteriori* as most proofs for God's existence in traditional (Christian) theology are.

The second candidate for the God of capitalism is money. As early as 1843, the British historian Thomas Carlyle wrote of the "invisible enchantment of Mammon," meaning by this the secular – or rather, covert – religion of modernity (McCarraher, 2019, p. 4). The same year the young Karl Marx wrote that "Money is the jealous god of Israel, beside which no other god may exist. Money abases all the goods of mankind and changes them into commodities" (Marx, [1843] 1978, p. 50). A year later, he also explicitly added the divine attribute of "omnipotence" in the *Economic and Philosophical Manuscripts* (Marx, [1844] 1978, p. 102). The superhuman power of money was exemplified by its capability to transform the human being:

> Thus, what I *am* and *am capable* of is by no means determined by my individuality. I am ugly, but I can buy for myself the most *beautiful* of women. Therefore I am not *ugly*, for the effect of *ugliness* – its deterrent

power – is nullified by money. I, in my character as an individual, am *lame*, but money furnishes me with twenty-four feet. Therefore I am not lame. I am bad, dishonest, unscrupulous, stupid; but money is honored, and therefore so its possessor. Money is the supreme good, therefore its possessor is good.

*(ibid., p. 103)*

In the 1850s, Marx's *Grundrisse* also called money "the god among the commodities": not just *one* object of worship, but *the* ultimate end of all human ambitions (Marx, [1857–58] 1973, pp. 221–222). The omnipresence of money hardly needs any further explication nor does its omniscience that determines the value of everything in an allegedly objective manner. It is at the same truly transcendent: banknotes, cards, or numbers on bank accounts are only symbols of it. These symbols express something that has no objective reality; it exists only to the extent that people believe in it. Money is credit and debt, promise and obligation: account books – as Philip Goodchild's *Theology of Money* says – are not descriptions of what there is but what we expect to be. The "real world" of money is nothing but a complicated network of imaginations, beliefs, hopes, or "shared fictions" (Goodchild, 2009, pp. 167–168). The paradox is that money nevertheless acts as a real God: its existence is spiritual and not merely psychological, for it creates true obligations and actually governs people's lives. It is the "animating spirit" of capitalism (McCarraher, 2019, p. 5).

It must be added that Marx sometimes spoke not only of money but of all commodities as metaphysical entities, full of "theological niceties." In the famous chapter of the *Capital*, "The fetishism of the commodity and its secret," he stated that the very moment a trivial object becomes a commodity, it "transcends sensuousness" and takes on mystical properties (like exchange value) that cannot be derived from its physical reality or use-value (Marx, [1867] 1976, pp. 163–165). This strange transformation is very similar to what happens in the case of religion, which is also nothing more than a fantastic projection of social relations. "In order, therefore, to find an analogy we must take flight into the misty realm of religion." One might therefore say that for Marx the worship of the commodity is not a "secular" religion but a real one; or one can just as well say that it is just as secular as th so-called real ones which are themselves nothing more than this-worldly, social phenomena. In a similar vein, Walter Benjamin also emphasized in a small fragment titled *Capitalism as Religion* in 1921 that capitalism was not like a religion or something conditioned *by* religion but an "essentially religious phenomenon" (Benjamin, [1921] 1996, p. 288). Although it looks more mundane, let us not forget that ancient religions were also not about anything "higher" or "transcendental" but served severely practical interests (ibid., p. 290).

Yet whether the market, money, or commodity fetishes are the ultimate objects of worship, the basic dogmas of capitalism remain unclear. Benjamin himself thought that there were none: capitalism was a "purely cultic" religion, a permanent celebration, a series of feast days commanding "the utter fealty of each worshipper" (ibid., p. 289). More recent authors, however, point out that capitalism does have a full theology, a teaching about the meaning of life (material prosperity), fundamental virtues (diligence, efficiency), or the course of history as a providential march toward a world of free markets. *Mercatus vult* ("the market wants it"), as American economist Paul Krugman ironically remarked, is a just as confident battle cry as the crusaders' *Deus vult* ("God wants it"), although the will of the market is about as well known by economists as the will of God by medieval warriors (Krugman, 2014).

The teaching is also laid down in sacred books and popular catechisms. Samuelson's *Economics* (the best-selling economics textbook of all time) is one of those sacred books that preaches the morals of an "implicit secular religion" (Nelson, 2001, p. 34). "Its moral and liturgical codes are contained in management theory and business journalism" (McCarraher, 2019, p. 5). The grand narrative underlying the articles of the *Wall Street Journal*, the *Financial Times*, or the *Economist* bears "a striking resemblance to Genesis, the Epistle to the Romans, and Saint Augustine's City of God" (Cox, 2016, p. 7). Which also suggests that there is a priesthood of economists with their academic "churches" and "denominations" (Nelson, 2001, pp. 113–114), and their sacred language of statistics and mathematics (ibid., p. 100). For popular religiosity, capitalism is represented by the "cathedrals" of consumption (Ritzer, 2005, p. 7) and the symbolism of brands that have in fact become more important in their transcendent reality than the old fetish of commodities: "Never again would the corporate world stoop to praying at the altar of the commodity market. From now on they would worship only graven media images . . . Brand! Brand!! Brand!!! That's the message" (Klein, 2002, p. 25).

The "religious" traits of either traditional or postmodern capitalism could be continued endlessly: its missionary zeal to unite the world ("One taste worldwide," as the McDonald's slogan says); the higher knowledge of its prophets ("a lot of people don't know what they want until you tell them," as Steve Jobs remarked); or the total personal conversion it demands from the individual who must literally "put on the new self" in the biblical sense of the word to be able to want what the market provides (Cox, 2016, pp. 205, 238, 193). It also has its own ideas of sin and punishment, its salvation history of "incessantly expanding production, trade, and consumption" (McCarraher, 2019, p. 5), and its eschatology which does not only describe a future ideal but makes faith in this ideal inherent in everyday life. It is most clearly visible in the case of money, which is always a credit, something to be fulfilled in the future: "Within the illusion of modernity, life is determined by eschatology" (Goodchild, 2009, p. 57).

Let us repeat once more that most works on the religion of capitalism explicitly call it "essentially religious" (Benjamin, [1921] 1996, p. 288), an "official religion" (Hinkelammert, 1986, p. xiv), a "modern religion" (Nelson, 2001, p. 10), or the "religion of modernity" (McCarraher, 2019, p. 11), adding that all this is not merely a "figure of speech" (Cox, 2016, p. 6). Even when some authors fall back on the vocabulary of "secular" or "ersatz" religions, it is somewhat reluctantly acknowledged that capitalism still "exhibits all characteristics of a classical faith" (ibid., p. 8). Regarding its religious roots and its explicitly religious endorsements in neoliberalism (Guest, 2022), one might even say that capitalism is not only one of the most widely discussed topics in the genre but also the one that most thoroughly undermines the secular/religious divide.

See also: Consumerism, Economics, Individualism, Marxism, Progress

## Sources

Benjamin, W. ([1921] 1996) 'Capitalism as Religion', in *Selected Writings, Volume 1: 1913–1926*, edited by Bullock, M., and Jennings, M. W. Cambridge: The Belknap Press of Harvard University Press, pp. 288–291.
Cox, H. (2016) *The Market as God*. Cambridge: Harvard University Press.
Goodchild, P. (2009) *Theology of Money*. Durham: Duke University Press.
Guest, M. (2022) *Neoliberal Religion: Faith and Power in the Twenty-First Century*. London: Bloomsbury.
Hinkelammert, F. J. (1986) *The Ideological Weapons of Death: A Theological Critique of Capitalism*. Translated by Berryman, P. Maryknoll: Orbis.
Klein, N. (2002) *No Logo*. New York: Picador.
Krugman, P. (2014) 'What Markets Will', *New York Times*, 16 October. Available at: https://www.nytimes.com/2014/10/17/opinion/paul-krugman-what-markets-will.html (Accessed: 1 December 2023).
Marx, K. ([1843] 1978) 'On the Jewish Question', in *The Marx-Engels Reader*, edited by Tucker, R. C. New York: W. W. Norton and Company, pp. 26–52.
Marx, K. ([1844] 1978) 'Economic and Philosophic Manuscripts of 1844', in *The Marx-Engels Reader*, edited by Tucker, R. C. New York: W. W. Norton and Company, pp. 66–125.
Marx, K. ([1857–58] 1973) *Grundrisse: Introduction to the Critique of Political Economy*. Translated by Nicolaus, M. New York: Vintage Books.
Marx, K. ([1867] 1976) *Capital: A Critique of Political Economy*, Volume 1. Translated by Fowkes, B. Harmondsworth: Penguin.
McCarraher, E. (2019) *The Enchantments of Mammon: How Capitalism Became the Religion of Modernity*. Cambridge: The Belknap Press of Harvard University Press.
Nelson, R. H. (2001) *Economics as Religion: From Samuelson to Chicago and Beyond*. University Park: The Pennsylvania State University Press.
Ritzer, G. (2005) *Enchanting a Disenchanted World*. Thousand Oaks: Pine Forge.
Smith, A. ([1776] 1981) *An Inquiry into the Nature and Causes of the Wealth of Nations*, Volume 1. Indianapolis: Liberty Fund.

**Celeb culture**

See Entertainment, Fandom.

**Climate activism**

See Ecology.

**Cloning**

Cloning may not be a full-fledged secular religion, but some of its mythical features may justify a separate discussion within the larger framework of genetics and biotechnology. The heart of the myth is the popular misbelief that genotypically identical biological organisms – including human beings – are in fact one and the same:

> This brings us to the fascination with the serial reproduction of the human in the form of the clone: the narcissistic fantasy of having a double, an echo of oneself that is the result of reproduction without sex – reproduction that is hygienic, purely technical and which takes place without a partner. That the history of the individual is that of the differentiating characteristics and that no individual, even a cloned individual, quite mirrors another is often forgotten, or even put forward as an argument for cloning.
>
> *(Le Breton, 2004, p. 4)*

In a similar fashion, cloning someone from a somatic cell after one's death would only create another person and not a "copy," let alone a "resurrected" individual. No matter how mistaken such beliefs might be, however, they have a real impact on the concept of the human being and the meaning of life: "The instrumentation of the clone, the feeling of not being a generic being in one's own right, but rather a double, is certainly not inconsequential" (ibid.). In Jean Baudrillard's words:

> Cloning is the final stage of the manipulation of the body whereby, reduced to its abstract and genetic formula, the individual is condemned to its own serial deceleration. We are taken back to what Walter Benjamin said about the work of art in the era of technological reproduction. What is lost in the work that is serially reproduced is its aura, the singular quality of the here and now.
>
> *(Baudrillard, 1981, pp. 151, 152)*

The myth of cloning thus has a transformative power, and the actual possibilities of cloning are also treated as part and parcel of this genetical utopia. As Lee M. Silver's *Remaking Eden* states:

> There is a final consequence of cloning that is more significant and powerful than any other use of the technology, one that has the potential to change humankind: the genetic engineering of human beings. Without cloning, genetic engineering is simply science fiction. But with cloning, genetic engineering moves into the realm of reality.
>
> *(Silver, 1998, p. 151)*

The reason is that the direct engineering of genes within an isolated embryo – destined to be a child – is not something that most people would readily accept, but multiple cells grown from a single embryo could perhaps be manipulated and selected without widespread opposition (ibid., p. 152). In this way, cloning can contribute to "gaining control" over our destiny, and Silver ultimately does not refrain from speaking of cloning in biblical terms, quoting Genesis 1:26: "Let us make man in our image, after our likeness." This suggests the replacement of God's image with our own, of course; so however secular such an attempt may seem, it hardly dispels the suspicion that it is an essentially religious one.

See also: Biotechnology, Genetics, Medicine, Scientism

## Sources

Baudrillard, J. (1981) *Simulacres et simulation*. Paris: Galilée.
Le Breton, D. (2004) 'Genetic Fundamentalism or the Cult of the Gene', *Body & Society*, 10(4), pp. 1–20. https://doi.org/10.1177/1357034X040478
Silver, L. M. (1998) *Remaking Eden: How Genetic Engineering and Cloning Will Transform the American Family*. New York: Avon Books.

## Colonialism

Colonialism is a strange case, even more paradoxical than other examples of secular religions. It seems rather a practical joke which suggests that for some people "on the left" (who rely on the "catechism" of anti-colonialism), colonialism has become an everlasting, "invisible but omnipresent" entity "like God" (Bruckner, 2020), against which an endless, ritual war is waged. So, although colonialism is described as a sort of negative deity, the real target of the irony is anti-colonialism and the decolonial movement. The French philosopher Pascal Bruckner, who criticizes ethnocentric multiculturalism and anti-Western prejudice from this angle, applies an abundance of religious phrases in his "The Flagellants of the Western World": the West as a "scapegoat," a daily practice of "repentance," people "beating their breasts," Europe being "messianic" in the inverted sense of the word, assuming all sins of the world on itself, or Africa as an "Eden" before it was spoiled by the West, for which only "a form of extreme unction" is now offered (ibid.). It is a good example of the journalistic use of religious terms, in which the multifaceted rhetoric aims to discredit its target because of its alleged systematic analogy to religion, using the word in a pejorative sense. This strategy at the same time presents the neoconservative outlook as an heir to the tradition of enlightenment secularism.

See also: Postmodernism, Racism, Wokeness

## Sources

Bruckner, P. (2020) 'The Flagellants of the Western World', *Tablet*, 12 November. Available at: https://www.tabletmag.com/sections/arts-letters/articles/postcolonial-western-guilt-pascal-bruckner (Accessed: 1 December 2023).

## Communism

Separating communism from socialism – even in the literature on secular religions – is highly problematic. In the beginning, the two were used more or less synonymously (even by Marx, who also experimented with other terms, Hudis, 2019, p. 757), and it was only after the Russian Revolution that communism established itself as the radical, revolutionary alternative to socialism or as the most developed socioeconomic system after capitalism and the transitory period of socialism. It is therefore only of anecdotic significance that the *Manifesto of the Communist Party*, written by Marx and Engels in 1848, started as a "creed" or literally as "a confession of faith" (*Glaubensbekenntnis*) for communists, only to be changed later, when its religious overtones became obvious for the authors (Koselleck, 2006, p. 47).

Words such as "communist" or "communism" were felt outdated even by Marxists toward the end of the 19th century (Steele, 1992, p. 44), and that is why most critics of secular religions concerned themselves with "socialism" or, after the 1917 revolution, with "Bolshevism," which they saw as a typically Russian form of socialism. Typical of this approach was Russian religious philosopher Nikolai Berdyaev, who first wrote *Catechesis of Marxism* (1905), *Socialism as Religion* (1906), *The Religious Foundations of Bolshevism* (1917), and finally *The Religion of Communism* (1931).

> [L]ike every religion, it carries with it an all-embracing relation to life, decides all its fundamental questions, and claims to give a meaning to everything; it has its dogmas and its dogmatic morals, publishes its

catechisms, has even the beginnings of its own cult; it takes possession of the whole soul and calls forth enthusiasm and self-sacrifice. Unlike most political parties, it will not admit secularized politics, divorced from an all-embracing *Weltanschauung*.

(Berdyaev, 1931, p. 56)

The wording unambiguously refers to a religion like any other, although the communist salvation story follows most closely the Christian example. History began with a paradisiacal state of equality that was destroyed by original sin, the appearance of private property and exploitation. This caused the moral and spiritual decay of humanity, "which infects all the history of the world, all classes of society, and disfigures all human beliefs" (ibid., p. 65). Humanity can thus only be saved by those who are innocent of original sin, in this case the proletariat, the "messianic class" (ibid., p. 67). This proletariat is not to be confused with the "empirical working class which we observe in actual life. It is a mythical idea, not an objective reality" (ibid., p. 68). Although Berdyaev at this point gets very close to speak explicitly of a secular religion, a "social idolatry" or worship of the "social collectivity which receives divine honors and steps into the place of both God and man" (ibid., p. 79), he ultimately confirms that it is a *real* religion, a rival of Christianity:

> It is impossible to understand Communism if one sees in it only a social system. But one can comprehend the passionate tone of anti-religious propaganda and persecution in Soviet Russia, if one sees Communism as a religion that is striving to take the place of Christianity. Only a religion is characterized by the claim to possess absolute truth; no political or economic movement can claim that. Only a religion can be exclusive. Only a religion has a catechism which is obligatory for everyone. Only a religion can claim to possess the very depths of the human soul. No political program or State can lay down such a claim. Communism persecutes all religions because it is itself a religion.
>
> (ibid., pp. 83–84)

The millenarian and messianic nature of communism was not Berdyaev's unique discovery. In 1920, German conservative journalist Fritz Gerlich already emphasized the same in his *Communism as the Theory of the Thousand-Year Empire*, and a slightly modified scheme would appear in 1946 in Bertrand Russell's *The History of Western Philosophy*, where Marx was called the Messiah and the Proletariat the Elect, while the Millennium remained "the Communist Commonwealth" (Russell, [1946] 2004, p. 338). Regarding "political messianism," Jacob Talmon's *The Origins of Totalitarian Democracy (1952)* traced back its origins to 18th century utopian thinkers (Mably and Morelly) and early communists (Babeuf and Buonnaroti), who established an "unbroken continuity as a sociological force for over a hundred and fifty years" (Talmon, 1952, p. 8).

> Jacobins may have differed from the Babouvists, the Blanquists from many of the secret societies in the first half of the nineteenth century, the Communists from the Socialists, the Anarchists from all others, yet they all belong to one religion.
> *(ibid., p. 12)*

Whether it was "a religion in the broadest sense" (ibid., p. 11) or a "secular religion" (ibid., pp. 12–13) nevertheless remained ambiguous. After all, as all religions, communism had its own "theological framework" which may have been "a marvel of logic, with syllogism following syllogism," but its "first premises" were "a matter of faith" which could "neither be proved nor disproved" (ibid., p. 12).

To separate communism from Marxism, Leninism, Bolshevism, socialism, anarchism, or totalitarian ideologies, in general, meant a terminological problem not only to Talmon but to almost everyone who wrote on communism as a religion. John Maynard Keynes' *A Short View of Russia* (1925) used interchangeably the phrases "communist faith" and Leninism as a "new religion," where the word "new" was almost synonymous with "fanatical":

> Like other new religions, Leninism derives its power not from the multitude but from a small minority of enthusiastic converts, whose zeal and intolerance make each one the equal in strength of a hundred indifferentists. . . . Like other new religions, it persecutes without justice or pity those who actively resist it. Like other new religions, it is unscrupulous. Like other new religions, it is filled with missionary ardour and oecumenical ambitions. But to say that Leninism is the faith of a persecuting and propagating minority of fanatics is, after all, to say no more nor less than it *is* religion and not merely a party, and Lenin a Mahomet, not a Bismarck.
> *(Keynes, [1925] 2010, pp. 256–257)*

Comparing communism to Islam was even more pronounced in Jules Monnerot's *The Sociology of Communism* (1949), the first part of which explicitly spoke of it as "The Twentieth-Century Islam." (For Bertrand Russell's similar description see "Bolsehvism" in the present volume.) It stemmed from an overarching doctrine which it transformed into an eschatological faith, while – especially in the case of Stalinism – it united all power in one hand, which ultimately served the aim of establishing the political rule of a new empire.

References to communism as either a genuine or secular religion have been so frequent ever since that citing further examples would be superfluous. As

Raymond Aron – who himself inverted Marx's famous description of religion as the "opium of the people" to apply it to communism as *The Opium of the Intellectuals* (1955) – noted, the term "secular religion" had by the time of the Cold War become "a commonplace," and it was no longer possible to tell whether communism was a secular or a genuine religion:

> In a sense, the quarrel is a verbal one. Everything depends on one's definition of the words involved. The doctrine provides true Communists with a global interpretation of the universe; it instils sentiments akin to those of the crusaders of all ages; it fixes the hierarchy of values and establishes the norms of good conduct. It fulfils, in the individual and in the collective soul, some of the functions which the sociologist normally ascribes to religions.
>
> *(Aron, [1955] 1962, p. 265)*

Or maybe not even that, for Aron – after writing almost three hundred pages on the "transfer of the sacred" (ibid., p. xiii), the "super-reality" invoked by communist show trials (ibid., p. 122), the "joys of theological argument" in Soviet academia (ibid., p. 228), or "dogmas," "myths," "idolatry," and "heretics" – finally refrains from calling communism a religion or even a secular religion: "Communism is thus not so much a religion as a political attempt to find a substitute for religion in an ideology erected into a State orthodoxy." Or rather a substitute for Catholicism: "an orthodoxy which goes on cherishing claims and pretensions abandoned by the Catholic Church" (ibid., p. 286).

Apart from its terminological difficulties, it is an undeniable merit of Aron's work that it was among the first that investigated examples outside the Western civilization, mainly in Asia, where the "communist religion" was an instrument of anti-colonialism, even though he maintained that "the doctrine in whose name they threw out the barbarians" belonged to the "very essence of the West" (ibid., p. 263). It may or may not be true, but this is a question to be tackled in other entries of this book, from Juche to Maoism.

See also: Anarchism, Bolshevism, Juche, Maoism, Socialism

## Sources

Aron, R. (1955 [1962]) *The Opium of the Intellectuals*. Translated by Kilmartin, T. New York: W. W. Norton and Company.

Berdyaev, N. (1905) 'The Catechesis of Marxism' (Катехизис Марксизма), *Вопросы жизни*, 2, pp. 369–379. Available at: https://www.berdyaev.net/1905/the-catechesis-of-marxism/ (Accessed: 1 December 2023).

Berdyaev, N. (1906) 'Социализм как религия', *Вопросы философии и психологии*, 17(5), pp. 508–545. Available at: http://relig-library.pstu.ru/catalog/35/book-35.pdf (Accessed: 1 December 2023).

Berdyaev, N. (1917) 'The Religious Foundations of Bolshevism' (Религиозные основы большевизма), *Русская свобода*, 8 August. Available at: https://www.1260.org/Mary/Text/Text_Berdyaev_The_Religious_Foundations_of_Bolshevism_en.htm (Accessed: 1 December 2023).
Berdyaev, N. (1931) *The Russian Revolution*. London: Sheed and Ward.
Gerlich, F. (1920) *Der Kommunismus als Lehre vom tausendjährigen Reich*. München: H. Bruckmann.
Hudis, P. (2019) 'Marx's Concept of Socialism', in *The Oxford Handbook of Karl Marx*, edited by Vidal, M., Smith, T., Rotta, T., and Prew P. Oxford: Oxford University Press, pp. 757–772.
Keynes, J. M. ([1925] 2010) 'A Short View of Russia', in *Essays in Persuasion*. Basingstoke: Palgrave Macmillan, pp. 253–271.
Koselleck, R. (2006) *Begriffsgeschichten: Studien zur Semantik und Pragmatik der politischen und sozialen Sprache*. Frankfurt: Suhrkamp.
Monnerot, J. (1949) *Sociologie du communisme*. Paris: Gallimard.
Russell, B. ([1946] 2005) *The History of Western Philosophy*. London: Routledge.
Steele, D. R. (1992) *From Marx to Mises: Post-Capitalist Society and the Challenge of Economic Calculation*. La Salle: Open Court.
Talmon, J. L. (1952) *The Origins of Totalitarian Democracy*. London: Secker and Warburg.

## Computer science

See Artificial Intelligence, Dataism, Scientism, Technology, Transhumanism.

## Constitutionalism

Constitutionalism has a special importance for the history of secular (or more precisely, political) religions, for it was the first modern ideology that was suspected of having hidden religious leanings during the French Revolution. Although the term "political religion" had a long ancestry (Seitschek, 2007), it originally meant the explicit use of an already existing tradition to legitimize political power and to provide social cohesion, while its modern sense, introduced by the liberal philosopher Condorcet in 1791, referred to a doctrine that was allegedly secular but, in reality, deplorably similar to former, religious creeds.

Condorcet's main concern was the new education plan of the French government that aimed to replace the catechism taught in religious (mostly Catholic) schools with its own, civil one, re-establishing an ideological hegemony that was thought to have been surpassed after the separation of church and state:

> It has been said that the teaching of the constitution of each country should be part of its national education. This is true, no doubt, if we speak of it as a fact; if we content ourselves with explaining and developing it; if, in teaching it, we confine ourselves to saying: *Such is the constitution established in the State to which all citizens must submit.*

But if we say that it must be taught as a doctrine in line with the principles of universal reason or arouse in its favor a blind enthusiasm which renders citizens incapable of judging it; if we say to them: *This is what you must worship and believe*; then it is a kind of political religion that we want to create. It is a chain that we prepare for the spirits, and we violate freedom in its most sacred rights, under the pretext of learning to cherish it.

*(Condorcet, [1791] 1989, p. 68)*

Condorcet's definition of religion thus involves reliance on a higher, transcendent authority (universal reason), a set of indisputable dogmas (principles that cannot be judged by laypersons), laid down in a holy scripture (the present constitution), and a fanatical devotion on part of the believer (a blind enthusiasm). All of which involve that "religion" is a negative word, a pejorative (a chain for the spirits), in contrast to some later authors who would criticize political religions because they are *political* and not because they are truly *religious*. For Condorcet, religion is bad enough, and its earthly copies are even worse.

It is, of course, highly dubious whether all religions have a transcendent absolute, a dogmatic system, and an officially adopted scripture, or whether the everyday practice of traditional religiosity is always characterized by an overwhelming enthusiasm. Even if Condorcet had Catholicism in mind (which was routinely called "fanaticism" in Enlightenment literature), he himself was not comfortable with his own terminology. For although political religion – exactly because it was "political" – was not a religion per se, he felt it necessary to add that it was not even a real political religion, only "a kind of" (*une espèce*) or a "sort of" (*une sort*) political religion, of which the English constitution was the best example:

Let the example of England become a lesson for other peoples: there, a superstitious respect for the constitution or for certain laws which supposedly serve national prosperity, a servile cult of a few maxims consecrated by the interest of the wealthy and powerful classes are part of the education; they are maintained for all those who want fortune or power; they have become a sort of political religion which makes almost impossible any progress towards the perfection of the constitution and the laws.

*(ibid., p. 70)*

This sort of political religion is thus linked to conservatism as the ideology of the ruling classes. Such criticism, however, blurs the line between religion, political religion, and political ideology, suggesting that the dividing line runs not between religion and non-religion but between tradition and progress, faith and reason, or blind obedience and critical thinking.

There are also a few scattered examples of the more positive use of the word "political religion" as reverence for the constitution. In the United States, an 1838 speech by Abraham Lincoln suggested that "support for the Constitution" should become the "political religion of the nation" (Lincoln, [1838] 1953, p. 112). Since, however, the text also added that politicians and preachers should work together to bring about this happy result, it is impossible to decide whether he meant a real religion or the mixture of a secular and a "real" one. Some authors therefore treat Lincoln's "political religion" as being synonymous with the American "civil religion" (Lenzner, 1999, p. 53), while others speak of an "almost sacred" obligation (Morel, 2007, p. 73) or a devotion to "republican ideals *instead* of God and scripture" (ibid., p. 88 n2).

Constitutional government was placed in a larger historical framework by Juan Donoso Cortés's 1850 *Discourse on the General Situation of Europe* in the Spanish parliament. According to Donoso, "religious affirmations and negations" all have their political counterparts. For instance, the religious affirmations:

1. "God exists and is everywhere"
2. "God reigns"
3. "God governs"

are analogous to the political affirmations:

1. "There is a king who is everywhere by means of his agents"
2. "The king reigns over his subjects"
3. "The king governs his subjects."
(Donoso Cortés, [1850] 2007, pp. 74–75)

The first religious negation is that of deism, which states that although God exists and reigns over the universe, He does not actually govern it. In other words, the fully transcendent creator of the world does not interfere in its subsequent operation. In the political world, the same idea is expressed by constitutionalism: the king – or any other authority – may create a constitution; it may pass laws, but from this very moment, laws take care of themselves. They are all there is, an absolute point of reference. In the 20th century, Carl Schmitt's *Political Theology* borrowed Donoso's scheme:

> The idea of the modern constitutional state triumphed together with deism, a theology and metaphysics that banished the miracle from the world. This theology and metaphysics rejected not only the transgression of the laws of nature through an exception brought about by direct

intervention, as is found in the idea of a miracle, but also the sovereign's direct intervention in a valid legal order.
*(Schmitt, [1922] 2006, pp. 36–37)*

The sacred status of the constitution and the laws, however, still suggests a personal authority. That is why, according to Schmitt, "the 'omnipotence' of the modern lawgiver, of which one reads in every textbook on public law, is not only linguistically derived from theology" (ibid., p. 38) but is an expression of the inevitably theological nature of politics. The connection between constitutionalism and legalism (belief in the laws or the rule of law) is also a close one. As more recent critics of American constitutionalism would say:

The United States Constitution became an icon through which one could worship in the legal faith. The court emerged as a crucial institution, and the courtroom trial, as observed in person and as re-enacted in newspapers and fiction, served as an important secular ritual. Most importantly, a belief in the rule of law became a central American commitment.
*(Papke, 1998, p. 3)*

Such criticism broadens the horizon of analogies to include institutions and rituals, so – in contrast to Schmitt – we can speak of a political or secular *religion* and not just a political *theology*. David Ray Papke's *Heretics in the Temple*, however, remains ambiguous about the terminology, when it says that the cult of the constitution is not a "conventional religion" because it lacks a "godhead," a "priesthood," and a "church," even though the constitution itself is a "totem" and the nation is its "veritable temple" (ibid., pp. 3–4). The description of ritual practices in fact perfectly fits a functionalist definition of religion: "seeing others perform the established rites provides reassurance that one belongs to a community of believers" (ibid., p. 8).

In the United States, the debates about constitutional originalism – the idea that the whole constitution must be interpreted based on its original understanding at the time it was adopted – remind some observers of theological disputes. "Defenses and criticisms of originalism have come to seem to me more like disputes among theologians than like other academic inquiries," as Mark Tushnet remarks (Tushnet, 2008, p. 623), meaning that such debates rely on absolute convictions ("taken-for-granted background facts") which remain in the final analysis a matter of choice, or rather, a matter of faith. In 2018, Eric Segall devoted a whole book to *Originalism as Faith*, where "faith" refers to a form of false consciousness: the mistaken supposition that courts decide cases under the law as an abstract rule, while it is in fact always the justices' personal values (their own "articles of faith") that determine the outcome (Segall, 2018). The analogy to the Protestant *sola scriptura* principle – which Adrian Vermeule uses in his own criticism of originalism (Vermeule, 2020) – thus proves to be a deceptive one. Constitutions may be cited as absolute points of reference, creating the illusion that a sort of "paper deity" rules over all things human, but it is always the judges' intentions and personal preferences that decide matters, regardless of what one cites as their ultimate justification.

See also: Revolution, Statism

## Sources

Condorcet, J. A. N. C. ([1791] 1989) 'Cinq mémoires sur l'instruction publique', in *Écrits sur l'instruction publique*, Volume 1. Paris: Edilig.
Donoso Cortés, J. ([1850] 2007) 'Discourse on the General Situation of Europe', in *Readings in Political Theory*, translated by McNamara, V., and Schwartz, M. Ave Maria: Sapientia Press of Ave Maria University, pp. 67–82.
Lenzner, S. J. (1999) 'Civil Religion', in *Encyclopedia of Religion in American Politics*, edited by Schultz, J. D., West, J. G., and Maclean, I. Phoenix: Oryx.
Lincoln, A. ([1838] 1953) 'Address before the Young Men's Lyceum of Springfield, Illinois (27 January 1838)', in *The Collected Works of Abraham Lincoln*, Volume 1, edited by Basler, R. P. New Brunswick: Rutgers University Press.
Morel, L. E. (2007) 'Lincoln's Political Religion and Religious Politics: Or What Lincoln Teaches Us about the Proper Connection between Religion and Politics', in *Religion and the American Presidency*, edited by Rozell, M. J., and Whitney, G. New York: Palgrave Macmillan, pp. 73–93.
Papke, D. R. (1998) *Heretics in the Temple: Americans Who Reject the Nation's Legal Faith*. New York: New York University Press.
Schmitt, C. ([1922] 2006) *Political Theology: Four Chapters on the Concept of Sovereignty*. Translated by Schwab, G. Cambridge: MIT Press.
Segall, E. J. (2018) *Originalism as Faith*. Cambridge: Cambridge University Press.
Seitschek, H. O. (2007) 'Early Uses of the Concept 'Political Religion'', in *Totalitarianism and Political Religions*, Volume 3, edited by Meier, H. New York: Routledge, pp. 103–113.
Tushnet, M. (2008) 'Heller and the New Originalism', *Ohio State Law Journal*, 69, pp. 609–624. Available at: https://core.ac.uk/download/pdf/159569111.pdf (Accessed: 1 December, 2023).
Vermeule, A. (2020) 'Common-Good Constitutionalism Interview', *Mirror of Justice*, 20 April. Available at: https://mirrorofjustice.blogs.com/mirrorofjustice/2020/04/common-good-constitutionalism-interview-english-translation.html (Accessed: 1 December 2023).

## Consumerism

In contemporary journalism it has become a cliché to call consumerism a new religion. Many texts compare shopping malls to churches, advertisement to preaching, shopping to rituals, companies to sects, CEOs to bishops, fans to crusaders, or shopping trips to pilgrimages (Echysttas, 2017). However, as skeptics of secular-religious comparisons may point out, if any place where people gather can be called a "church," any persuasion a "sermon," any regular activity a "ritual," any community a "sect," any opinion leader a "bishop," any sufficiently enthusiastic person a "fanatic," and any considerably long voyage a "pilgrimage," then every human activity can be labeled religious. Moreover, such rhetoric uses the word "religion" in a less descriptive than derogatory fashion, leaving open the question whether traditional "organized" religions are more destructive than their new, consumerist counterparts. It is also a matter of debate whether capitalism is the same as consumerism or something different from it. "Religion" often seems hardly more than a clickbait term in the titles of articles that otherwise make no serious attempt to draw concrete analogies and change their wording from religion to "ideology" whenever they feel it is more suitable (Grafstrom, 2017).

Some authors, however, maintain that consumerism is indeed a religious phenomenon (even if a false one, a misguided "theodicy," Jackson and Pepper, 2011) or a "secular folk religion" (which is in turn both "transcendent" and "quasi," Varul, 2015, p. 449 and 458). Sometimes the ambiguity goes as far as saying that consumerism is in many respects the opposite of religion ("As I researched the relationship between the two, I began to realize that consumerism and religion have many conflicting ideas"), which nevertheless does not prevent it from becoming "a religion of its own" (Rajendran, 2019).

It is thus better to say that consumerism blurs "the boundaries between the religious and secular spheres, to the extent that the religion/secular distinction becomes increasingly impotent," which, however, does not necessarily mean that consumerism itself is a religion; it is rather the cultural context that transforms every religious practice – including traditional ones – to its own de-institutionalized and event-based image (Gauthier, 2017). De-institutionalized does not simply mean individualistic, however. As two Finnish authors argue:

> Consumerism effectively binds the individual to the existential process of shared meaning-making in inescapable ways, and thus connects people together to form ever-expanding consumer societies prone to support the ideals of consumer culture. We also argue strongly against claims that consumerist lifestyles are inherently hollow, worthless, and purposeless. Instead, the perspective of religion reveals a most definite quest for the meaning of life and the construction of individual value – both claims directed outwards into the community in order to be validated externally.
> *(Kurenlahti and Salonen, 2018)*

In other words, the similarity of consumerism to religion may not be a bad thing, after all.

See also: Capitalism, Entertainment, Fandom

**Sources**

Echysttas, A. (2017) 'Consumerism as Religion', *Mentatul*, 24 March. Available at: https://mentatul.com/2017/03/24/consumerism-as-religion/#comments (Accessed: 1 December 2023).

Gauthier, F. (2017) 'Religion Is Not What It Used to Be: Consumerism, Neoliberalism, and the Global Reshaping of Religion', *LSE Blogs*, 6 October. Available at: https://blogs.lse.ac.uk/religionglobalsociety/2017/10/religion-is-not-what-it-used-to-be-consumerism-neoliberalism-and-the-global-reshaping-of-religion/ (Accessed: 1 December 2023).

Grafstrom, S. L. (2017) 'Money as God, Consumerism as Religion', *Uttryck Magazine*, 30 June. Available at: https://www.uttryckmagazine.com/money-as-god-consumerism-as-religion/ (Accessed: 1 December 2023).

Jackson, T., and Pepper, M. (2011) 'Consumerism as Theodicy', in *Religion, Consumerism, and Sustainability*, edited by Thomas, L. London: Palgrave, pp. 17–36.

Kurenlahti, M., and Salonen, A. O. (2018) 'Rethinking Consumerism from the Perspective of Religion', *Sustainability*, 10, p. 2454. https://doi.org/10.3390/su10072454

Rajendran, N. (2019) 'Consumerism: A New Religion?', *LinkedIn*, 25 March. Available at: https://www.linkedin.com/pulse/consumerism-new-religion-nethra-rajendran/ (Accessed: 1 December 2023).

Varul, M. Z. (2015) 'Consumerism as Folk Religion: Transcendence, Probation and Dissatisfaction with Capitalism', *Studies in Christian Ethics*, 28(4), pp. 447–460. https://doi.org/10.1177/0953946814565984

## Critical race theory

See Postmodernism, Racism, Wokeness.

## Cultural Marxism

See Marxism, Multiculturalism, Postmodernism, Socialism, Wokeness.

# D
## DATAISM

"Dataism" is described as a religion (the "data religion") in Yuval Noah Harari's best-selling book *Homo Deus*, which states that treating all organisms as bundles of information or mere algorithms is an "all-encompassing dogma" (Harari, 2015, p. 462). It profoundly transforms our views of the human being, the meaning of life, and world history, which hereafter becomes not one determined by ideas or ideologies but by the competition of "data-processing systems" (ibid., p. 430). Since all these features (and others like dataism's prophecies, moral commandments, or missionary zeal, ibid., p. 445) are reliant on the concept of progress in artificial intelligence, science, and technology, its effects are discussed in more detail in the latter entries.

See also: Artificial Intelligence, Posthumanism, Scientism, Technology

### Sources

Harari, Y. N. (2015) *Homo Deus: A Brief History of Tomorrow*. London: Vintage.

### Darwinism

See Evolutionism.

### Democracy

The most obvious sign of the religious character of modern democracy is the unquestionable principle of popular sovereignty which its early critics like Alexis de Tocqueville explicitly called a "dogma." The term occurs more than fifteen times in Tocqueville's *Democracy in America* which also states that "The people rule the American political world as God rules the universe. They are the cause and end of all things; everything arises from them, and everything is absorbed by them" (Tocqueville, [1835] 2010, p. 97). The French original, where *le peuple* is in the singular, makes the analogy with God even more palpable.

The people, at the same time, do not exist as an objective reality. As the Russian religious philosopher Nicolai Berdyaev said, "The people is not a class, nor an estate. The people is not and cannot be an arithmetic combination of individual wills. . . . The people, as a reality, is a certain mystical organism" (Berdyaev, 1906, pp. 36–37). Or, as the Italian sociologist Vilfredo Pareto remarked in his *The Mind and Society*:

> We must not be led astray by the term "people," which seems to designate a concrete thing. Of course, the sum of the inhabitants of a country might be called a "people," and a "people" in such a case is a real, concrete thing. But only in virtue of an abstraction wholly foreign to reality can such an aggregate be regarded as a person possessing a will and the power to express it.
> 
> *(Pareto, [1916] 1935, p. 972)*

That is why the people's will is usually replaced by the will of the majority. As Tocqueville observed, the majority is thereby endowed with a series of divine attributes: it is omnipotent ("The very essence of democratic governments is that the dominion of the majority be absolute" Tocqueville, [1835] 2010, p. 403), omnipresent (ibid., p. 329), and perfectly good ("The French, under the old monarchy, held as a given that the king could do no wrong . . . Americans have the same opinion about the majority," ibid., p. 405). Its power – the power of public opinion – is more spiritual than physical ("Princes had, so to speak, materialized violence; the democratic republics of today have made violence as entirely intellectual as the human will that it wants to constrain," ibid., p. 418). Its perfect qualities are inseparable from each other, showing something like divine simplicity and unity in Christian theology:

> It is true that courtiers, in America, do not say: Sire and Your Majesty, a grand and capital difference; but they talk constantly about the natural enlightenment of their master. They do not raise the question of knowing which one of the virtues of the prince most merits adoration; for they assert that he possesses all virtues, without having acquired them and, so to speak, without wanting to do so.
> 
> *(ibid., p. 423)*

The identification of the majority with the people (the part with the hole) is obviously groundless: "Evidently the will of the majority is the will of the majority and not the will of 'the people.' The latter is a mosaic that the former completely fails to represent," as Joseph Schumpeter would say in the 20th century (Schumpeter, [1942] 2003, p. 272). Moreover, the majority has no more objective reality than the people, especially if its will is expressed by an elected body, in which case different electoral systems can produce totally different majorities (Nyirkos, 2018, pp. 116–122). To think that parliaments still express the will of the community is not something we *know* but something we are compelled to *believe* in. As Herbert Spencer said:

> The great political superstition of the past was the divine right of kings. The great political superstition of the present is the divine right of parliaments. The oil of anointing seems unawares to have dripped from the head of the one on to the heads of the many and given sacredness to them also and to their decrees.
>
> *(Spencer, [1884] 1960, p. 174)*

Or as Italian political scientist Gaetano Mosca remarked:

> A conscientious observer would be obliged to confess that, if no one has ever seen the authentic document by which the Lord empowered certain privileged persons or families to rule his people on his behalf, neither can it be maintained that a popular election, however liberal the suffrage may be, is ordinarily the expression of the will of the people, or even the will of the majority of a people.
>
> *(Mosca, [1896] 1939, p. 71)*

Although today it sounds outrageous to call democratic belief irrational, the first half of the 20th century was full of such allegations. In 1934, the president of the American Political Science Association, Walter J. Shepard noted that the democratic dogma of the people's wisdom rested on the assumption that people made their own decisions independently and rationally, which in the age of pressure groups and propaganda was mere fiction: "We have learned much since the Age of Reason regarding the phenomena of social psychology" (Shepard, 1935, p. 7). Or, as Ralph Henry Gabriel's *The Course of American Democratic Thought* put it in 1940: "The persistence of the democratic faith in an age of science is a phenomenon of significance. The essence of the formula is faith. Not one of its doctrines can be proved in any scientific sense" (Gabriel, 1940, p. 382). Conservative author Erik von Kuehnelt-Leddihn gave a list of no less than seventeen unscientific "dogmas" of democracy, most of which concerned equality ("All human beings are equal," "Everybody is able to judge every political question," "The functional value of the ignorant and the learned are the same"), the majority principle ("One human being can err, the majority of a group never," "Majorities are the better part of the whole," "A majority suppressing a minority is a lesser evil than a minority dominating a majority"), and social psychology ("The masses value liberty more than everything else" (Kuehnelt-Leddihn, 1943, p. 104).

The vexing contradiction between the fundamental dogma of democracy (the existence of autonomous individuals capable of making their own decisions) and scientific doubts about free will and independent motivation has not disappeared ever since. What happened instead was that political declarations have been isolated from the findings of brain studies and social psychology. This outcome had also been predicted by historians such as Crane Brinton in the mid-20th century:

> Democracy, in short, is in part a system of judgments inconsistent with what scientists hold to be true. This inconsistency would not create difficulties – or at least would not create some of the difficulties it now creates – were the democratic able to say that his kingdom is not of this world, able to say that his truth is not the kind that is in the least tested by the scientist, any more than the truth of the Catholic doctrine of the Eucharist is tested by the chemical analysis of the bread and wine. Such a solution of the democrat's intellectual quandary is not a happy one, but it is not altogether inconceivable. Democracy may become a genuinely transcendental faith, in which belief is not weakened by lack of correspondence between the propositions it lays down and the facts of life on this earth. . . . In short, democracy may be able to take its promised heaven out of this world, and put it in the world of ritual performed, of transcendental belief, or vicarious satisfactions of human wants, may keep it an ideal not too much sullied by the contrast with the spotted reality.
> *(Brinton, 1950, p. 549)*

The ritual manifestations of democracy may nowadays be less frequent than in earlier ages when elections were preceded by ritual processions and ballot boxes were placed upon altars flanked with republican symbols (as during the first French general elections in 1848, Rosanvallon, 2006, pp. 108–109), but they are not entirely absent. As Elias Canetti remarked, "the moment in which he [the elector] casts his vote is almost sacred; the sealed boxes which hold the ballot papers are sacred; and so is the count" (Canetti, [1960] 1981, p. 190). Elections continue to be seen as the celebrations of democracy, new voters are greeted with special ceremonies in several countries, and democratically elected politicians are inaugurated into office by highly formal liturgical procedures. Where democracy is new or non-existent, its worship may take extreme forms. During the 1989 student protests on Tienanmen Square in Beijing, a statue of the "Goddess of Democracy" was erected and greeted with something like a religious sermon:

> Democracy, how long has it been since we last saw you . . .? You are the Chinese nation's hope for salvation! Today, here in the People's Square,

the people's Goddess stands tall and announces to the whole world: A consciousness of democracy has awakened among the Chinese people! The new era has begun! From this piece of ancient earth grows the tree of democracy and freedom, putting forth gorgeous flowers and a bountiful harvest of fruit. The statue of the Goddess of Democracy is made of plaster, and of course cannot stand here forever. But as symbol of the people's hearts, she is divine and inviolate . . . We have strong faith that that day will come at last. We have still another hope: Chinese people arise! Erect the statue of the Goddess of Democracy in your millions of hearts.

*(cited by Deneen, 2005, p. xv)*

Obviously, the religious vocabulary (salvation, Goddess, divine, and faith) does not refer to the reality of existing democracies struggling with voter apathy, corruption, or the hidden power of lobbies. Democratic faith is not about this-worldly democracy but its celestial copy: a world of equality and freedom that remains the promise of the future ("a new era"). In other words, it is no longer seen as a form of government among others, but as the last best hope of humanity, to which no justifiable alternative exists.

The nomenclature of comparing democracy to religion nevertheless remains vague. Tocqueville himself – despite all the analogies he listed – finally refrained from calling democracy a religion; Spencer only spoke of a "political superstition"; Mosca of an "in a sense religious" phenomenon which was at the same time "shorn of strictly theological elements" (Mosca, [1896] 1939, p. 166). Pareto, on the other hand, systematically used the word "democratic religion," although the analogy was drawn almost exclusively with Christianity:

The many varieties of Socialism, Syndicalism, Radicalism, Tolstoyism, pacifism, humanitarianism, Solidarism, and so on, form a sum that may be said to belong to the democratic religion, much as there was a sum of numberless sects in the early days of the Christian religion. We are now witnessing the rise and dominance of the democratic religion, just as the men of the first centuries of our era witnessed the rise of the Christian religion and the beginnings of its dominion. The two phenomena present many profoundly significant analogies.

*(Pareto, [1916] 1935, p. 1294)*

This also means that democracy is an overarching category whose name can be used by any political ideology with an egalitarian or emancipatory agenda. What makes this possible is the ever-growing vagueness of the term. The German legal scholar Erich Küchenhoff already complained in 1967 that democracy became an "all-embracing idol concept," referring to its mutually exclusive uses from people's democracies to liberal or Christian democracies, and its nevertheless unquestionable status as the highest political and social ideal (Küchenhoff, 1967, p. 653). By the 2000s, the Romanian historian Lucian Boia could write in his *Myth of Democracy* that the meaning of the word has become so manifold as to express nothing else than the "good" form of government and society (Boia, 2002, p. 98). Others prefer to speak of a *Democratic Faith*, either in a critical way as American conservative author Patrick Deneen or in a more positive sense that tries to avoid the negative connotations of "religion" or "myth" (Schwartz, 2006; Rothman, 2016; Kahn, 2017; Sniderman, 2017; Rockefeller, 2020). The fact that we need "faith" in democracy nevertheless indicates a profound uncertainty about its this-worldly character and scientifically proven superiority above all other forms of social and political organization.

See also: Constitutionalism, Liberalism, Progress, Revolution

## Sources

Berdyaev, N. (1906) 'Concerning the Will of the People'. Available at: https://www.berdyaev.net/1906/concerning-the-will-of-the-people/ (Accessed: 1 December 2023).
Boia, L. (2002) *Le mythe de la démocratie*. Paris: Belles Lettres.
Brinton, C. C. (1950) *Ideas and Men*. New York: Prentice-Hall.
Canetti, E. ([1960] 1981) *Crowds and Power*. Translated by Stewart, C. New York: Continuum.
Deneen, P. J. (2005) *Democratic Faith*. Princeton: Princeton University Press.
Gabriel, R. H. (1940) *The Course of American Democratic Thought*. New York: The Ronald Press.
Kahn, J. S. (2017) 'The Virtue of Democratic Faith: A Recovery for Difficult Times', *Political Theology*, 18(2), pp. 137–156. https://doi.org/10.1080/1462317X.2016.1224136
Küchenhoff, E. (1967) *Möglichkeiten und Grenzen begrifflicher Klarheit in der Staatsformenlehre*, Teil I. Berlin: Duncker & Humblot.
Kuehnelt-Leddihn, E. R. (1943) *The Menace of the Herd, or Procrustes at Large*. Milwaukee: The Bruce Publishing Company.
Mosca, G. ([1896] 1939) *The Ruling Class*. Translated by Kahn, H. D. New York: McGraw-Hill.
Pareto, V. ([1916] 1935) *The Mind and Society*. Translated by Bongiorno, A., and Livingston, A. New York: Harcourt, Brace and Company.
Rockefeller, S. C. (2020) 'Renewing the American Democratic Faith', *State of American Democracy*, 16 September. Available at: https://stateofamericandemocracy.org/renewing-the-american-democratic-faith/ (Accessed: 1 December 2023).
Rosanvallon, P. (2006) 'The Republic of Universal Suffrage', in *Democracy Past and Future*, translated by Mason, L. New York: Columbia University Press, pp. 98–114.
Rothman, J. (2016) 'How to Restore Your Faith in Democracy', *The New Yorker*, 11 November. Available at: https://www.newyorker.com/culture/persons-of-interest/how-to-restore-your-faith-in-democracy (Accessed: 1 December 2023).
Schumpeter, J. ([1943] 2003) *Capitalism, Socialism and Democracy*. New York: Routledge.
Schwartz, E. (2006) 'A Democratic Faith', *Journal of Law and Religion*, 21(2), pp. 407–412. Available at: http://www.jstor.org/stable/30040592

Shepard, W. J. (1935) 'Democracy in Transition', *The American Political Science Review*, 29(1), pp. 1–20.
Sniderman, P. M. (2017) *The Democratic Faith: Essays on Democratic Citizenship*. New Haven: Yale University Press.
Spencer, H. ([1884] 1960) *The Man versus the State*. Caldwell: Caxton. Available at: http://www.jstor.org/stable/30040592
Tocqueville, A. ([1835] 2010) *Democracy in America*. Translated by Schleifer, J. T. Indianapolis: Liberty Fund.

## DNA

See Genetics.

# E
# ECOLOGY

Ecology (understood not as an academic discipline but as an ideology and movement, sometimes also called "ecologism," Vincent, 2010, p. 198) is one of the least secular of the so-called secular religions. There are overtly religious (Christian, Buddhist, etc.) versions of ecological thought; some speak of "Mother Nature" or "Gaia" in an explicitly (albeit not traditionally) religious language, treating nature as a living and life-giving female deity; several currents of deep ecology remain embedded in a more impersonal, yet still religious (pantheistic) metaphysics; finally, some self-professedly secular beliefs and practices are regularly unmasked by skeptics as being covertly religious.

What advocates and critics both point out is that the "ecological religion" does treat nature as an absolute. Not in its present form, though, but as it should be, or as it was before humanity appeared, which suggests a sort of transcendence and salvation history. In the beginning there was a golden age, of which there are still remnants in the so-called untouched areas such as the "churches" of the forests or the "cathedrals" of the wilderness, as John Muir, founder of Sierra Club liked to say (Nelson, 2010, p. 14). At the beginning of history, even human beings were innocent of the sins of their descendants:

> Early humans (some would go so far as to say "before industrialization") had a much more responsive and caring view of the world around them. The impression is that pre-industrial or primal peoples implicitly respected nature and only took from it what they needed; whether they were hunter-gatherers or market gardeners, their more animistic perspective led them to care for nature.
> 
> *(Vincent, 2010, p. 200)*

DOI: 10.4324/9781003471257-6

Celts, native Americans, or early Buddhists are also often presented as "an example of a life in harmony with nature in its original form" (Ferry, 1995, p. 70). Their earthly paradise was only corrupted later by the "original sin" of human exploitation, which shows that despite appearances, the ecological religion still stands closer to Christianity than to paganism or Buddhism. More exactly, the moral relentlessness of radical ecologism, the whipping of human pride and arrogance, the juxtaposition of God (or, in this case, nature), and the corrupt human being rather fit into the Puritan tradition. Original sin is not a personal act but something embedded in human existence: it is humanity as a whole that is the "cancer of the earth" as David Brower, executive director of Sierra Club and Dave Foreman, founder of Earth First! said (Nelson, 2010, pp. 81 and 121) or the "AIDS of the earth" as Paul Watson, one of the founders of Greenpeace, put it (Watson, 1988).

There are "infidels" (like climate skeptics) who entirely reject this narrative, but there are also "heretics" who only dispute some of its elements, suggesting that global warming might also have positive effects, opening new areas for settlement and agriculture (Nelson, 2010, p. 11). Economist William Nordhaus carried out detailed cost-benefit calculations on how much it is worth investing in mitigating the effects of climate change and how this compares to the results expected from such an investment. His calculations were at the same time outrageous for those who saw nature as a value in itself and considered saving habitats, plants, and animals an absolute duty. As American physicist Freeman Dyson replied to Nordhaus: care for nature is not a scientific issue, but an expression of moral responsibility (Dyson, 2008). Theologians such as Holmes Rolston even called the economic development of the past four centuries "demonic," a "Faustian bargain" that led to a disaster whose "most sure sign is the ecological crisis" (Rolston, 2006, p. 309). This is also why authors like Robert Nelson speak of "new holy wars" between the "economical" and the "environmental" religion (which is not the best term, however, for radical ecology respects nature more than just the "environment" of humanity). Although more recent years saw the rise of "green capitalism," a transition to more nature-friendly products and technologies in the private sector, this, too, was immediately denounced by radical ecologists as a fraud or "myth," since the "entire capitalist system is premised on the privatization of gains and the socialization of losses" (Pistor, 2021), which makes any reconciliation between the two worldviews impossible.

Others, like political scientist Roger Pielke, argue for the exact opposite: that "climate heretics" like him are persecuted by both ecologists and big business (Pielke, 2016). "Heretic" in this case means the same as in theology: someone who dissents from one or more dogmas while trying to remain inside the church. (Pielke disputed that the frequency of storms was actually growing during the past few decades, while he never denied climate change itself.) He may have been wrong, but – as other critics remark – it is always problematic to treat scientific claims as dogmas, and even more problematic when the objectivity of science is extended to the field of morality. From the scientific fact that climate change is real, it does not automatically follow that people must behave in a certain way or another. "For there is always considerable danger that a new dogmatism will resurface when one claims to have found 'natural,' thus 'objective,' models of behavior, and to be able to decide *more geometrico* where good and evil lie" (Ferry, 1995, p. 84).

Reference to science is, of course, mandatory for everyone in our age who wants to appear modern, but the relationship between ecology and science is much more controversial. Aldo Leopold, the father of deep ecology, often criticized the "high priests of progress" and those "apostles" for whom "the only creed is salvation by the machine" (Nelson, 2010, p. 177), while many other authors (Michel Serres, Bill Devall, or Neil Everndon) condemned not only technological progress but also rationality and science that made it possible: "Ecology undermines not only the growth addict and the chronic developer, but science itself" (Everndon, 1978, cited by Devall and Sessions, 1985, p. 48).

The fundamental contradiction, however, is not between scientism and anti-scientism but between the doctrines of deep ecology and the facts of modern biology. When someone sees "untouched" ecosystems as the reflection of the divine, a world of undisturbed harmony, an end in itself, this is sharply contrary to the Darwinian image of nature, in which there is no harmony or teleology, only a struggle for survival, regardless of the "value" of one being or another (Nelson, 2010, p. 173). It is also dubious whether any part of the planet has remained untouched by human activity, regardless of what the justifications of environmental policies claim (Botkin, 1990, p. 194). As for the concept of "ecosystem," it is a theoretical construction without a fixed essence: ecosystems are what one perceives them to be, and their boundaries are drawn where the ecologist draws them. Their number is potentially infinite: a dunghill can be an ecosystem just as much as a forest or the whole Earth (Fitzsimmons, 1999, pp. 29–30). Words like "maturation," "cooperation," or "mutual benefits" of ecosystems (e.g., in Eugene Odum's 1953 classic textbook *The Fundamentals of Ecology*) say more about our belief in them than their objective reality.

In addition to soteriological and ontological dogmas, ecology also has practical moral commandments. The most important is asceticism or self-denial. Not only humanity is expected to renounce certain material goods such as mineral resources but also the individual should reject animal products (as in the case of ethical veganism) or the procreation of children to save the planet (Fleming, 2018). The exercise of monastic virtues (poverty and chastity) is supplemented with the *vita activa* of demonstrations, for example, attacks on artworks in museums around the world which went viral in

2022 and became a highly formalized ritual repeating the same chants and gestures (Benzine, 2022).

Sacred symbols of the ecological movement are also many and varied: from more traditional ones like the "Ecology Flag" to more postmodern ones like the icons of Greta Thunberg or "prayer candles" with her image (Amazon, 2022). This shows that an element of saint-worship is also present: in the case of Greta Thunberg, some even suspect the revival of the cult of "child saints" (Grant, 2019; Voshell, 2019). The label is not flat out rejected by the saint's followers or even the saint herself, who once called her own mental "difference" (Asperger's syndrome) a "superpower" (Thunberg, 2019). The mental and moral superiority of climate activists is also shown by their efforts to guide less developed people toward salvation. Robert Nelson calls this the "Save Africa from the Africans!" project, exemplified by the displacement of indigenous people from the Ngorongoro and Serengeti national parks to recreate a mystical vision of a pristine Garden of Eden (Nelson, 2010, p. 257).

The idea of a divine absolute, the full-fledged doctrine of sin and salvation, the part dogmatic, part mystical way of thinking, the rituals, the symbols, and the worship of saints all suggest that – at least a certain type of – ecological thought and practice can be called religious without restraint. Indeed, some of its own adherents call it a "religious" worldview. As the Norwegian philosopher Arne Naess who coined the term "deep ecology" said:

> Insofar as these deep feelings are religious, deep ecology has a religious component, and those people who have done the most to make societies aware of the destructive way in which we live in relation to natural settings have had such religious feelings.
>
> *(Bodian, 1982)*

Bill Duvall and George Sessions, who quote Naess approvingly, add that deep ecology is a "comprehensive religious and philosophical worldview" (Devall and Sessions, 1985, p. 65).

Others more modestly (and less coherently) speak of an "earthbound but transcendental" moral obligation, the reconciliation of religion and science, as the ecologist E. O. Wilson did in his *Creation* (Wilson, 2006, p. 168).

Words like "quasi-religion" are also used in both a positive and negative sense: as a German newspaper said, "The climate movement has been accused of being too preachy, quasi-religious and irrational. This is the best that can happen to it," meaning that without a positive utopia, a belief in a "paradise planet," and an emotional appeal the struggle against climate change will remain fruitless (Arzt, 2019). Interestingly, however, the same author also uses the word "religion," just as those criticisms that alternately call climate activism a "quasi-religious fervor" and a "religion" without adjective (Grant, 2019). "Secular religion" also appears in the discourse (Baker, 2019;

Drobinski, 2019) just as "secular eschatology" (Kuehn, 2019), showing the same uncertainty of authors as in all other cases of religious/secular parallelisms. Sometimes the same author uses as many different phrases as "pantheism," "dogmatism," "fundamentalism," or the "divinization of nature," which nevertheless leaves the biosphere as "quasi-divine," etc. (Ferry, 1995, pp. 79, 130, 134).

It thus remains problematic what ecology (or ecologism) really is. It is an obvious mistake of much of the literature that it does not distinguish rational, pragmatic, scientifically based environmentalism from the metaphysical claims of deep ecology or the exaggerations of ecological radicalism. But with the deepening of the climate crisis, the most radical ("religious") approach will predictably become more manifest even in those branches of the movement that do not explicitly call themselves "deep ecological."

See also: Animal rights, Capitalism, Economics, Scientism, Veganism

## Sources

Amazon (2022) 'Greta Thunberg Celebrity Prayer Candle'. Available at: https://www.amazon.com/Greta-Thunberg-Celebrity-Prayer-Candle/dp/B085S7WSGV (Accessed: 1 December 2023).

Arzt, I. (2019) 'Klima unser im Himmel', *Die Tageszeitung*, 26 September. Available at: https://taz.de/Klimaschutz-als-Religion/!5626370/ (Accessed: 1 December 2023).

Baker, G. (2019) 'St. Greta Spreads the Climate Gospel', *Wall Street Journal*, 20 September. Available at: https://www.wsj.com/articles/saint-greta-spreads-the-climate-gospel-11568989306 (Accessed: 1 December 2023).

Benzine, V. (2022) 'Here Is Every Artwork Attacked by Climate Activists This Year from the Mona Lisa to Girl with a Pearl Earring', *Artnet*, 31 October. Available at: https://news.artnet.com/art-world/here-is-every-artwork-attacked-by-climate-activists-this-year-from-the-mona-lisa-to-girl-with-a-pearl-earring-2200804 (Accessed: 1 December 2023).

Bodian, S. (1982) 'Simple in Means, Rich in Ends: A Conversation with Arne Naess', *Ten Directions*, Summer/Fall, pp. 10–15. Available at: https://openairphilosophy.org/wp-content/uploads/2019/02/OAP_Naess_Int_Bodian.pdf (Accessed: 1 December 2023).

Botkin, D. B. (1990) *Discordant Harmonies: A New Ecology for the Twenty-first Century*. Oxford: Oxford University Press.

Devall, B., and Sessions, G. (1985) *Deep Ecology: Living as If Nature Mattered*. Salt Lake City: Gibbs M. Smith.

Drobinski, M. (2019) 'Wenn Protest zur Säkular-Religion wird', *Süddeutsche Zeitung*, 21 September. Available at: https://www.sueddeutsche.de/politik/klimadebatte-wenn-protest-zur-saekular-religion-wird-1.4607802 (Accessed: 1 December 2023).

Dyson, F. (2008) 'The Question of Global Warming', *New York Review of Books*, June 12. Available at: http://www.nybooks.com/articles/2008/06/12/the-question-of-global-warming/ (Accessed: 1 December 2023).

Everndon, N. (1978) 'Beyond Ecology: Self, Place, and the Pathetic Fallacy', *North American Review*, 263(4), pp. 16–20. Available at: http://www.jstor.org/stable/25118053

Ferry, L. (1995) *The New Ecological Order*. Translated by Volk, C. Chicago: The University of Chicago Press.
Fitzsimmons, A. K. (1999) *Defending Illusions: Federal Protection of Ecosystems*. Lanham: Rowman and Littlefield.
Fleming, A. (2018) 'Would You Give Up Having Children to Save the Planet? Meet the Couples Who Have', *Guardian*, 20 June. Available at: https://www.theguardian.com/world/2018/jun/20/give-up-having-children-couples-save-planet-climate-crisis (Accessed: 1 December 2023).
Grant, M. (2019) 'Greta Thunberg Is the First Saint of Our Cruel Environmental Religion', *Telegraph*, 28 September. Available at: https://www.telegraph.co.uk/environment/2019/09/28/greta-thunberg-first-saint-cruel-new-environmental-religion/ (Accessed: 1 December 2023).
Kuehn, E. F. (2019) 'Is the Climate Crisis a Secular Eschatology?', *The University of Chicago Divinity School*, 3 October. Available at: https://divinity.uchicago.edu/sightings/articles/climate-crisis-secular-eschatology (Accessed: 1 December 2023).
Nelson, R. H. (2010) *The New Holy Wars: Economic Religion vs. Environmental Religion in Contemporary America*. University Park: The Pennsylvania State University Press.
Odum, E. (1953) *Fundamentals of Ecology*. Philadelphia: W. B. Saunders Company.
Pielke, R. Jr. (2016) 'My Unhappy Life as A Climate Heretic', *Wall Street Journal*, 2 December. Available at: https://www.wsj.com/articles/my-unhappy-life-as-a-climate-heretic-1480723518 (Accessed: 1 December 2023).
Pistor, K. (2021) 'The Myth of Green Capitalism', *Project Syndicate*, 21 September. Available at: https://www.project-syndicate.org/commentary/green-capitalism-myth-no-market-solution-to-climate-change-by-katharina-pistor-2021-09 (Accessed: 1 December 2023).
Rolston, H. III (2006) 'Caring for Nature: What Science and Economics Can't Teach Us but Religion Can', *Environmental Values*, 15(3), pp. 307–313. Available at: https://www.jstor.org/stable/30302158
Thunberg, G. (2019) Available at: https://twitter.com/GretaThunberg/status/1167916177927991296 (Accessed: 1 December 2023).
Vincent, A. (2010) *Modern Political Ideologies*. Malden: Wiley-Blackwell.
Voshell, F. (2019) 'Greta Thunberg: History's Warning about Secular Child Saints', *American Thinker*, 1 October. Available at: https://www.americanthinker.com/articles/2019/10/greta_thunberg_historys_warning_about_secular_child_saints.html (Accessed: 1 December 2023).
Watson, P. (1988) 'On the Precedence of Natural Law: Speech to the Sixth Western Public Interest Law Conference at the University of Oregon Law School', *Journal of Environmental Law and Litigation*, (3), pp. 79–90.
Wilson, E. O. (2006) *The Creation: An Appeal to Save Life on Earth*. New York: W. W. Norton and Company.

## Economics

The only reason this book treats economics as a separate "secular religion" is that several other works do the same. The difference from the secular religion of capitalism is that in such works economics as a social science becomes the decisive element, the effective creator, and operator of the whole belief system. This also means that not only "capitalist" economics may play such a role but in principle any other, regardless of its ideological context. Since, in this approach, economics appears as a theological way of reasoning, its institutions and representatives are also viewed as churches and priests, making it a highly institutionalized, "clerical" secular religion.

The fundamental dogma of economic theology is that the ultimate cause of all human misery is scarcity, and therefore redemption must also be economic in nature. Carl Schmitt's *The Age of Neutralizations and Depoliticizations* (1929) describes European history from the 16th to the 20th century as four distinct epochs in which the center of intellectual life gradually shifted from theology to metaphysics, then to morality, and finally, to "economism" as the final stage of secularization. Although Schmitt speaks of secularization, he implicitly admits (referring to Marx) that this final stage has its own transcendental point of reference: "It holds that economics is the basis and foundation of everything intellectual and spiritual" (Schmitt, [1929] 2007, p. 84). As more recent authors like Robert Nelson in his *Economics as Religion* note, this is exactly what makes economics a religion: "To the extent that any system of economic ideas offers an alternative vision of the 'ultimate values,' or 'ultimate reality,' that actually shapes the workings of history, economics is offering yet another grand prophesy in the biblical tradition" (Nelson, 2001, p. 23).

This means that economics is first and foremost a soteriological religion and – despite the word "religion" – it is more closely related to the Judeo-Christian tradition than to religion in general. The different schools of economics only represent different visions within this tradition. The prophecies of salvation, for instance, may take two different forms: in the "pre-millennial" form, the golden age of humanity will be preceded by a last great cataclysm (a revolution, as in Marx), while in the "post-millennial" one (represented by Keynes) we are already witnessing the beginning of the new era, in which only an endless improvement of conditions will follow (ibid., pp. 30–31).

In both cases, the religion of economics is closely connected to the religion of progress and the religions of science and technology. In the American progressive movement, faith in economic progress is also accompanied by faith in democracy and in America as a "promised land" (ibid., pp. 38–39). This feature of the progressive movement is in fact so obvious that its historians regularly use words like "gospel," "crusade," or "religious awakening" (ibid., p. 46).

Later schools of economics (the neoclassical, the Keynesian, or the subsequent generations of the Chicago school) differ from each other like Christian denominations do. With some wit, one can even draw analogies between the optimism of Keynes, who believed that the laws of economy were rationally calculable, and the Catholic optimism about the intelligibility of natural law (ibid., pp. 101–103) or between the "revolt" of the Chicago school against such optimism and the Protestant Reformation, which are also similar in their emphasis on the individual instead of institutions (ibid., pp. 113–114). Or, as John Rapley's *The Twilight of the Money Gods* suggests, Keynes's

"Catholicism" was already a response to the former "Protestantism" of the neoclassical school:

> His new doctrine was effectively to neoclassical economics a bit what Catholicism was to Protestantism: against the neoclassical belief in the need for individuals to find their own way to heaven, Keynes called for the community to be lifted as one.
> *(Rapley, 2017a, p. 173)*

The historical analogy thereby becomes somewhat strained, as if Protestantism was followed by Catholicism and the latter by Protestantism once again. Especially if parallels with Judaism are also involved, when the founder of the Chicago school, Frank Knight, is described as a Jewish patriarch: "As Paul Samuelson declared: 'Knight was the founder of the Chicago School in economics; if he was Abraham, Henry Simon was Isaac, and Milton Friedman was Jacob' to the Chicago gospel" (Nelson, 2001, p. 114). The presence of Abraham, Isaac, and Jacob in a gospel sounds strange enough, but when the same chapter also calls them the "Gods of Chicago," the analogies become so blurred as to be almost incomprehensible.

In any case, the different schools also resemble different Christian denominations because their dogmas cannot be empirically verified:

> For instance, when it had to decide who would win the 2013 Nobel Prize in Economics, the Swedish Central Bank was torn between [Robert] Shiller's claim that markets frequently got the price wrong and [Eugene] Fama's insistence that markets always got the price right, so it opted to split the difference and gave both men the medal – a bit of Solomonic wisdom that would have elicited howls of laughter had it been a science prize (just imagine the sort of headline that might have followed: "Evolutionary Biologist and Intelligent Design Creationist Share Prestigious Science Prize"). In economic theory, very often, you believe what you want to believe – and as with any act of faith, your choice of heads or tails will as likely reflect sentimental predisposition as scientific assessment.
> *(Rapley, 2017a, p. 402)*

That is why economists need to establish schools and gain followers before they can exert influence, "as happens with preachers who gather a congregation" (Rapley, 2017b). Comparing economists to preachers, prophets, or priests is indeed pervasive in the literature on economic religion. According to Robert Nelson, the "basic role of economists is to serve as the priesthood of a modern secular religion of economic progress that serves many of the same functions in contemporary society as earlier Christian and other religions did in their time" (Nelson, 2001, p. xv). Or, as Rapley says, "Over time, successive economists slid into the role we had removed from the churchmen: giving us guidance on how to reach a promised land of material abundance and endless contentment" (Rapley, 2017b).

Apart from the functional analogy, economists are also expected to behave entirely differently than ordinary people do. Participants in the market follow their self-interest, while economists and economic decision-makers act in a public-spirited way. Almost as though we had "two species of human beings, one for the marketplace and one for the public sector" (Nelson, 2001, p. 99). All this is very similar to the distinction of lay people and priesthood in Catholicism. Most people cannot be expected to live their lives according to the same high standards as God's representatives on earth: the most they can do in a fallen and sinful world is to obey economic incentives. The work of priests and monks, in contrast, should never be motivated by self-interest.

Although Nelson refers here to those who believe in central planning and government regulation, the other (libertarian) party behaves in a no less priestly manner. The latter, as Nelson assumes, does nothing more than legitimize the individualistic trends prevalent in America since the 1960s:

> A modern priesthood is giving its approval in a new artistic imagery of economic "science." Chicago economists blessed the new changes in the technical language of economic efficiency, still the leading moral arbiter of good and evil, the most powerful source of social legitimacy in American life today.
>
> *(ibid., pp. 195–196)*

In the more sarcastic style of Paul Krugman (himself a Nobel Memorial Prize winner economist), free market economists are like holy warriors who have a just as confident knowledge about the working of the market as their predecessors about God's will:

> In the Middle Ages, the call for a crusade to conquer the Holy Land was met with cries of "Deus vult!" – God wills it. But did the crusaders really know what God wanted? Given how the venture turned out, apparently not. Now, that was a long time ago, and, in the areas I write about, invocations of God's presumed will are rare. You do, however, see a lot of policy crusades, and these are often justified with implicit cries of "Mercatus vult!" – the market wills it. But do those invoking the will of the market really know what markets want? Again, apparently not.
>
> *(Krugman, 2014)*

"Mercatus vult" is in Latin, the language of medieval clerics, but today's economists also have their own sacred language that separates them from the laity. According to Nelson, the mathematical and statistical formulas of modern economics are no more understandable to ordinary people than Latin used to be:

> It all served to convey an aura of majesty and religious authority – as does the Supreme Court in the United States, still sitting in priestly robes. In employing an arcane language of mathematics and statistics, Samuelson and fellow economists today seek a similar authority in society.
> *(Nelson, 2001, p. 100)*

Economics also has its sacred scriptures (the most famous being Samuelson's *Economics* that saw twenty editions until 2020 and was translated into more than forty languages) and its theological seminaries that were either transformed from former religious universities like Harvard and Yale or newly created as Chicago, Cornell, or Johns Hopkins. Some economists like George Stigler even compare the university community to a medieval monastery (ibid., p. 164).

Stigler also published a collection of essays titled *The Economist as Preacher*, in which, however, he made it clear that by "preaching" he only meant "a clear and reasoned recommendation (or, more often, denunciation) of a policy or form of behavior" (Stigler, 1982, p. 3). What he nevertheless realized was that any such preaching presupposes an ethical basis. This, however, also means that economists must become advocates of cultural change, especially in less developed countries, which stands very close to a religious mission: "In practice, organizations such as the World Bank and International Monetary Fund are routinely engaged in proselytizing efforts of this kind, seeking to teach 'modern' values" (Nelson, 2001, p. 260).

Because of such features (theological speculations, salvation histories, denominational differences, priests with their own sacred language and scriptures, seminaries and monasteries, or even missionary zeal), some authors speak simply of "religion" (Rapley, 2017a), while others remain more ambiguous, alternately using "religion" and "secular religion," for which the only explanation seems to be that their religious message is "implicit" (Nelson, 2001, p. 50) or that this message is more humanistic than theistic: "The place of the Christian God in explaining the workings of the world has been taken by the workings of the economic drive for individual gain (broadly conceived)" (ibid., p. 185).

Sometimes even economists speak of themselves in religious terms. Samuelson, as we have seen, called Eric Knight "Abraham," Stigler called him a "prophet" (ibid., p. 164), while in 1950, Knight himself called his own presidential speech at the AEA a "sermon" (ibid., p. 120), which, however, never prevented him from criticizing others using the same language: he repeatedly explained that nowadays science has become a religion and even named "scientific" socialism a secular equivalent of Christianity (ibid.,

p. 124). Such half-serious, half-ironical remarks nevertheless indicate that economists themselves are aware of the ambivalence of their science which is as much a prophecy about the advent of another world as a description of the present one.

See also: Capitalism, Marxism, Scientism

## Sources

Krugman, P. (2014) 'What Markets Will', *New York Times*, 16 October. Available at: https://www.nytimes.com/2014/10/17/opinion/paul-krugman-what-markets-will.html (Accessed: 1 December 2023).

Nelson, R. H. (2001) *Economics as Religion: From Samuelson to Chicago and Beyond*. University Park: The Pennsylvania State University Press.

Rapley, J. (2017a) *Twilight of the Money Gods: Economics as a Religion and How It All Went Wrong*. London: Simon and Schuster.

Rapley, J. (2017b) 'How Economics Became a Religion', *The Guardian*, 1 June. Available at: https://www.theguardian.com/news/2017/jul/11/how-economics-became-a-religion (Accessed: 1 December 2023).

Schmitt, C. ([1929] 2007) 'The Age of Neutralizations and Depoliticizations (1929)', in *The Concept of the Political*. Translated by Konzen, M., and McCormick, J. P. Chicago: The University of Chicago Press.

Stigler, G. J. (1982) *The Economist as Preacher and Other Essays*. Chicago: The University of Chicago Press.

## Electism

"Electism" is John McWhorter's former word for "woke racism," both of which he compared to religion in the wake of the 2020 BLM protests (McWhorter, 2021). The word here refers to the alleged elitism of the movement's leaders who see themselves as a sort of chosen people, more enlightened than the rest of humanity which they are thereby entitled to lead out of darkness. Although McWhorter later devoted a whole book to the (renamed) phenomenon, it is remarkable that already here, he speaks of no "analog" but a "straight-up religion." As it turns out, the main point of identity is not even the idea of the chosen people but

> that religion typically includes a wing of belief that must stand apart from empiricism . . . religious belief requires a person to sequester a part of their cognition for a kind of belief that is not based on logic.

The irony is that this is also true of all kinds of reasoning, as critics had pointed out long before: "It is idle to talk always of the alternative of reason and faith. Reason is itself a matter of faith. It is an act of faith to assert that our thoughts have any relation to reality at all" (Chesterton, 1909, p. 56). No wonder that skeptics criticized empirical knowledge already in antiquity, and after the rise of empiricism as an "ism" their descendants never failed to emphasize that its own first principle "only those propositions are meaningful that can be supported by empirical evidence" cannot be supported by empirical evidence. Which would, of course, lead to the more profound question of how to distinguish scientific first principles from religious ones, but McWhorter proudly declares that he has not studied religion. And perhaps only slightly more deeply science.

See also: Anti-racism, Wokeness

## Sources

Chesterton, G. K. (1909) *Orthodoxy*. London: John Lane.
McWhorter, J. (2021) 'Is It Just Hype to Call Electism a Religion?', 26 June. Available at: https://johnmcwhorter.substack.com/p/it-is-just-hype-to-call-electism (Accessed: 1 December 2023).

## Enlightenment

In Hans Kelsen's *Secular Religion*, a whole section is devoted to allegations which state that the so-called Enlightenment, despite its apparent irreligious or anti-religious traits, was in fact a large-scale attempt to create a new religion in place of Christianity. Kelsen himself rejected this view (as well as the very notion of "secular religion"), but the list of prominent authors who raised such allegations is worth a deeper look.

As Ernst Cassirer's *The Philosophy of the Enlightenment* noted, "The strongest intellectual forces of the Enlightenment do not lie in its rejection of belief but rather in the new form of faith which it proclaims, and in the new form of religion which it embodies" (Cassirer, [1932], 2009, pp. 135–136). This new form of religion may even be called a super-religion in the sense that it does not concern itself with this or that problem of traditional religions but with the very foundations of religion itself:

> The more insufficient one finds previous religious answers to basic questions of knowledge and morality, the more intensive and passionate become these questions themselves. The controversy from now on is no longer concerned with particular religious dogmas and their interpretation, but with the nature of religious certainty; it no longer deals with what is merely believed but with the nature, tendency, and function of belief as such.
>
> *(ibid., p. 136)*

The religious character of the Enlightenment thus consists in its quest for ultimate meaning and explanation and not in any formal practice or institutional arrangement. Similar views are manifested in Carl L. Becker's *The Heavenly City of the Eighteenth-Century Philosophers*, which claimed that "the

Philosophers were more akin to the religious than they knew" (Becker, 1932, pp. 41–42). Their battle cries against the tyranny of priests and for the liberation of humanity only dispensed with one form of enthusiasm to replace it with another, and this was not only a question of style or manners. It in fact suggested a prophetic vision; they knew "beforehand that the truth would make them free," even if this supposedly absolute truth later turned out to be no more than a "special brand of truth" that fitted their own purposes (ibid., p. 42). Becker in fact saw the Cult of the Supreme Being, introduced by Robespierre in 1794 during the French Revolution a logical outcome of the Enlightenment and not its aberration.

The religion of the Enlightenment is therefore not only a theoretical "supertheology" as Cassirer would have it, but (at least in some cases) a full-fledged cult with its symbolic and ritual elements. The mention of the "Heavenly City" refers to the even more important, salvation-historical element that is present in any progressive line of thought. The very word "Enlightenment" suggests that there is a necessary progress from darkness toward light, from ignorance toward knowledge, and from a valley of tears toward an earthly paradise. All these, however, presuppose a higher knowledge or a higher post of observation from which not only the past but also the future is visible. Or even more paradoxically, it presupposes a position from which our own position is also visible; otherwise, we might always fall victim to the prejudice of our own age that naturally sees itself more advanced than earlier ones.

"Enlightenment" is, of course, a very broad term that is sometimes used as a synonym for modernity, thereby encompassing other, "progressive" forms of secular religion. Although some authors (such as American historian Crance Brinton) are reluctant to use the term "religion," they also confirm that all such "worldviews" show a remarkable analogy with it:

> Since words like "religion" and "theology" applied, say, to modern Western nationalism, or to Marxism, or to any form of Enlightenment clearly do offend many Christians, I shall reluctantly fall back at times on that horrid Germanism "world view" (Weltanschauung).
>
> *(Brinton, 1959, p. 29)*

A few pages later, however, Brinton himself returns to the terminology of secular religions ("our own secular religions like nationalism, Marxism, the various positivist or rationalist beliefs stemming mostly from the eighteenth-century enlightenment," ibid., p. 39), secular churches ("the secular surrogate churches of the enlightenment," ibid., p. 191), faiths ("feminism as a faith is a product of the eighteenth-century enlightenment," ibid., p. 167), heresies ("rationalist enlightenment" as the "heretical belief that men are by nature good," ibid., p. 175), or even "the religion of the Enlightenment" without adjectives (ibid., pp. 163 and 266).

The enlightenment thus proves to be rather a complex of religions than just one religion: an umbrella term for "rationalism, humanism, scientism, naturalism, secularism, evolutionism, positivism, ethical culture" or "modern democracy," "belief in progress," and "Communism" (ibid., p. 275); the perhaps most overarching of them all.

See also: Atheism, Democracy, Evolutionism, Feminism, Humanism, Marxism, Nationalism, Progress, Revolution, Scientism

## Sources

Becker, C. L. (1932) *The Heavenly City of the Eighteenth-Century Philosophers*. New Haven: Yale University Press.
Brinton, C. (1959) *A History of Western Morals*. New York: Harcourt, Brace and Company.
Cassirer, E. ([1932] 2009) *The Philosophy of the Enlightenment*. Translated by Koelln, F. C. A., and Pettegrove, J. P. Princeton: Princeton University Press.
Kelsen, H. (2012) *Secular Religion: A Polemic against the Misinterpretation of Modern Social Philosophy, Science, and Politics as "New Religions."* Vienna: Springer.

## Entertainment

To call entertainment a "religion" already suggests that it is more than just a way of having fun or spending one's free time. As many authors assert, since the emergence of welfare societies in the second half of the 20th century, it has become a fundamental part of life, a source of meaning, and an instrument of re-enchanting a largely disenchanted world. The very concept suggests that it stands outside the realm of everyday routine, offering an escape to a more interesting, more colorful, perhaps even more real world than the ordinary. This idyllic sphere also has its transcendent inhabitants, the stars or celebrities as "super-personalities" (Morin, 1972), whose transcendence consists in the fact that with the help of modern technology they can overcome their physical limitations:

> The film amplifies the expressive intensity of the actor, particularly the beauty of their face; the disc and the radio permit the singer's voice to circulate without physical limits; the microphone liberates the artist and highlights the nuances of their personality.
>
> *(Piette, 1993, p. 59)*

And all this was written in the 1990s; today's technology is indeed capable of transforming the original qualities of the performer or creating virtual personalities with or without the original (see, e.g., the "new" Beatles songs of 2023 or shows such as "Abba Voyage"). The cult of the star and especially the celebrity is at the same time a more democratic phenomenon than that of the "genius" in romantic art, as the model it offers is allegedly available to everyone. Although the promoted lifestyle is an idealized one, a sort of heaven in which existence is a "permanent celebration" (Piette, 1993, p. 47), the sermon never ceases to suggest that what the stars or celebrities achieved by their own effort can be achieved by their admirers as well. The very concept of the "celeb" (which does not presuppose any special qualities other than being popular) best exemplifies this tendency.

The cult of entertainment is nevertheless a close relative of the cult of art as it emerged in the 19th century, with some minor varieties. If the artist was like a prophet or a savior, the stars or celebrities are more like saints who have their own hagiography (a life story constructed to inspire followers), their established iconography, their shrines (from Elvis Presley's Graceland to Jim Morrison's grave in the Père Lachaise), or their relics collected by the most devout followers. In some cases, the religious analogy is truly striking, for instance, when a star's relics are treated in the exact same way as those of

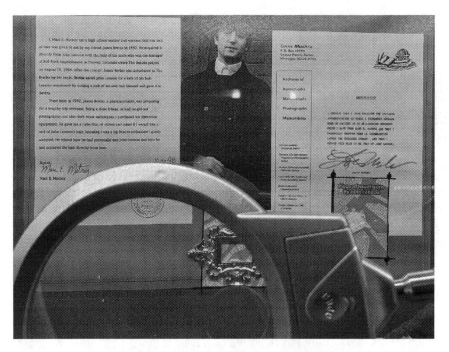

**FIGURE 1**   Officially authenticated relics of John Lennon in the Egri Road Beatles Museum, Eger, Hungary

*Source:* Egri Road Beatles Museum, Eger, Hungary, permission provided by the Museum

a medieval saint, with an official confirmation of authenticity issued by the appropriate authority.

As for the Beatles, Timothy Leary (American psychologist best known for his advocacy of psychedelic drugs in the 1960s) even called the members of the Beatles "St. Paul, St. John, St. George, and St. Ringo," the four evangelists inspired by the "big vibration" (ibid., p. 74).

Whether such analogies are only ironic or should be taken at face value is disputable, but the presence of full-fledged cults related to books, movies, TV shows, or computer games from *Harry Potter* and *Star Wars* to *Buffy the Vampire Slayer* and PlayStation's *Spider-Man* (Burton, 2020, pp. 63–90) suggests that there is in fact an entire universe of meanings and symbols that create actual communities centered around an imagined sacred. It is not even certain that the re-enchantment that such "religions" offer is as individualized as it is sometimes supposed. Since mass entertainment itself is a product of the entertainment industry, it has the same unifying tendency as capitalism or consumerism. As Ernest Gellner remarked, "Max Weber thought that rational industrial production brought with it the cold 'disenchanted' vision of the world," but what in fact happened was that industrial societies produced "more consumers, fewer producers; less time at work, more at leisure," and in consumption, everything tended "toward ease and facility rather than rigor and coldness." In our advanced societies, "re-enchantment itself is now mass-produced, standardized, and rationalized" (Gellner, 1979, pp. 61–64).

While some later accounts of the re-enchantment of the world emphasize the explicitly religious traits of such efforts (e.g., Ritzer, 1999), others maintain that it is exactly secularization that enchants, at least in the sense of revitalizing "magic" in a postmodern era (Josephson-Storm, 2017, pp. 35–36). Regardless of how we categorize entertainment (a secular religion, a remixed religion, or a form of magic), it remains true that in a functional sense it shows similar features as any traditional religion. It has a sense of transcendence (overcoming the boundaries of the here-and-now); an idea of the holy (holy persons, objects, or places); sacred scriptures (or, in a more advanced setting, audio-visual representations); a promise of salvation from the vale of tears, work, fatigue, and everyday routine; an often fanatical commitment to one's ideals or idols (see fandom); and a sense of community with those who share the same commitment.

See also: Art, Capitalism, Consumerism, Fandom, Rock

## Sources

Abba Voyage (2023) Available at: https://abbavoyage.com/. (Accessed: 1 December 2023).
Burton, T. I. (2020) *Strange Rites: New Religions for a Godless World*. New York: Public Affairs.

Gellner, E. (1979) *Spectacles and Predicaments: Essays in Social Theory*. Cambridge: Cambridge University Press.
Josephson-Storm, J. Ã. (2017) *The Myth of Disenchantment: Magic, Modernity, and the Birth of the Human Sciences*. Chicago: The University of Chicago Press.
Morin, E. (1972) *Les stars*. Paris: Seuil.
Piette, A. (1993) *Les religiosités séculières*. Paris: Presses Universitaires de France.
Ritzer, G. (1999) *Enchanting a Disenchanted World: Revolutionizing the Means of Consumption*. Thousand Oaks, CA: Pine Forge Press.

## Environmentalism

Since the word "environmentalism" suggests that nature is only important as the environment of human beings and thereby retains an anthropocentric outlook, the more radical (and thereby allegedly "religious") forms of the ecological movement are discussed under the more general heading of ecology.
See: Ecology.

## Evolutionism

The theory of biological evolution is more than just a scientific doctrine. As British philosopher Mary Midgley argues in her book *Evolution as a Religion*, it is "a powerful folktale about human origins" with a "symbolic force," something that has the capacity to replace the "theistic drama" with another, in which the human being appears as a lonely hero "challenging an alien and meaningless universe" (Midgley, 1985, p. 1). Or rather, as someone who creates a new meaning, for scientists themselves have a "very strong guiding imaginative system," a "world-picture," which is not a mistake but the very foundation of true scientific enquiry: "Merely to pile up information indiscriminately is an idiot's task. Good scientists do not approximate to that ideal at all" (ibid., p. 3). The only question is whether these worldviews remain connected to science, or become distortive "myths," as in the "cosmic pessimism" of social Darwinism and racism, or in the "cosmic optimism" of progressive ideologies (ibid., p. 7).

Those myths already belong to the realm of secular religions, and it should also be noted that the idea of an ongoing war between (evolutionary) science and (traditional) religion is a myth of relatively recent origin. The early debates about Darwinism

> did not appear at the time as raging between science and religion, but as cutting straight across both. Darwin's most serious opponents by far were the official scientific establishment of his day and many of his supporters, such as Charles Kingsley and H. G. Baden-Powell, were clergymen.
> *(ibid., p. 10)*

According to Midgley, it was Thomas Henry Huxley, Darwin's main popularizer ("Darwin's bulldog"), who first created the myth of a "holy war" between evolutionary science and the Christian church, while in doing so, he himself implicitly acknowledged that the spheres of science and religion could not be fully separated:

> His thoughts ranged remarkably widely, and he certainly saw no need to draw a sharp line between even their widest ranges and his scientific views. He thought as a whole person, a person who was a scientist. And it seemed to him that it was essentially scientific business which brought him into conflict with religion. But on the narrower notions of science which have come out of his work, this can scarcely be right.
> 
> *(ibid., p. 12)*

By the early 20th century, it became customary to speak of Darwinism as a new worldview that dealt with the same existential questions as traditional religions and with the same authority. As Gilbert Keith Chesterton wrote in the *Illustrated London News* in 1922, "In the outer courts the statue of Darwin is still the statue of a god," only to add that while in science Darwin's theory had already been profoundly modified, some of its original claims were still popularized as a sort of orthodoxy:

> Evolution has become not a perception but a prejudice; because it is not an invention, which most people can touch and even tinker with, but an origin, which most people prefer to leave undisturbed . . . In all these abstract or aboriginal problems, therefore, men do not seek the stimulus or progress which is sought in applied science; they rather seek the repose that is sought in religion.
> 
> *(Chesterton, 1922, p. 496)*

Chesterton thus identified the main religious features of evolutionism as the blind veneration of a holy person, an established orthodoxy with its dogmas about origins and principles, and the emotional comfort that all these provided to simple believers by offering an overarching explanation of the meaning of life. The popular form of evolutionism had also established its own sacred spaces by then, for instance, the Natural History Museum in London (opened in 1881), which is sometimes still presented as a "cathedral" of evolutionary science, alongside medieval churches such as the Laon cathedral (Ruse, 2003).

Evolutionism has also been compared to other "secular faiths": those of humanity, democracy, art, medicine, economics, money, or Marxism (Midgley, 1985, p. 15), all of which show a more profound analogy with "real" religions than it is usually supposed. "It is not like saying that golf is someone's religion, which is probably just a joke, and at most means only that it is the most important thing in his life, the thing to which the rest gives place." In secular faiths, we "find priesthoods, prophecies, devotion, bigotry, exaltation, heresy-hunting and sectarianism, ritual, sacrifice, fanaticism, notions of sin, absolution and salvation, and the confident promise of a heaven in the future" (ibid., pp. 15–16).

Whether all these are found in evolutionism remains dubious, however. Midgley herself scarcely writes about popularizers as priests; somewhat more about prophecies (of a higher form of consciousness, for instance, the "Omega Man"); or genetic engineering as the exaltation of the human condition (ibid., p. 33). The main object of her criticism is the unfounded belief in progress ("the irresistible escalator") that seems all the more religious since it is connected to the no less unfounded belief in "Life," a clandestine supernatural entity that fills the role of God. "References to it cannot really be taken as pure metaphor, because its function as unfailing planner is needed to guarantee that the future part of the escalator is solid and reliable" (ibid., p. 62). As for heresy-hunting and fanaticism, it is enough to look at the opening or closing chapters of popular science books, which regularly transcend scientific argument. As Midgley remarks,

> When I have complained of this sort of thing to scientists, I have sometimes met a surprising defence, namely, that these remarks appear in the opening or closing chapters of books, and that everybody knows that what is found there is not to be taken literally; it is just flannel for the general public. The idea seems to be that supplying such flannel constitutes a kind of a ritual. If so, it must surely strengthen our present unease, since addiction to ritual is another fault supposed to be the mark of religion.
> 
> *(ibid., p. 67)*

Let us note once again that neither Midgley nor Chesterton, let alone more recent authors like Michael Ruse, have ever been "enemies" of evolution as a scientific theory. Midgley's book is dedicated "To the memory of Charles Darwin who did not say these things," Chesterton said that Darwin was "a great man who sought and served knowledge with all the sincerity of a stronger generation," and Ruse made it clear in the introduction to his book *The Evolution-Creation Struggle* that he was a "committed evolutionist, an ardent Darwinian." What these – and many other, certainly non-creationist authors – emphasize is that a simplistic understanding of evolutionism has always showed a tendency to become a just as dogmatic system with its sacred scriptures, moral precepts, saints, prophets, priests, churches, and symbols as any other, allegedly non-scientific worldview. Whether to call it an "ideology" or a "religion" nevertheless remains dubious:

> An ideology, to be sure. But would the term "religion" also be appropriate? Considering the nature of the beast, it truly seems so. The concept of

a religion is notoriously hard to define, but one thinks in terms of a world picture, providing origins, a place (probably a special place) for humans, a guide to action, a meaning to life. . . . Rather than getting too flustered by counterexamples, let us allow the oxymoron "secular religion" and cast our question in these terms. And the answer does seem positive. Popular evolution – evolutionism – offered a world picture, a story of origins, and a special place for humans in the scheme of things. At the same time, it delivered moral exhortations, prescribing what we ought to do if we want things to continue well . . . In asking about origins, evolutionism was answering a question posed by Christianity (and Judaism before this), and in focusing on the status and obligations of humans, evolutionism was trying deliberately to do better than Christianity.

*(Ruse, 2005, p. 122)*

In other words, evolutionism still appears as a surrogate of Christianity or Judaism and not of religion in general. "Without Providence, without God's grace, we have nothing. No hope, no joy, no genuine relationships with our Maker and with ourselves. We have come a full circle and are back where we started" (Ruse, 2017, p. 279).

See also: Biotechnology, Progress, Scientism

## Sources

Chesterton, G. K. (1922) 'Our Notebook', *The Illustrated London News*, 8 April, p. 496.

Midgley, M. (1985) *Evolution as a Religion: Strange Hopes and Stranger Fears*. London: Methuen.

Ruse, M. (2003) 'Is Evolution a Secular Religion?', *Science*, 299 (7 March), pp. 1523–1524. https://doi.org/10.1126/science.1082968

Ruse, M. (2005) *The Evolution-Creation Struggle*. Cambridge, MA: Harvard University Press.

Ruse, M. (2017) *Darwinism as Religion: What Literature Tells Us About Evolution*. Oxford: Oxford University Press.

# F

## FANDOM

Fandom is an umbrella term for the cults of sport, film, literature, music, or any other branch of entertainment. As American screenwriter and producer Joss Whedon once said, fandom is "The closest thing to religion that isn't actually a religion" (Rogers, 2012).

Others, however, argue that it actually is. Being a fan gives meaning to one's life, offering a complete framework of myths, mythical heroes, and symbols for the interpretation of an otherwise meaningless world. In this sense, the imaginary world of fandom is even more authentic than the one we live in, just as in many ancient metaphysical traditions the "other world" was the real one and ours its second-rate copy (Molnar, 1988, p. 26).

In many films, TV shows, and books the topics themselves are metaphysical or supernatural:

> Today's mass culture – the strongest shaper of social imagination – is full of visions showing the intertwining of paranormal phenomena and the technological society that manipulates its members, from vampire movies to the X-files. "The truth is out there," as we all know.
>
> *(Kovács, 2021, p. 115)*

Even the works of "angry atheists" such as Joss Whedon are so full of "religious" themes that whole books can be written about them (Mills, Morehead, and Parker, 2013).

Endowing the world with meaning is also "a mechanism for collective identity-making and reinforcement," which Tara Isabella Burton calls "the very definition of a Durkheimian religion" (Burton, 2020, p. 67). It is not an exaggeration to speak of a spiritual community: "fans, while obviously not claiming to experience a revelation from God, are nevertheless claiming to experience a new and special relationship to another with whom they have not had any conventional contact or interaction" (Cavicchi, 1998, p. 52).

Identity-making is also closely connected to the moral guidance provided by the example of heroes, be they real or imagined. As Daniel Cavicchi writes in his book on Bruce Springsteen fandom:

> as Christians' ongoing, daily life of devotion to God involves interpretation of the Bible and thinking about how God's will is revealed in their lives, so fans' ongoing, daily life of devotion to music involves interpretation of Springsteen's songs and puzzling over how the music addresses their experiences.
>
> *(ibid., p. 186)*

Fans of any rock star know very well that a sufficiently complex oeuvre can serve as a complete guide (a collection of sacred scriptures) throughout one's life.

All this entails a strong enthusiasm originally associated with things divine; let us not forget that the word "fan" itself is an abbreviation of "fanatic," which in turn comes from the Latin word *fanum* (temple or sanctuary). And just as in temples, certain rituals and symbols are applied to sustain devotion, along with a specific (sacred) language: "The most successful fandom properties have been those that offer not just unity among their admirers but a coherent language for talking about the world" (Burton, 2020, p. 69).

Despite all similarities and the abundance of literature on them, however, some authors still insist that fandom is *not* a religion:

> Such interpretations miss the point. Fans' use of religious language in explaining and thinking about fandom and the clear parallels between their behavior and that of Christian believers do not mean that fandom is a religion; rather, they point to the fact that both fandom and religion are addressing similar concerns and engaging people in similar ways.
>
> *(Cavicchi, 1998, p. 187)*

By a closer look, however, it only implies that fandom is not Christianity and not that it is not a religion. In most cases, it is only the fans' self-perception that is different from that of a self-professedly religious person:

> All sorts of things fill in for religion for people who do not go to church, and music is certainly one of those things for me, and I definitely do feel as if I've been to a "spiritual revival" after a Bruce show, but it is very difficult to explain that to folks who have not experienced that feeling.
>
> *(ibid.)*

Those who reject the word "religion" often do it only because of its negative ring while happily accepting some other label, of which "spiritual" is the most fashionable. It nevertheless remains true that the comparison of fandom and religion is rarely followed with analytical rigor. As Michael Elliott observes:

> First and foremost, the specific meaning of religion tends to be assumed rather than defined, which makes the comparison unclear and difficult to scrutinize. Second, scholars can also cherry-pick one or two prominent features of religion that are clearly associated with fan behaviour and then claim equivalence between the two, which glosses over the complexity of religion and simplifies the comparison. Third, this comparison gets more confusing when scholars (a) are not clear about whether fandoms are *equivalent to* religion, *similar to* religion or *substitutes for* religion, (b) use other terms interchangeably with religion (e.g. cult, sacred, spiritual) or (c) introduce a plethora of hyphenated terms that are related to, but also distinct from, religion (e.g. para-religion, neo-religion, quasi-religion, implicit religion).
> *(Elliott, 2021, p. 119)*

Yet if one chooses a phrase "sacred but not religious" (or literally, "a *sacred* form that is based in a *secular* world" that is "not devoted to something supernatural or superhuman," ibid.) the whole problem of secular religions returns, for the "sacred" is by its very definition something beyond the natural or the human. A "profane sacred" is just as oxymoronic as a secular religion.

See also: Entertainment, Rock

## Sources

Burton, T. I. (2020) *Strange Rites: New Religions for a Godless World.* New York: Public Affairs.
Cavicchi, D. (1998) *Tramps Like Us: Music and Meaning among Springsteen Fans.* Oxford: Oxford University Press.
Elliott, M. A. (2021) 'Fandom as Religion: A Social-scientific Assessment', *Journal of Fandom Studies*, 9(2), pp. 107–122. https://doi.org/10.1386/ jfs_00036_1.
Kovács, G. (2021) *A kiborg és az emberi állapot.* Budapest: Liget.
Mills, A. R., Morehead, J. W., and Parker, J. R. (eds.) (2013) *Joss Whedon and Religion: Essays on an Angry Atheist's Explorations of the Sacred.* Jefferson: McFarland.
Molnar, T. (1988) *Twin Powers: Politics and the Sacred.* Grand Rapids: Eerdmans.
Rogers, A. (2012) 'Joss Whedon on Comic Books, Abusing Language and the Joys of Genre', *Wired*, 3 May. Available at: https://www.wired.com/2012/05/joss-whedon/. (Accessed: 1 December 2023).

## Fascism

Italian fascism – and not fascism in general, which is a more imprecise category – was originally difficult to distinguish from the religions of nationalism and patriotism, or the cult of the state that promoted them. These had a long prehistory in Italy, which can be traced back to the time of the Risorgimento (the unification of Italy in the 19th century), and have always had an overtly religious character. Leaders of the movement like Giuseppe Mazzini talked about Italy as a "religious idea," monuments were erected to the "immortal Fatherland," martyrs were remembered by solemn rituals like the roll call of fallen soldiers (Severino, 2017), holy days were celebrated by mass parades, and veterans of the war of independence and later the First World War acted like a true priesthood, preaching devotion to the nation and the country (Gentile, 1996, pp. 1–18).

Fascism was a direct continuation of this tradition. It did not have to be "uncovered" as a religion, for it openly declared what it was: "I recalled one of the mottoes flung high on the Rome Fascisti headquarters – '*Italia è una religione*' (Italy is a religion), and I could not help but see Mussolini in the light of a political Messiah – a super-Nationalist," as an American journalist wrote in the New York Times as early as 1922 (Rohe, 1922). In 1924, the philosopher and minister of education Giovanni Gentile confirmed the same connection between patriotism, fascism, and religion: "The *patria* is law and religion, which requires the subjection of the particular to a general and perennial interest, to an ideality superior to everything that has been and that is" (Gentile, 1924, p. 24). As he added, it was not even a secular, this-worldly religion but a real one: "the religion of the spirit that has not fallen into the abject blindness of materialism" (ibid., p. 36).

The difference between traditional patriotism and fascism (according to Emilio Gentile's *The Sacralization of Politics in Fascist Italy*) consisted in the extremely militant and intolerant character of the latter, a sacralization and mythologization of violence. For many fascists, it was a "way of continuing the war, of transforming its values into a civic religion." It turned the patriotic movement into an "armed militia" that was "determined to impose its religion on all Italians, and to deal with opponents unwilling to convert as reprobates, as the damned, as enemies who should be persecuted, punished, and exiled from the national community" (Gentile, 1996, pp. 20, 21).

Another special feature of fascism was its totalitarian nature, which was often described using Catholic analogies:

> One cannot be a fascist in politics and non-fascist . . . in school, non-fascist in one's own family, non-fascist in one's workshop. Just as the Catholic . . . if he is truly Catholic and has a religious sense will always remember his highest vocation to work and think and pray and meditate and feel as a Catholic; so the fascist, whether he is in the parliament or in the Fascio, whether he writes for the newspapers or reads them, whether he sees to his private life or talks to others, looks to the future or remembers his past and the past of his people, must always remember to be a fascist.
> 
> *(Gentile, 1924, p. 38)*

Catholicism was thus both a rival and a model for fascism: as Mussolini remarked as early as 1921, it was "the only universal idea surviving in the Rome of today" and a spiritual power of which Italians should be proud, a power that could "be used for national expansion" (Gentile, 1996, p. 53). While he maintained that fascist nationalism was itself a religion (Ellery, 1926, p. 668), Mussolini never hesitated to use the reverse, secularist argument against his adversaries. When asked about the Catholic priest and opposition politician Luigi Sturzo, he replied: "Priests should only say mass; they should not mix in profane affairs – like politics" (Rohe, 1922). Fascism, in other words, was only "secular" in the sense of not being Catholic; in any other context, it acted in a self-consciously religious way.

It also belonged to the unique character of the fascist religion that it developed a formerly unknown, large-scale worship of the leader. The 1926 party statute already called Mussolini the "Supreme Guide"; the word "Duce" was required to be written in capital letters; rituals such as the "Salute to the Duce" were created; through images and radio speeches modern technology made him omnipresent; and, ultimately, he was not just sanctified as a prophet, the savior of Italy, or the creator of fascism but literally deified as a God. As the fascist journalist Asvero Gravelli wrote: "God and history today mean Mussolini" (Gentile, 1996, pp. 135–137).

Regarding the overtly religious features of fascism, it is somewhat odd to call it a secular religion. Emilio Gentile's work itself vacillates between "religion," "secular religion," "political religion," "civic religion," and the "sacralization of politics." Of contemporary observers the Catholic theologian Novello Papafava spoke of a "new religion" (that also had dogmas, sacraments, and an infallible leader like Catholicism) but immediately added that it had no recourse to any revelation or divine anointment, so it was rather a false religion (Papafava, 1923). The liberal politician Giovanni Amendola – after speaking of the "crusade," the "baptism," and the "credo" of fascism – remained similarly ambiguous when stating that "fascism makes the same claims as a religion," which may have meant either that it was a religion or that it was deceptively similar to it (Amendola, [1923], 1960, pp. 193–194).

Others compared fascism to the civil religion of the French Revolution with its "altars of the fatherland," "tablets of law," and "civil processions" (De Nolva, 1924). The German legal scholar Hermann Heller compared it to "polytheistic paganism" in which "church and state were one" but also called it an "inverted religion" (Heller, 1929, p. 14), before ultimately admitting that "all normative concepts and imperatives of fascism, like religion, hierarchy, authority, discipline, state, law" were essentially empty (ibid., p. 63). American scholars Herbert Schneider and Shepard Clough, on the other hand, called fascism a "genuine religion" (Schneider and Clough, 1929, p. 189).

The scope of possibilities comes to an end here. What the example of fascism seems to illustrate is that some modern ideologies – especially with the help of technology and mass psychology – can become even more totalitarian than any of the traditional religions. It is no accident that the first use of the term "secular religion" was referring to this feature of modern dictatorships:

> It is true . . . that the dictators of the present are not lineal descendants of the despots and tyrants of the past, that those of today have a new and powerful technique in mass control through propaganda by radio, movie, press, education, and a secular religion of their own making.
> *(Ford, 1935, p. vii)*

See also: Nationalism, Nazism, Patriotism, Statism

## Sources

Amendola, G. ([1923] 1960) *La democrazia italiana contro il fascismo (1922–1924)*. Milano: Ricciardi.
De Nolva, R. (1924) 'Le mysticisme et l'esprit révolutionnaire du fascisme', *Mercure de France*, 1 November.
Ellery, E. (1926) 'Italian People under New Fascist Discipline', *Current History*, 24(6), pp. 966–969.
Ford, G. S. (ed.) (1935) *Dictatorship in the Modern World*. Minneapolis: University of Minnesota Press.
Gentile, E. (1996) *The Sacralization of Politics in Fascist Italy*. Translated by Botsford, K. Cambridge: Harvard University Press.
Gentile, G. (1924) *Che cosa è il fascismo: discorsi e polemiche*. Firenze: Vallecchi.
Heller, H. (1929) *Europa und der Fascismus*. Berlin: Walter de Gruyter.
Papafava, N. (1923) 'Il fascismo e la costituzione', *La Rivoluzione Liberale*, 28 August.
Rohe, A. (1922) 'Mussolini, Hope of Youth, Italy's Man of Tomorrow', *New York Times*, 5 November.
Schneider, H. W., and Clough, S. B. (1929) *Making Fascists*. Chicago: The University of Chicago Press.
Severino, V. S. (2017) 'Reconfiguring Nationalism: The Roll Call of the Fallen Soldiers (1800–2001)', *Journal of Religion in Europe*, 10(1–2), pp. 16–43. https://doi.org/10.1163/18748929-01002002

## Feminism

Some forms of feminism are described as a secular religion both by conservative critics and by feminists who criticize this or that "irrational" or "fundamentalist" trait of feminism. As for the first, a typical example is Roger Scruton's *The West and the Rest*, which speaks of a "covert appeal to the religious":

> Feminism claims, like Marxism, to be a political movement, but it is in fact a movement against politics, just as Marxism has been. It seeks to replace or rearrange the core experience of social membership and therefore has

the ambitions of a monotheistic faith, offering a feminist answer to every moral and social question, a feminist account of the human world, a feminist theory of the universe, and even a feminist reading of the Goddess. It drives the heretics and half-believers from its ranks with a zeal that is the other side of the inclusive warmth with which it welcomes the submissive and the orthodox. And it stands implacably opposed to the old order, in something like the way that Protestantism stood opposed to the Roman Catholic Church during the Renaissance.

*(Scruton, 2002, p. 72)*

The existence of an overarching moral (or even metaphysical) doctrine that separates true believers from heretics, creating a community of the faithful, indeed stands very close to the classic Durkheimian definition of religion. Religious "zeal" at the same time evokes the characteristics of new religious movements or rather sects that distinguish themselves from established churches in the Weberian sense of the term. In Scruton's account – and in many others' who oppose feminism as a threat to the traditional sources of identity – the feminist movement is also part of the even more overarching category of "political correctness," which in turn includes anti-racism, multiculturalism, or the postmodernism of Foucault, Derrida, and Rorty. Each of those, as the argument goes, implies "a kind of religious faith: faith in the relativity of all opinions, including this one. For this is the faith on which a new form of membership is founded – a first-person plural of denial" (ibid., p. 74).

The interesting fact is that similar issues are also raised by feminist authors. Janet Radcliffe Richards' *The Sceptical Feminist* insists that there is a "feminist dogma" that goes beyond the rationally defensible proposition that "women suffer from systematic social injustice because of their sex" (Richards, 1980, p. 1). To say that all moral questions should be reduced to the question of "what is, or is not, good for women" or that sexual oppression is "the only form of oppression" (and not only the worst among many, which may be true) are absolutistic claims that exclude any other conception of justice:

> No matter how great the suffering of an oppressed group, and no matter how much it will have to be given before justice is done, its advantage can never be the same thing as justice. To identify the two is to allow for the possibility of the oppressed group's being given too much, and to set out on a path which leads to injustice, injustice according to the very principles by which it was established that women were oppressed in the first place. The heavenly city is being built with stones stolen from its own foundations.

*(ibid., p. 10)*

In other words, the absolutization of sexual oppression is but an inversion of similarly dogmatic statements made in earlier ages about the natural subjection of women; one that may in turn lead to a similarly oppressive outcome, even against women who do not share the radical feminist's views on what women ought or ought not to do (ibid., p. 14). Moreover, radicals are inclined to see the oppression of women in the trivia of everyday life, in much the same way as the religious believer who sees the "hand of God" in what is to the atheist the unremarkable course of nature. It is a "common religious view that since the truth is manifest, the fallen state of the heathen can be imputed only to Sin, or, in this case, vested interests and conditioning" (ibid., pp. 268–269).

Words like "dogma," "heavenly city," "the hand of God," "fallen state," "heathen," or "Sin" all imply a strong reliance on religious analogies, to which Christina Hoff Sommers adds that although Richards' argument sounds convincing, there is also an "interesting difference in the public testimony of the adherents. The devout tend to confess their sins. By contrast, the feminist ideologue testifies relentlessly to how she has been sinned *against*" (Sommers, 1994, p. 27). What Sommers – who defines herself as an "equity feminist" – calls "gender feminism" thus proves to be not even a secular religion but an inverted one which nevertheless shares the dogmatic character of its traditional counterparts. She even cites Roger Scruton's account of "indoctrination" in this regard, asserting that such indoctrination is based on a "unified set of beliefs," a "Closed System" that is immune to criticism:

> In a term made popular by Sir Karl Popper, gender feminism is *non-falsifiable*, making it more like a religious undertaking than an intellectual one. If, for example, some women point out that *they are* not oppressed, they only confirm the existence of a system of oppression, for they "show" how the system dupes women by socializing them to *believe* they are free, thereby keeping them docile and cooperative.
>
> *(ibid., p. 96)*

The idea that gender feminists (also called "new feminists" or "doctrinaire feminists") betray the original aims of feminism by making it a religious undertaking is a topos that is also present in other examples of the contemporary literature on secular religions. (Compare the title of Sommers' book: *Who Stole Feminism? How Women Have Betrayed Women* with that of John McWhorter's *Woke Racism: How a New Religion Betrayed Black America*.) Such works also share the conviction that being religious is something "bad" or "irrational" to which more reasonable alternatives exist. On the other side, traditional (Christian) authors criticize feminism not because it is religious but because it is not truly so: it has a false (self-appointed) priesthood of gender theorists, a false idea of original sin (that of "male privilege" for which no redemption is available), a false idea of martyrdom (which anyone can attribute to herself), and a set of self-contradicting sacred scriptures that have as many interpretations as there are different versions of feminism (Kersten, 1994).

This, however, also confirms that there is no such thing as "feminism" either as a secular or a negative religion. All we can say is that there are "feminisms," some of which might be suspected of "religious" leanings (belief in an ultimate truth, a set of theoretical dogmas, an idea of original sin, an unquestionable moral code, the establishment of church-like institutions, an anointed priesthood, a variety of sacred scriptures, etc.), but any further generalization should be treated as a rhetorical whim and not as an analytical approach.

See also: Multiculturalism, Political Correctness, Postmodernism, Racism, Wokeness

### Sources

Kersten, K. (1994) 'How the Feminist Establishment Hurts Women', *Christianity Today*, 20 June. Available at: https://www.christianitytoday.com/ct/1994/june-20/how-feminist-establishment-hurts-women.html (Accessed: 1 December 2023).
Richards, J. R. (1980) *The Sceptical Feminist: A Philosophical Enquiry*. New York: Routledge.
Scruton, R. (2002) *The West and the Rest: Globalization and the Terrorist Threat*. Wilmington: ISI Books.
Sommers, C. H. (1994) *Who Stole Feminism? How Women Betrayed Women*. New York: Simon and Schuster.

### Fitness

See Wellness.

### Food

"Eating and food choice has become a secular religion," as Australian nutritionist Catherine Lockley once wrote in a LinkedIn article.

> If you utilize social media, you'd be hard pressed to go a single day without one of your friends or acquaintances posting an attractively designed meme relating to food. People, having been "illuminated" into a particular "food-religion" feel compelled to proselytize, to help others that have not yet been enlightened.
>
> *(Lockley, 2017)*

The term "food religion" is used here as a comprehensive metaphor, encompassing a "sea of shifting dietary recommendations," all of which are promoted by media nutritionist "gurus" ("a word meant to denote a spiritual leader") whose message, like a religious sermon, "helps people make sense of a chaotic world." It is not even necessary that the message should be a positive one: to preach that "the world is full of evil toxins, chem-trails, and 'deathly' industrial additives" or that those who "eat wrong" are "inherently sinful" and must be "saved" at least offers a clear-cut knowledge of what the toxins are and how to avoid them. The redemptive message (with all its negative positivity) is thus akin to the Christian idea of Paradise lost:

> We ate the "wrong" or "forbidden" food in paradise and subsequently fell from Grace. The notion that everything "past" (and therefore "purer") is best can be seen in the fear and anger displayed at the marriage of technology and food ("Organic," "Non-GMO").

And finally, joining a particular "food religion" also confers a "sense of belonging" to a community of like-minded believers that prevents critical thinking and making one's own choices.

Individual examples of "food religions" (thinness, veganism, vegetarianism) are discussed in other entries of this book, but there are other cases like raw food diet, which is sometimes described in similar terms:

> This food practice is based on the idea of finding salvation, but for this to happen, one must find its nature. The raw food leaders promise a revolutionary diet that could cure disease and guarantee the return to Adam and Eve's natural paradise. By condemning a cultural symbol such as cooking, they claim to have the key to escape the degenerative modernity. They seduce and convert a cult of followers in Western countries. The dichotomies on which the norms of this diet are based refer to the notions of the pure and the impure, of the good and the bad. They divide up the world according to moralistic binaries.
>
> *(Thircuir, 2019)*

In such descriptions, "food practices" appear as "recompositions of new religious actions," which use a "religious and moral vocabulary, referring to great dichotomies (good/bad, natural/non-natural, pure/impure), prohibitions and sins" (ibid.), and the same is true of books about *The Gluten Lie*, which Alan Levinovitz calls a "myth," adding further examples like sugar-free eating as "a form of secular puritanism" (Levinovitz, 2015).

At the other extreme, cooking or gastronomy may also be described as a secular religion. Jean Anthelme Brillat-Savarin's famous *The Physiology of Taste* in the early 19th century already contained *Meditations on Transcendental Gastronomy* (Brillat-Savarin, [1825] 2009), presenting an amalgam of scientific and religious views on gastronomy. Eating had always been a "ritual" throughout history (ibid., pp. 81, 292, 341), and this was what separated the human being from animals: "Animals feed themselves, men eat; but only wise men know the art of eating" (ibid., p. 15).

In addition to the ritual and metaphysical aspects of gastronomy, one might suggest that it also has its sacred books. Brillat-Savarin's work itself is still often called the "bible of gastronomy" (Physiologie de Goût, 2002), but other "bibles" are also available, from the *Larousse Gastronomique* (Bruno, 2020) to Julia Child's *Mastering the Art of French Cooking* (Cordon Blue, 2012). All these might be little more than advertising clichés, but the most often cited example of a gastronomical bible, the *Michelin Guide* (Ganley and Badias, 2023), is indeed the work of a magisterial office whose decisions are unquestionable; or, if someone does question them because of their "unreasonable" and "restrictive" character (Escoffier, 2022), it amounts to something like a heresy, the rejection of dogmatic requirements.

Searching for further parallels between the "church of gastronomy" and traditional religions (great cooks as priests, restaurants as temples, tables as altars, culinary festivals as religious celebrations, etiquette as liturgy, etc.) would be hardly more than a frivolous overstretching of the analogy. What nevertheless remains defensible is the claim that food and eating had already been a central concern of the so-called genuine religions, a corporeal as well as spiritual experience, the traces of which are still found in the "secular" religions of diets, meal regulations, and gastronomies.

See also: Thinness, Veganism, Vegetarianism, Wellness

## Sources

Brillat-Savarin, J. A. ([1825] 2009) *The Physiology of Taste, or Meditations on Transcendental Gastronomy*. Translated by Fisher, M. F. K. New York: Alfred A. Knopf.

Bruno, M. (2020) 'Larousse Gastronomique: The Bible of Gastronomy Uncovered', *Fine Dining Lovers*, 27 August. Available at: https://www.finedininglovers.com/article/larousse-gastronomique-uncovered (Accessed: 1 December 2023).

Cordon Bleu (2012) 'From Le Cordon Bleu to TV and Movies, Julia Child Inspires New Cookers Until Today'. Available at: https://www.cordonbleu.edu/news/julia-child-inspires-new-cooks/en (Accessed: 1 December 2023).

Escoffier (2022) 'How Restaurants Get Michelin Stars: A Brief History of the Michelin Guide', *Auguste Escoffier School of Culinary Arts*, 1 September. Available at: https://www.escoffier.edu/blog/world-food-drink/a-brief-history-of-the-michelin-guide/ (Accessed: 1 December 2023).

Ganley, E., and Badias, J.-F. (2023) 'Self-taught Chefs Win Coveted Stars from Michelin Guide', *AP News*, 6 March. Available at: https://apnews.com/article/michelin-guide-chefs-stars-awards-france-cooking-e02e09e2a0904bbf08a774eec8b419f2 (Accessed: 1 December 2023).

Levinovitz, A. (2015) *The Gluten Lie and Other Myths about What You Eat*. Collingwood: Nero.

Lockley, C. (2017) '"Give Us This Day Our Daily Bread:" Food and Religion in the Modern Dietary Landscape', *LinkedIn*, 9 July. Available at: https://www.

linkedin.com/pulse/give-us-day-our-daily-bread-food-religion-modern-dietary-lockley/?trk=articles_directory (Accessed: 1 December 2023).

Physiologie du Goût (2002) Available at: https://rmc.library.cornell.edu/food/gastronomy/Physiologie_du_Gout_L.htm (Accessed: 1 December 2023).

Thircuir, S. (2019) 'I Eat Therefore I Believe: The Raw Food Diet, a Believing Solution for Healing', *The International Journal of Religion and Spirituality in Society*, 9(1), pp. 41–55. https://doi.org/10.18848/2154-8633/CGP/v09i01/41-55

## Football

Different sports are often called secular religions, but football (especially "association football" or soccer) as the most popular one deserves a separate discussion. Bombastic claims such as "In Italy, football is a religion" (Cannavaro, 2020), "In Argentina we say football is a religion" (Times, 2021), or "For Sunderland fans, football is a religion" (Graham, 2023) have few counterparts in other sports, and academic literature on the religious aspects of sports also often cites football as the prime example of a new "civil" religion (Xifra and Ordeix, 2008).

Although the former may be seen as rhetorical exaggerations that only express a strong commitment, some authors confirm the existence of a more substantial analogy. Adopting a morphological analysis of religion, as David Chidester notes, it may be said that football-worship also has its "prayers, curses, hymns, vestments, transcendent gods, and sacrificial rituals," as well as a "sacred center" that "must be visited at least once in a lifetime," the FIFA World Cup that moves to a different location every four years but retains "its structural role as the central shrine of the religion of football" (Chidester, 2018, p. 49, quoting Schechter, 2010). According to a functional analysis of religion, it may even be suggested that football is a "better" religion than traditional ones, because it provides the world "with a genuine ritual of social solidarity," regardless of the denominational differences of its adherents. As *Guardian* commentator Theo Hobson remarked:

> The desire for society to be united in common ritual expression, or worship, is basic to religion, and perhaps politics too, but all actual realizations of this ideal should be viewed with suspicion . . . We should be grateful for a harmless version of this deep-rooted instinct.
> *(ibid., p. 50, quoting Hobson 2010)*

Similar views are expressed by statements like "In Nigeria, I was told that football is a religion, but it is a lie. It is more than that. In Nigeria, football is life," as FIFA President Gianni Infantino said, thus attributing a sort of "super-religious" status to football (Premium Times Nigeria, 2018).

In sum, football is usually compared to religion because:

1. It has a transcendent absolute. Either "football" itself is the ultimate object of worship or a given football team (be it the national one or a given football club), none of these are empirical entities but ideas that have no existence outside the human mind. To worship the game is not to like this or that football match but to see the latter as the temporary manifestation of an eternal essence. To be a fan of the Nigerian national team or FC Barcelona is not to sympathize with the eleven players currently on the field but to be dedicated to the idea of Nigerian or Catalonian football, its history, its past, present, and future heroes – something that is beyond the scope of any momentary experience.
2. It is also obvious that – although they are often called "gods" in figurative speech – football heroes are more like "saints," exemplars of outstanding virtue, whose pictures are omnipresent in public and private shrines, whose personal objects are worshipped as relics, and whose words are cited as sacred texts even when their origins become obscure and their meaning dubious (like Diego Maradona's "Football, it's a religion" or Pelé's "Football is like a religion to me, I worship the ball and treat it like a god").
3. The worship of football and footballers also naturally involves sacred places like stadiums; sacred symbols like flags and coats of arms, often worn on the liturgical dress of adherents (scarves, caps, and t-shirts); and liturgical hymns and chants, sometimes combined with the likewise liturgical cursing of other denominations. The liturgy takes place on holy days – in earlier times, football matches were usually held on Saturdays and Sundays – and although more recently any day can become such a holy day, it does not alter the fact that all these represent an exception from everyday routine, a sort of transcendent celebration.
4. At the same time, the idea of the sacred and its corresponding rituals all serve the purpose of creating a moral community, a "church" in the Durkheimian sense of the word, which can be institutionalized on a local, national, or international level. Football clubs, national leagues, or organizations like the UEFA or the FIFA are certainly not the same as the communities of believers but may be viewed as a higher hierarchy, often endowed with the task of defining theoretical dogmas, disciplinary rules, and conditions of belonging.

Those who think that all this is an over-extension of the category of religion should remember once again that nowadays no definition treats "belief in one God" or "attending a church" in the traditional sense as a necessary condition of being religious. What is truly problematic is not why football should be seen as a *religion* but why a cultural phenomenon that is sometimes openly called as such and in fact presents many traits of the former (belief in an absolute, saint-worship, sacred places, symbols, rituals, liturgical calendars, the idea of a moral community, and its institutional hierarchy) should be called *secular*.

See also: Entertainment, Fandom, Sports

## Sources

Cannavaro, F. (2020) 'Il calcio in Italia è una religione, deve ripartire', *Il Napolista*, 20 May. Available at: https://www.ilnapolista.it/2020/05/cannavaro-il-calcio-in-italia-e-una-religione-deve-ripartire/ (Accessed: 1 December 2023).

Chidester, D. (2018) 'Interreligious Football: Christianity, African Tradition, and the Religion of Football in South Africa', in *Global Perspectives on Sports and Christianity*, edited by Adogame, A., Watson, N. J., and Parker, A. New York: Routledge, pp. 47–63.

Graham, M. (2023) 'Niall Quinn: For Sunderland Fans Football is a Religion – It's Extraordinary', *Sports Illustrated*, 17 February. Available at: https://www.si.com/soccer/sunderland/news/niall-quinn-for-sunderland-fans-football-is-a-religion (Accessed: 1 December 2023).

Hobson, T. (2010) 'The World Cup: A Ritual that Works', *Guardian*, 12 June. Available at: www.guardian.co.uk/commentisfree/belief/2010/jun/12/world-cup-ritual-religion (Accessed: 1 December 2023).

Premium Times Nigeria (2018) 'Football Is More Than a Religion in Nigeria – FIFA President', 20 February. Available at: https://www.premiumtimesng.com/news/top-news/259289-football-religion-nigeria-fifa-president.html?tztc=1 (Accessed: 1 December 2023).

Schechter, D. (2010) 'The Religion of Football', *CNN Belief Blog*, 4 June. Available at: http://religion.blogs.cnn.com/2010/06/04/the-church-of-football/ (Accessed: 1 December 2023).

The Times (2021) 'In Argentina We Say That Football Is a Religion and Its God Is Diego Maradona – Inside the Church of Maradona', 25 November. Available at: https://www.thetimes.co.uk/article/in-argentina-we-say-football-is-a-religion-and-its-god-is-diego-maradona-kzgzsrcb6 (Accessed: 1 December 2023).

Xifra, J., and Ordeix, E. (2008) 'Global Corporate Public Relations and Sport's Culture: A Civil Religion Approach to Nation-Building', in *Estableciendo puentes en una economia global – Building Bridges in a Global Economy*, edited by Pindado, J., and Payne, G. Madrid: ESIC, p. 270.

# G

## GENDER

See Feminism, Wokeness.

### Genetics

Genetics becomes a religion or a "cult of the gene" (Le Breton, 2004) when it offers a complete metaphysics, presenting the scientific method it applies (reducing every living being to pieces of information) as if it were the ultimate explanation of life.

That the latter is indeed a metaphysical idea is best seen when it is compared to traditional views of the human being and the biological world. Not only religions like Christianity mark off the human being as the center of creation but all forms of "secular" humanism that suggest something like a human essence, or at least a human "existence," the capability of free choice, autonomy and responsibility that distinguish humans from the rest of the natural world. In contrast, genetics offers a universal leveling:

> Living things are no longer perceived as birds and bees, foxes and hens but as bundles of genetic information. All living beings are drained of their substance and turned into abstract messages. Life becomes a code to be deciphered. There is no longer any question of sacredness or specialness.
> *(Rifkin, 1998, p. 214)*

Although at first sight this seems the exact opposite of a religion (the absence of any divine or natural essence, a total profanation of the world, and even the lack of any morality, for being a bundle of information precludes that anyone could be held responsible for their acts), the case is more complex. Speaking of the gene as a source of one's existence and properties is only another sort of essentialism, not without theological antecedents. As Dorothy Nelkin and Susan Lindee put it:

> The modern cultural concept of genetic essentialism draws much of its power from such theological roots. The gene has become a way to talk about the boundaries of personhood, the nature of immortality, and the sacred meaning of life in ways that parallel theological narratives. Just as the Christian soul has provided an archetypical concept through which to understand the person and the continuity of the self, so DNA appears in popular culture as a soul-like entity, a holy and immortal relic, a forbidden territory. The similarity between the powers of DNA and those of the Christian soul, we suggest, is more than linguistic or metaphorical. DNA has taken on the social and cultural functions of the soul.
> 
> *(Nelkin and Lindee, 2004, pp. 41–42)*

Let us also not forget that the soul was originally conceived as a creation and reflection of God, one that miraculously preserved this divine essence even after belief in God disappeared from the minds of secular humanists. To say that DNA or the genome is like the soul, it is to attribute to them the same divine attributes, and this is what a certain genetic essentialism and determinism does. In this conception the gene is indeed something absolute: omnipotent, omnipresent, all-wise; perhaps not "all-good" but still no questions should be asked about its goodness. It is also transcendent in the sense that most believers have never seen a gene, they only accept by authority what their priests (scientists and science popularizers) have to say about it. "And certain biologists are vying to be the privileged administrators of this DNA, setting themselves up as the priests of this new discourse," as David Le Breton says (Le Breton, 2004, p. 4).

In practice, geneticists may even act as lords of life and death, for

> the identification of a genetic illness which is currently untreatable leads potentially to the decision to carry out a therapeutic abortion, and in this way a drift occurs, whereby medicine moves away from a therapeutic role to the project of eliminating that which it cannot treat.
> 
> *(ibid., p. 5)*

The problem is that all this relies on dogmas, most of which are not scientific (hence the word "genetical fundamentalism"). Monogenic illnesses are extremely rare, and a genetic predisposition is usually not a destiny but rather an indication of probability. "Not only is it the case that environmental factors might prevent the disease from developing, but other genes may have an effect, all of which contributes to the uncertainty" (ibid., p. 6).

Regardless of which, as can be seen, theoretical dogmas are often translated into moral precepts. It is not morality or ethics that a thoroughly genetic outlook will eliminate, it is only those forms of it that are incompatible with the higher morality of the gene. As E. O. Wilson said, "Human behavior – like the deepest capacities for emotional response which drive and guide it – is the circuitous technique by which human genetic material has been and will be kept intact. Morality has no other demonstrable ultimate function" (Wilson, 1978, p. 167). This also means that perhaps "the time has come for ethics to be removed temporarily from the hands of the philosophers and biologicized" (Wilson, 1975, p. 562).

This sort of biologicized or scientific ethics also has a social impact or even a program of social transformation. Although traditional eugenics (the selective "breeding" of certain people or groups with presumably advantageous hereditary traits) has become discredited by the similar efforts of Nazi Germany, "new eugenics" still holds that human capacities may be enhanced by the use of reproductive technology and genetic engineering. This in turn suggests a sort of salvation history, the liberation of humanity from evil:

> With as much conviction as the first Christians waiting for the Messiah or communists waiting for collective happiness, they are convinced all that is bad in the world stems from "bad" genes and that it "suffices" to eradicate them in order to create a humanity without evil. Genetic fundamentalism offers a discourse of salvation that fascinates a number of intellectuals who come from other disciplines.
> 
> *(Le Breton, 2004, p. 16)*

It thus comes as no surprise when a book on genetic engineering (Lee M. Silver's *Remaking Eden*) not only chooses a religious metaphor as its title but is in fact full of religious references, starting each part with a biblical citation (mostly from Genesis but also from the Gospels or the Book of Revelation), suggesting that the historical vision of "reprogenetics" (the use of genetics in reproduction) is in fact a modern-day substitute for the traditional story of creation, fall, and redemption.

Describing genetics or molecular biology as an attempt to find the "Holy Grail" (as it has often been done by renowned scientists from Walter Gilbert and Leroy Hood to the propagators of the Human Genome Project) is itself a sign of religious devotion, or rather, of a mystical religiosity. As American geneticist Richard Lewinton ironically noted, it is somewhat curious that an otherwise atheistic community of scientists "has chosen for its central metaphor the most mystery-laden object of medieval Christianity" (Lewontin, 2000, p. 137). Let us repeat, however, that all this has nothing to do with genetics as a scientific undertaking that has always rejected not only genetic determinism but also its conflation with metaphysical, let alone religious ideas (if by religion one means a quest for the meaning of life):

> If we take seriously the proposition that the internal and external codetermine the organism, we cannot really believe that the sequence of the human genome is the grail that will reveal to us what it is to be human, that it will change our philosophical view of ourselves, that it will show how life works.
>
> *(ibid., p. 149)*

In other words, genetic determinism or fundamentalism is not even a religion (although it has its own absolute, its dogmas and moral commandments, and its priests and simple believers who regularly use phrases like "it's in my genes" as if they knew what a gene was) but rather a modern superstition.

See also: Biotechnology, Cloning, Medicine, Posthumanism, Scientism, Technology

## Sources

Le Breton, D. (2004) 'Genetic Fundamentalism or the Cult of the Gene', *Body & Society*, 10(4), pp. 1–20. https://doi.org/10.1177/1357034X04047853

Lewontin, R. (2000) *It Ain't Necessarily So: The Dream of the Human Genome and Other Illusions*. New York: The New York Review of Books.

Nelkin, D., and Lindee, M. S. (2004) *The DNA Mystique: The Gene as a Cultural Icon*. Ann Arbor: University of Michigan Press.

Rifkin, J. (1998) *The Biotech Century: Harnessing the Gene and Remaking the World*. New York: Jeremy P. Tarcher / Putnam.

Silver, L. M. (1998) *Remaking Eden: How Genetic Engineering and Cloning Will Transform the American Family*. New York: Avon Books.

Wilson, E. O. (1975) *Sociobiology: The New Synthesis*. Cambridge, MA: The Belknap Press of Harvard University Press.

Wilson, E. O. (1978) *On Human Nature*. Cambridge, MA: The Belknap Press of Harvard University Press.

# H

## HEALTH

See Beauty, Medicine, Wellness.

### Hip Hop

Hip Hop music is not a widely discussed case of "secular religions," but there are some references to it in the literature as a "new" religion, which in turn suggests that it is not a religion in the traditional sense; it is rather something between the categories of the religious and the secular. As Monica Miller's *Religion and Hip Hop* argues, the conventional approaches to religion as a "quest for meaning" or "ultimacy" miss the point entirely, because they fail to define what kinds of meaning count as religious and non-religious (Miller, 2013, p. 60, citing Asad, 1993, p. 45). The many references to Talal Asad's *Genealogies of Religion* in the book make it abundantly clear that the whole distinction of the religious and the secular is rejected by the author, after which it is also natural that a Hip Hop artist like KRS-One will appear not as the representative of either "real" or "secular" religion but as someone who "uses the capital associated with 'God' talk to establish the 'realness' of Hip Hop culture" (Miller, 2013, p. 60). Even when he writes a *Gospel of Hip Hop* and says that "Our culture is our religion, and our religion is our culture" (KRS-One, 2009, p. 26), it does not mean that there is a functional or substantive analogy between religion and Hip Hop culture; only that the artist builds "his gospel upon the *already* established, lived, and authenticated power of religion in the world, as well as theological codes and grammar that ground such talk" (Miller, 2013, p. 62).

When RZA of the Wu-Tang Clan writes of the Tao (which seems a just as religious idea as KRS-One's gospel), it is more like a "spiritual autobiography through the heuristics of wisdom seeking," and not a legitimation of either Hip Hop culture or religion (ibid., p. 64). He rather "uses religion, philosophy, spirituality, and popular culture as a means by which to construct a more pragmatic philosophy of life based on *tactics* and *strategies*" (ibid., p. 69). To ask what all this means is itself a mistake: "the use of religion in these works doesn't *mean* anything in the strict sense. Rather religion *functions* as a means by which to *authorize* particular social interests" (ibid.). Or, as Tupac Shakur said:

> I'm the religion that to me is the realist religion there is. I try to pray to God every night unless I pass out. I learned this in jail, I talked to every God [member of the Five Percent Nation] there was in jail. I think that if you take one of the "O's" out of "Good" it's "God," if you add a "D" to "Evil," it's the "Devil." I think some cool motherf**ker sat down a long time ago and said let's figure out a way to control motherf**kers.
> 
> *(ibid., p. 177)*

The only reason why this part individualistic, part political, and part explicitly religious mixture might still be called a secular religion is that it has its own symbols, signifying tattoos, communities, and even occasional shout-outs to a God of its own making, while lacking a "singular confessional approach" (ibid., p. 180). A thorough analysis of Hip Hop lyrics would perhaps lead to other conclusions, but – as Miller never fails to remind us – searching for the meaning of those would never reveal what Hip Hop is all about.

> The uses of religion within Hip Hop material productions remind the scholar of religion that we must get beyond our modernist lenses of religion as feeling, and get up to speed with religion as effect, strategy, and manufacturing of social, cultural, and political interests. Chasing meaning is like chasing waterfalls – it is an impossible and endless task.
> 
> *(ibid., p. 70)*

Hip Hop culture, in other words, is the best indicator of the "fractured life-worlds of the postmodern condition," something that might be called a religion, a secular religion, or a fully secular phenomenon. "The stylings and uses of religion within the living-out of Hip Hop material culture are cutting back through the dimensions, and the scholar setting out to locate religion may find that 'religion' has reposited the locus of study" (ibid., p. 180).

See also: Entertainment, Postmodernism, Rock

## Sources

Asad, T. (1993) *Genealogies of Religion: Discipline and Reasons of Power in Christianity and Islam*. Baltimore: Johns Hopkins University Press.
KRS-One (2009) *The Gospel of Hip Hop: The First Instrument*. Brooklyn: Powerhouse Books.
Miller, M. R. (2013) *Religion and Hip Hop*. New York: Routledge.

## History

See Enlightenment, Progress, Revolution.

## Human rights

The belief in human rights is one of the rare examples that have been explicitly called a "secular religion" by both its advocates and its critics. Although it played some part in the orations and liturgies of the French Revolution already (the Constitution was often called the "daughter" of the Declaration of the Rights of Man and Citizen, while the tables of the latter were carried around in revolutionary processions, Ozouf, 1988, p. 67), a full-fledged, independent cult only appeared with the Universal Declaration of Human Rights in 1948.

As for religious self-references, already the preamble to the UDHR talked about the "advent" of a new world, a "faith" in fundamental human rights, and a "pledge" to the promotion of something "universal." And this was no metaphorical language. As Earl Warren, Chief Justice of the United States Supreme Court, asserted in 1968, the UDHR was an expression of "our faith in humanity, the kind of faith based on things not seen" (Warren, 1969, p. 45). The reference was to Hebrews 11:1 from the Bible: "Now faith is the substance of things hoped for, the evidence of things not seen." A similar statement was made in 1980 by Vratislav Pechota, former Chairman of the United Nations Committee on Legal Affairs: "A universal human rights culture based on faith in the dignity and worth of the human person" (Pechota, 1980, p. 468). American law scholar Paul Brietzke similarly wrote in 1985 about "faith" in human rights as the basis for such additional rights as the right to development (Brietzke, 1985, p. 600; for more examples, see Traer, 1991, pp. 209–211).

In these cases, the notion of "faith" was used in a positive sense, but in another parallel narrative, faith or belief appeared as a proof of irrationality or theoretical unfoundedness. Alasdair MacIntyre's *After Virtue* claimed that the modern notion of rights (including human rights) had no counterparts in premodern cultures, and all references to the latter were based on a kind of superstition-like belief in witches and unicorns:

> The best reason for asserting so bluntly that there are no such rights is indeed of precisely the same type as the best reason which we possess for

asserting that there are no witches and the best reason which we possess for asserting that there are no unicorns: every attempt to give good reasons for believing that there *are* such rights has failed.... In the United Nations declaration on human rights of 1949 what has since become the normal UN practice of not giving good reasons for *any* assertions whatsoever is followed with great rigor. And the latest defender of such rights, Ronald Dworkin (*Taking Rights Seriously*, 1976) concedes that the existence of such rights cannot be demonstrated, but remarks on this point simply that it does not follow from the fact that a statement cannot be demonstrated that it is not true (p. 81). Which is true but could equally be used to defend claims about unicorns and witches.

*(MacIntyre, [1981] 2007, pp. 69–70)*

As Malcolm D. Evans puts it, faith in human rights is not only a dogmatic but an "intolerant faith." When certain UN human rights documents assert that full religious freedom does not apply to those who violate the rights of others, it means that the idea of human rights "is itself as intolerant of other forms of value systems which may stand in opposition to its own central tenets as any of those it seeks to address" (Evans, 1997, p. 260). Others nevertheless maintain that this is a "secular" and not a "religious" faith. In Cornelius Murphy's words, "the Declaration can be viewed as the expression of a common secular faith in the worth of the human person" (Murphy, 1972, p. 290). Or, as Michael Ignatieff more critically says, the idea of human rights "has become the major article of faith of a secular culture that fears it believes in nothing else" (Ignatieff, 2001, p. 53). Ignatieff also uses the terms "idolatry" and "secular religion." The latter is based on Elie Wiesel's famous claim in the volume celebrating the fiftieth anniversary of the UDHR, which calls human rights the "world-wide secular religion of today" (Wiesel, 1999, p. 3; for a similar terminology, see Cotler, 2007, p. 22 and Julius, 2010, p. 453). Even those who speak of an "ideology" instead (such as Torkel Opsahl, member of the European Commission of Human Rights, or Louis Pettiti, judge of the European Court of Human Rights) acknowledge that this ideology can at least be a substitute for religion (Traer, 1991, p. 210).

The common element of all such talk is that the idea of human rights – exactly because it is an *idea* – has nothing to do with the physical description of the world. Moreover, as a *normative* idea, it tells us not how things are but how they should ideally be. The adjective "human" also does not refer to anything empirical: in its metaphysical generality, it is just as transcendent as the gods of traditional religions. We are yet to see the human being as such, its common essence, not to mention its "freedom" or "dignity." We are nevertheless obliged to believe in these ideas as absolutes, as many UN documents confirm. The 2000 Millennium Declaration speaks of all "principles" of the UN Charter as "timeless and universal," while the 2005 World Summit Outcome specifically mentions human rights, saying that their "universal nature" is "beyond question" (UN, 2005, §120). This is, however, not a description of the state of the field (for the same document acknowledges the possibility of controversies, see §121) but a magisterial decision rejecting further argument, at least about the essential universality of human rights. The 2015 Sustainable Development Framework (or Agenda 2030) does not even refer to controversies but takes the previous documents, the Charter, the UDHR, the Millennium Declaration, and the Summit Outcome as its scriptural foundations. This "sola scriptura" approach is important because any deeper investigation of the historical or philosophical origins of human rights would threaten its global acceptability. As Jacques Maritain put it when he and his colleagues – coming from diverse cultural and philosophical traditions – drafted the Universal Declaration of Human Rights: "We agree about the rights, but on condition that no one asks us why" (Maritain, 1949, p. i).

More recently, the radical critics of human rights as a secular religion (e.g., French legal historian Jean-Louis Harouel) view it as part of the much broader religion of humanity, a continuation of the religions of progress, socialism, Marxism, or French republicanism (Harouel, 2016). The common roots of this secular (political, civil, lay, etc.) religion are Gnosticism and millenarism, so – as in many other cases – the analogy is not with religion as such but with these "great falsifications of Christianity." The essence of the falsification consists not only in the deification of the human being and the historical mechanism but also in the denial of the Christian separation of church and state, reintroducing a "state church" of universalism. The latter, however, remains ambiguous, for it only forbids Europeans to cultivate their own identity but remains a promoter of multiculturalism in the case of immigrants. The comparison with religion thus returns to the negative (intolerant, anti-democratic, totalitarian) connotations of the word, of which only an idealized Christianity remains an exception. Or perhaps not even that, because Harouel himself cites many examples from the Christian Middle Ages to the contrary.

See also: Humanism, Multiculturalism, Progress, Revolution, UN

## Sources

Brietzke, P. (1985) 'Consorting with the Chameleon, or Realizing the Right to Development', *California Western International Law Journal*, 15(3), pp. 560–601.
Cotler, I. (2007) 'The New Anti-Semitism', in *Anti-Semitism: The Generic Hatred*, edited by Fineberg, M., Samuels, S., and Weitzman, M. London: Vallentine Mitchell, pp. 15–32.
Evans, M. D. (1997) *Religious Liberty and International Law in Europe*. Cambridge: Cambridge University Press.
Harouel, J.-L. (2016) *Les droits de l'homme contre le people*. Paris: Desclée de Brouwer.
Ignatieff, M. (2001) *Human Rights as Politics and Idolatry*. Princeton: Princeton University Press.

Julius, A. (2010) *Trials of the Diaspora: A History of Anti-Semitism in England*. Oxford: Oxford University Press.
MacIntyre, A. ([1981] 2007) *After Virtue: A Study in Moral Theory*. Notre Dame: University of Notre Dame Press.
Maritain, J. (1949) *Human Rights: Comments and Interpretations*. New York: Columbia University Press.
Murphy, C. (1972) 'Ideological Interpretations of Human Rights', *DePaul Law Review*, 21(2), pp. 286–306. Available at: https://via.library.depaul.edu/law-review/vol21/iss2/2 (Accessed: 1 December 2023).
Ozouf, M. (1988) *Festivals and the French Revolution*. Translated by Sheridan, A. Cambridge: Harvard University Press.
Pechota, V. (1980) 'East European Perceptions of the Helsinki Final Act and the Role of Citizen Initiatives', *Vanderbilt Journal of Transnational Law*, 13(2), pp. 467–500. Available at: https://scholarship.law.vanderbilt.edu/vjtl/vol13/iss2/13/ (Accessed: 1 December 2023).
Traer, Robert (1991) *Faith in Human Rights: Support in Religious Traditions for a Global Struggle*. Washington, DC: Georgetown University Press.
UN (2000) 'United Nations Millennium Declaration'. Available at: https://www.ohchr.org/en/instruments-mechanisms/instruments/united-nations-millennium-declaration (Accessed: 1 December 2023).
UN (2005) 'Resolution adopted by the General Assembly on 16 September 2005'. Available at: https://undocs.org/en/A/RES/60/1 (Accessed: 1 December 2023).
UN (2015) 'Transforming our World: The 2030 Agenda for Sustainable Development'. Available at: https://sustainabledevelopment.un.org/post2015/transformingourworld (Accessed: 1 December 2023).
Warren, E. (1969) 'Address', in *The International Observance: World Law Day – Human Rights 1968*. Geneva: World Peace Through Law Centre, pp. 44, 45.
Wiesel, E. (1999) 'A Tribute to Human Rights', in *The Universal Declaration of Human Rights: Fifty Years and Beyond*, edited by Danieli, Y., Stamatopoulou, E., and Dias, C. Amityville: Baywood, pp. 3, 4.

# Humanism

The "secular" adjective of secular religions is often understood simply as "human," something that celebrates the human being and its creations instead of worshipping the God(s) of traditional religions. In this sense, almost every entry in this book may be about a "humanistic" religion, but there is a more concrete sense in which the word has been used since the 19th century.

One of the first mentions of the "religion of humanity" – in the works of Claude Henri de Saint-Simon after the French Revolution – presented it as an elimination of transcendence, making it a truly *secular* but at the same time more *perfect* expression of the essence of religion than any of its previous manifestations. Although the idea of God, as Saint-Simon remarked (from ancient Egypt and Rome to the various sects of Christianity), "lacks unity," it does not mean that the idea itself should be abandoned: "the idea of God should not be used in the physical sciences, but I do not say it should not be used in political matters." Politics cannot do without a unifying principle, but it should be a truly universal one, which – at least for the time being – should also be "clothed in forms which make it sacred" (Saint-Simon, [1808] 1964, p. 20). In this sense, the religion of humanity is rather the religion of an invented God, a primitive form of political religion to serve the common good.

It was Saint-Simon's disciple, Auguste Comte, who – in his *System of Positive Polity* – went one step further and modified the definition of religion to comply with his own concept of the religion of humanity. According to this new definition (which would also have an impact on Durkheim and other later sociologists), religion has nothing to do with the concept of God; it is rather an expression of "a state of complete harmony peculiar to human life" or a sort of "moral and physical health." That is also why there are no "religions," only one, for it is "as impossible to speak of several religions as of several healths" (Comte, [1852] 1875, p. 8).

The new religion has only two goals – moral or individual and political or social – to "regulate each personal life" and to "combine different individual lives" (ibid.). Another important feature of the religion of humanity is its connection to science. As Saint-Simon said as early as 1803, "spiritual power" should be placed "in the hands of the scientists, and temporal power in the hands of the property-owners" (Saint-Simon, [1803] 1964, p. 11). In contrast, Comte's "scientists" are both priests and political leaders, teachers and catechumens (Comte, 1858, p. 22), polyhistors with "encyclopedic" knowledge (from arithmetic to medicine), and moral experts, who are aware of the "the necessary participation of the heart and the intellect respectively, in reference to the synthetical state, or unity, of the individual and the society" (ibid., p. 51). The queen of sciences is sociology that absorbs all other forms of inquiry from biology to moral studies (ibid., p. 187), while society is elevated to the rank of a new absolute: an "immense and eternal being," the "real Great Being," or "Supreme Being" (ibid., pp. 63–64).

This elevation at the same time deprives society of its empirical character. If humanity is "the whole of human beings, past, present, future," then it is a no more physical reality than Yahweh or Allah. Not only because such a whole is obviously *more* than the sum of existing individuals, but also because it is *less*:

> you must not take in all men, but those only who are really capable of assimilation, in virtue of a real co-operation on their part in furthering the common good . . . mere digesting machines are no real part of Humanity.
> *(ibid., pp. 74–75)*

Humanity is, in other words, a normative idea and not something the existence of which can ever be "proven" by any branch of science. Even less will it ever be scientifically explained why this abstract idea of humanity or human society should be respected, worshipped, or obeyed as the highest authority (see Comte's frequent and not in the least negative references to "sociolatry" or "sociocracy," ibid., pp. 96, 118, 126, 136).

While the "secular" nature of Comte's religion may be disputed, its "religious" character is beyond doubt. In addition to the fully otherworldly idea of humanity it also has its dogmas (ibid., pp. 58, 63, 70, 79, 162, 212), sacraments (ibid., pp. 128–136), temples (ibid., p. 140), sacred symbols (ibid., p. 142), and its fully-fledged liturgical calendar (ibid., p. 433), most of which are admittedly borrowed from Catholicism.

The fundamental dogma is that of unity: "the universal religion, then, adopts, as fundamental dogma, the fact of the existence of an order, which admits of no variation, and to which all events of every kind are subject" (ibid., p. 58). The sacraments are also familiar from Catholicism, only their number is not seven but nine. The "consecration of birth" is the equivalent of baptism; the rites of "initiation" and "admission" are very similar to the Christian rite of confirmation; and the same holds for the sacrament of marriage. Comte's additions only concern some special celebrations of "destination" (choosing a profession), "maturity" (reaching the age of 42), and "retirement" (at the age of 63) while the sacrament of "transformation" (a euphemism for dying) is once again the parallel of the Catholic sacrament of extreme unction. At this point, Comte explicitly admits that he took the idea from Catholic practice:

> It is to be the substitute for the horrible ceremony of the Catholic ritual. Catholicism, free from all check on its anti-social character, openly tore the dying person from all his human affections and made him stand quite alone before the judgment-seat of God. In our transformation, the priesthood mingles the regrets of society with the tears of his family and shows it has a just appreciation of the life that is ending.
>
> *(ibid., p. 135)*

The last sacrament, that of "incorporation," is also said to be borrowed from Catholicism ("an idea, which, in its germ, sociocracy borrows from theocracy"): an equivalent of canonization, the veneration of the dead who serve as an example for later generations, having their tombs "ornamented with a simple inscription, a bust, or a statue, according to the degree of honor awarded" (ibid., p. 136).

Speaking of busts and statues it is also not difficult to recognize the similarity of Catholic and humanistic symbolism: "In painting or in sculpture, equally, the symbol of our Divinity will always be a woman of the age of thirty, with her son in her arms" (ibid., p. 142). Moreover, the picture of this Comtian Madonna should be carried around in "solemn processions" just like in its Catholic counterparts, while the temples of humanism should also appropriate old – presumably Catholic – church buildings: "Provisionally, then, we shall have to use the old churches, in proportion as they fall into disuse" (ibid., p. 140).

Looking back from the 21st century, it is almost incomprehensible how this strange bricolage of Catholic allusions and pseudo-scientific rhetoric could ever appear as the religion of the future. The fact is that it did not, at least not for most of Comte's contemporaries. After the publication of the *System of Positive Polity* and especially the *Catechism of Positivism*, it became customary to distinguish between a "good" Comte, the author of such early sociological and philosophical works as the *Course on Positive Philosophy*, and a "bad" one who later turned his science and philosophy into religion (Bourdeau, 2022).

Although later versions of humanism kept trying to abandon the religious overtones of Comtism, they never fully succeeded in doing so. In 1933, the Humanist Manifesto returned to the phrase "new religion" in very much the same way as other secular religions do. It was exactly this wording that Corliss Lamont (himself a humanist but in a more radically secular sense) criticized in 1949:

> As for the word *religion*, I think that current redefinitions of it are particularly confusing, since they bring under the heading of religion such very different and in some cases positively irreligious phenomena as nationalism, communism and even atheism . . . It is evident that the *Manifesto* makes religion cover practically everything that men do.
> *(Lamont, [1949] 1997, p. 157)*

Lamont thus rejected not only that humanism should be a secular religion but also that other ideologies belonged to the same – and certainly blurry – category. What is doubtful is whether there exists any form of humanism that can be isolated as purely secular. After all, to say that the human being is the ultimate point of reference is to make an absolute claim. To cite Swinburne's "Glory to Man in the highest! For Man is the master of things" (ibid., 77) is not to prove a scientific observation but to announce a dogma. In addition, Swinburne is not the only dubiously secular character in Lamont's *The Philosophy of Humanism*, which also includes Buddha and Jesus Christ, making the separation of secular and religious just as arbitrary as in any other version of humanistic thought.

Humanism also possesses a vision about the earthly paradise brought about by the "person of autonomy, freedom, creativity, applying reason and science to human problems, enjoying the beauties of nature and culture, free of superstition . . . a lover of peace and concord" (Smith, 1994, p. 42). Self-salvation, at the same time, is just as religious an idea as salvation, and belief in it requires a good deal of resistance to facts. Let us not forget that the first Humanist Manifesto was drafted in 1933, at the time of Hitler's rise to power in Germany, the great famine in Stalin's Soviet Union, a civil war in China, and only a few years before the biggest war in history. Although the second Manifesto in 1973 had to acknowledge that the expectations of the first were "far too optimistic," it ultimately maintained the belief that war and poverty could be eliminated, showing once again that this had more to do with faith in the "things unseen" (Heb 11:1) than with historical experience.

The Manifestos themselves may be seen as sacred scriptures or creeds, parts of a larger tradition with its own martyrs and prophets from Socrates to Giordano Bruno, Galileo, or Darwin, including even heretics or "detractors" who "pollute" the meaning of humanism (Kurtz, 1973, p. 177). To safeguard the true faith against non-believers is one task of the official churches of humanism such as the American Humanist Association or the Academy of Humanism (Smith, 1994, p. 37). Some authors go as far as suggesting that rituals should also become part of the humanist worship:

> An essential function for artists and writers in a Humanist society will be to work out rituals and ceremonies that are consistent with the central tenets of Humanism. Such ceremonies should appeal to the emotions as well as the minds of the people, capturing their imagination and giving an outlet to their delight in pomp and pageantry. Present-day Humanists regard a festival like Christmas, which has already become secularized to a large extent in the United States, as a folk day symbolizing the joy of existence, the feeling of human kinship, and the ideal of democratic sharing. However, during the year's most intensive holiday season, many Humanists prefer to put their stress on New Year's Day rather than Christmas. Easter can be humanistically utilized to celebrate the re-birth of the vital forces of Nature and the renewal of our own human energies. In fact, according to the anthropologists, Easter probably originated in just such a way. Humanism will likewise naturally make much of the birthdays of outstanding leaders of the human race, and of other important anniversaries.
> 
> *(Lamont, [1949] 1997, p. 302)*

Despite such features and the fact that "temples of humanity" still exist in Brazil, India, the United States, or Canada, most critics of humanism refrain from calling humanism a religion in the full sense of the term. As John E. Smith says:

> I call Humanism a quasi-religion but not a religion proper . . . I employ the term "quasi-religions" as the best way of pointing up the similarities and analogies involved between certain movements and the religions proper while at the same time staying clear of the charge that one calls any

of these movements a "religion" merely as an act of what one writer has called "terminological aggression."

*(Smith, 1994, pp. 23–24)*

Whether the same charge cannot be raised against the terminology of "quasi-religion" (as something which is not even a "real" religion, only a second-class substitute for it) is another question to be answered by those who use the word.

See also: Atheism, Individualism, Scientism

## Sources

Bourdeau, M. (2022) 'Auguste Comte', in *The Stanford Encyclopedia of Philosophy*. Available at: https://plato.stanford.edu/Archives/win2022/entries/comte/ (Accessed: 1 December 2023).

Comte, A. ([1852] 1875) *System of Positive Polity or Treatise on Sociology, Instituting the Religion of Humanity, Volume 2*. Translated by Harrison, F. London: Longmans, Green and Co.

Comte, A. (1858) *The Catechism of Positive Religion*. Translated by Congreve, R. London: John Chapman.

Kurtz, P. (ed.) (1973) *The Humanist Alternative*. London: Pemberton Books.

Lamont, C. ([1949] 1997) *The Philosophy of Humanism*. Eighth, revised edition. Amherst: Humanist Press.

Saint-Simon, C.-H. ([1803] 1964) 'Letters from an Inhabitant of Geneva to His Contemporaries', in *Social Organization, the Science of Man and Other Writings*, translated by Markham, F. New York: Harper and Row, pp. 1–11.

Saint-Simon, C.-H. ([1808] 1964) 'Introduction to the Scientific Studies of the 19th Century', in *Social Organization, the Science of Man and Other Writings*, translated by Markham, F. New York: Harper and Row, pp. 12–20.

Smith, John E. (1994) *Quasi-Religions: Humanism, Marxism, and Nationalism*. New York: Macmillan.

# 1
# INDIVIDUALISM

At a closer look, many of the secular religions discussed in this book have some connection to the worship of the individual. Anarchism, the cult of beauty, capitalism, entertainment, the idea of human rights, liberalism, psychology, selfism, or wellness culture all suggest an elevation of the individual to the rank of an absolute. As the French sociologist of religion Émile Durkheim predicted as early as 1898, the "cult of the individual" would be the religion of the modern age, something he did not even call "secular," for it fulfilled every criterion of a real religion:

> a religion does not necessarily imply symbols and rites, properly speaking, or temples and priests. This whole exterior apparatus is only the superficial part. Essentially, it is nothing other than a body of collective beliefs and practices endowed with a certain authority.
> *(Durkheim, [1898], 1973, pp. 50–51)*

Moreover, as a result of modernity's more developed division of labor (when "each mind finds itself oriented to a different point on the horizon") and urbanization (which weakens social control), members of the group now "have nothing in common among themselves except their humanity" (ibid., p. 51). In a historical sense, this paradoxical new religion – in which belief in the individual should become the basis of community – is not even a complete break with Christianity, which itself contributed to its birth by transporting the center of moral life from the external to the internal, and "the individual was thus elevated to be sovereign judge of his own conduct, accountable only to himself and his God" (ibid. p. 52). Individualism is also not irreconcilable with collective ideologies (political religions) like nationalism. The fact that everyone has a similar view of the importance of the individual is in fact the "last reserve of collective ideas and feelings which is the very soul of the nation" (ibid., p. 54).

What remains problematic is the hierarchy of religions in such an individualistic society, which is purportedly tolerant and pluralistic but still strives to maintain unity. For no matter how tolerant it attempts to be, it cannot help granting individualism a privileged status in the social framework of "primary and secondary ordered religious values, in which the truth and moral claims of the cult of the individual take precedence over those of traditional religions" (Carls, 2019, p. 293).

Traditional religions, according to Durkheim, are disappearing, anyway: "the former gods are growing old or dying, and others have not yet been born" as he writes elsewhere (Durkheim, [1912] 1995, p. 429). This remains dubious, however, since traditional religions are still with us more than a hundred years later, and new religions are also constantly being born. Durkheim may have thought he was living in a transitory period, but his was in fact fully continuous with the French Revolution and has not ended until the present day. Contrary to what he suggested, the revolutionary cults of homeland, nation, progress, and constitutions are still alive, just as the cult of the individual, even if regularly challenged by other, collectivist, or trans- and post-humanist secular religions.

The most frequent objection against calling individualism a "religion" is the lack of a transcendent being as the object of worship. Let us note, however, that the concept of the "individual" is just as transcendent as that of any God. Neither science nor everyday experience informs us of its existence, only of its various manifestations; in other words, it is a metaphysical concept, the meaning of which differs from one culture (or one philosopher) to the other. According to some, modern neuroscience in fact disproves the existence of an "individual self" (Harari, 2015, p. 338), but even if we are convinced that we have something like an individual mind, we can never be certain that others also do, as the "problem of other minds" shows in philosophy. Since philosophical problems are by their very nature insoluble, the existence of individuals always remains a matter of belief, which some philosophers of religion such as Alvin Plantinga, not without reason, compared to belief in God (Plantinga, 1967).

The other objection is less powerful, for Durkheim himself asserted that symbols, rites, priests, and temples do not necessarily belong to the essence of religion. Yet symbols or rites, and feast days or myths can also be present in one's own personal self-worship, even if in a necessarily individual sense. As for priests and temples, some authors suggest that modern psychology is itself a church of individualism or rather "selfism" (Vitz, 1993), just as modern entertainment and consumerism with their emblematic figures and institutions may be described as a priesthood and church preaching self-adoration.

Or perhaps the whole modern world as such has become one big megachurch of individualism.

See also: Consumerism, Entertainment, Humanism, Psychology

## Sources

Carls, P. (2019) 'Modern Democracy as the Cult of the Individual: Durkheim on Religious Coexistence and Conflict', *Critical Research on Religion*, 7(3), pp. 292–311. https://doi.org/10.1177/2050303218823069

Durkheim, É. ([1898] 1973) 'Individualism and the Intellectuals', in *On Morality and Society: Selected Writings*, translated by Traugott, M. Chicago: The University of Chicago Press, pp. 43–57.

Durkheim, É. ([1912] 1995) *The Elementary Form of Religious Life*. Translated by Fields, K. E. New York: The Free Press.

Harari, Y. N. (2015) *Homo Deus: A Brief History of Tomorrow*. London: Vintage.

Plantinga, A. (1967) *God and Other Minds: A Study of the Rational Justification of Belief in God*. Ithaca: Cornell University Press.

Vitz, P. C. (1993) *Psychology as Religion: The Cult of Self-Worship*. Grand Rapids: Eerdmans.

# J
# JUCHE

North Korea's official ideology of self-reliance is another good example of how problematic the distinction of the religious and the secular is. Juche is sometimes described as a socialist ideology (Znamenski, 2021), sometimes as a form of nationalism (Shin, 2006b), a political religion or a quasi-religion (Armstrong, 2013), a substitute religion (Holmes and Hong, 2022), an "intentional religion," or an "ideology that morphed into a religion" (Widjaja et al., 2021), while others dispute that it is an ideology or belief system at all (Myers, 2014).

Those who accept that Juche has religious traits are also divided on the exact character of this religiosity. Some suggest that it is a totalitarian transformation of Confucianism (Yüksel, 2015); others find its roots in Japanese state Shinto (Halpin, 2015); while still others argue that it combines elements of Christianity, Chondoism, and Confucianism (Jung, 2013). Since the latter are usually accepted to be "religions" in the full sense of the word, it is almost impossible to decide where Juche stands on the overlapping fields of secularity, secular religiosity, and religiosity as such.

The concrete features that are usually listed as proofs of its religious character are:

- the worship of the nation as an "indivisible and deified sacred entity," an organic unity without which (whom?) the individuals are "not worthy of living" (Cumings, 2003, p. 159)
- the worship of the leader who is the highest expression, the literally "immortal" "brain" of the national organism (Jung, 2013, p. 96)
- the hagiography of the Kim family with all its mystical elements (Kim Il-sung's long ancestry of freedom fighters and martyrs, Kim Jong Il's

birth at the holy mountain of Paektu and the prophecies about him as the future savior, or Kim Jong-un's extraordinary abilities as a child, Richardson, 2016)
- the visual manifestations of the worship, such as the mausoleum of Kim Il-sung and Kim Jong Il, their public icons and statues, or Juche Tower, the monument of Juche ideology itself
- liturgical feasts such as Sun Day, the birthday of Kim Il-sung (Shin, 2006a, p. 519), or the Arirang Mass Games celebrating the birth of the nation after a history of oppression and suffering (Jung, 2013)
- even the introduction of a new era starting with 1912, the birth of Kim Il-sung:

The Juche era is a symbol of the eternal harmony of the Korean people with the President. With its institution, our nation and humankind can always live in Kim Il-sung's era, in the history of the sun. It is an immortal milestone symbolic of the immortality of the era of Juche created by the President.

*(cited in Shin, 2006a, p. 519)*

What remains difficult to tell is why such a full-fledged system of dogmas, sacred texts, shrines, symbols, and rituals that most authors call "transcendent" or "other-worldly" should still be treated as a *secular* religion. The sole reason might be that official documents still speak of Juche as an atheistic philosophy (ibid.), which, however, only confirms the suspicion that in such cases the adjectives "secular" or "atheistic" simply mean "non-traditional" or "not explicitly assumed."

See also: Atheism, Communism, Nationalism, Socialism

## Sources

Armstrong, C. (2013) 'The Role and Influence of Ideology', in *North Korea in Transition: Politics, Economy, and Society*, edited by Park, K.-A., and Snyder, S. Lanham: Rowman and Littlefield, pp. 3–18.

Cumings, B. (2003) *North Korea: Another Country*. New York: The New Press.

Halpin, D. P. (2015) 'North Korea's Kim Family Cult: Roots in Japanese State Shinto?', *NK News*, 19 February. Available at: https://www.nknews.org/2015/02/north-koreas-kim-family-cult-roots-in-state-shinto/ (Accessed: 1 December 2023).

Holmes, R., and Hong, E. (2022) 'Perceptions of Juche ideology by expats in North Korea: A Qualitative Study', *Missiology: An International Review*, 50(4), pp. 362–373. https://doi.org/10.1177/00918296211064294

Jung, H. J. (2013) 'Jucheism as an Apotheosis of the Family: The Case of the Arirang Festival', *Journal of Korean Religions*, 4(2), pp. 93–122. Available at: http://www.jstor.org/stable/23943356

Myers, B. R. (2014) 'Western Academia and the Word "Juche"', *Pacific Affairs*, 87(4), pp. 779–789. Available at: http://www.jstor.org/stable/43592450

Richardson, C. (2016) 'Hagiography of the Kims and the Childhood Saints', in *Change and Continuity in North Korean Politics*, edited by Cathcart, A., Winstanley-Chesters, R., and Green, C. K. London: Routledge, pp. 109–135. https://doi.org/10.4324/9781315545646

Shin, E.-H. (2006a) 'The Sociopolitical Organism: The Religious Dimensions of Juche Philosophy', in *Religions of Korea in Practice*, edited by Buswell, R. E. Princeton: Princeton University Press, pp. 517–533.

Shin, G.-W. (2006b) *Ethnic Nationalism in Korea: Genealogy, Politics, and Legacy*. Stanford: Stanford University Press.

Widjaja, F. I., Boiliu, N. I., Simanjuntak, I. F., Gultom, J. M. P., and Simanjutak, F. (2021) 'The Religious Phenomenon of Juche Ideology as a Political Tool', *HTS Teologiese Studies/Theological Studies*, 77(4). https://doi.org/10.4102/hts.v77i4.6324

Yüksel, C. D. (2015) 'Confucianism and Juche Ideology: An Analysis of the Manipulation of Confucianism for the Creation of a Political Religion', in *New Europe College Yearbook 2014–2015*, edited by Vainovski-Mihai, I. Bucharest: New Europe College, pp. 403–423.

Znamenski, A. (2021) *Socialism as a Secular Creed: A Modern Global History*. Lanham: Lexington Books.

# K
# KUNG FU

Although Kung Fu and other martial arts are sometimes called secular religions, the use of the term raises the same difficulties as in many other cases. On the one hand, it is not at all clear whether a claim like "Kung Fu is my religion" means anything more than "it is very important to me," applying a casual metaphor to express a deep devotion (Jennings, Brown, and Sparkes, 2010, p. 539) or suggesting an actual analogy. Or, if we do accept that Kung Fu and other martial arts have a religious backdrop, the word "secular" becomes problematic since they explicitly rely on the religious traditions of Buddhism, Taoism, or Confucianism, even if the latter are reinvented and conflated in a popular, often obfuscated, "unsystematic manner" (McFarlane, 1991, p. 357).

As for Kung Fu, articles titled "It Can Be a Religion If You Want: Wing Chun Kung Fu as a Secular Religion" reflect the same ambiguity: "Of course, in conventional academic terms, this martial art is clearly not a religion" (Jennings, Brown, and Sparkes, 2010, p. 538). After which, however, the same article lists all those features that make it explicitly religious: the Buddhist shrine at the center of the training space decorated with the portrait of the Great Grandmaster and the flags of other martial arts schools; the requirement that students must wear a sort of liturgical dress, an "appropriate attire"; the "formal patterns" of ceremonies with which classes are started and finished; the unquestionable authority of the master and his teaching; or the collective enthusiasm of fellow martial artists (ibid., pp. 539–540). An element of asceticism is also present: as the master himself admits, he was sometimes mocked by others who thought that because of constant training, he did not have the time to get a girlfriend, to which he replied that it was an act of self-denial: "To become good, I had to sacrifice many other things" (ibid., p. 542).

DOI: 10.4324/9781003471257-12

Such a sacrifice or "monastic devotion" (also observed in the case of other, Western types of "martial arts" such as boxing, Wacquant, 2004, p. 60) is once again difficult to describe as purely secular. Especially when the master himself speaks of a "church," a "religion," or a "transcendental path" to achieve unity with the "universe or whatever that is" (Jennings, Brown, and Sparkes, 2010, pp. 542–544). It is also notable that the Durkheimian definition of religion that such accounts routinely use will not distinguish between secular and religious forms of the sacred: the moral community they create, the "solidarity system of beliefs and practices" is the same in both cases (Wacquant, 2004, p. 100).

In conclusion, the description of Kung Fu and other martial arts as secular religions fails not because it rests on a superficial analogy. Quite to the contrary: it fails because it cannot explain why a system of beliefs and practices that is profoundly similar (and also genetically connected) to what is usually called a "religion" should nevertheless be treated as secular.

See also: Boxing, Sport, Wellness

## Sources

Jennings, G., Brown, D., and Sparkes, A. C. (2010) '"It Can Be a Religion If You Want:" Wing Chun Kung Fu as a Secular Religion', *Ethnography*, 11(4), pp. 533–557. https://doi.org/10.1177/1466138110372588

McFarlane, S. (1991) 'The Mystique of Martial Arts: A Reply to Professor Keenan's Response', *Japanese Journal of Religious Studies*, 18(4), pp. 355–368. Available at: http://www.jstor.org/stable/30233452

Wacquant, L. (2004) *Body and Soul: Notebooks of an Apprentice Boxer*. Oxford: Oxford University Press.

# L

# LEGALISM

See Constitutionalism.

## Leninism

To distinguish "Leninism" from "Bolshevism" or from "Communism" (not to mention the even more overarching category of "Socialism") is mostly artificial, but some authors – especially during the first few decades after the Russian Revolution – insisted on using this term to separate it either from the communist ideology of earlier times or from Stalinism which followed it.

In 1925, the American economist John Maynard Keynes remarked that many regarded Leninism as a "new religion" because of its intolerance of other faiths, its missionary ardor, and its ecumenical ambitions (Keynes, [1925], 2010, pp. 256–257). In 1936, the Swiss Protestant theologian Adolf Keller called Leninism a "camouflaged secular religion" because of its "Messianism without a Messiah (unless Lenin himself takes His place)" and its "ardent chiliasm," which, however, expected not a "new heaven but a new earth" (Keller, 1936, p. 69). In 1952, the French Catholic philosopher Étienne Gilson included Leninism in his *The Metamorphoses of the City of God*, although only as a temporary form between Marxism and Stalinism, which nevertheless professed the same controversial belief in the "scientific dogma" of progress, a secular version of the Christian salvation story: "an obstinate effort to make a temporal city of this eternal city, by substituting for faith any conceivable natural bond as the unifying force of this society" (Gilson, [1952] 2005, pp. 232–233).

While all the above emphasize the utopian character of Leninism as a worldwide missionary movement, some ambiguous remarks (like Keller's) also refer the cult of Lenin as an extraordinary – almost superhuman – personality, of which the later embalming of Lenin's body and its placement in the Mausoleum as a site of pilgrimage are the visible signs. The analogy with the cult of Christian saints (whose bodies in glass coffins are still venerated in Catholic churches in Italy, France, and other countries) was also amended by works of hagiography (e.g., the miraculous revelations of the "child Lenin") and liturgical exclamations such as "Lenin lived, Lenin lives, Lenin will live on" (taken from Vladimir Mayakovsky's famous poem "Vladmir Illich Lenin" of 1925).

In other words, Leninism as an ideology and Leninism as a cult of the person are two different, although related phenomena. The first is mostly discussed by secular religions' literature as an example of historical theology that offers an ultimate explanation for world history, a final goal for humanity, and a set of unquestionable dogmas to believe in; all this with a missionary zeal and an institutionalized priesthood of missionary elites

**FIGURE 2** The statue of Lenin showing the way to the future in Memento Park, Budapest, Hungary

*Source:* Photograph by Ferran Cornellà, Wikimedia Commons, https://commons.wikimedia.org/wiki/File:Lenin_statue_from_Csepel,_Memento_park_4.JPG, used under license CC BY-SA 3.0 DEED

(party officials and intellectuals). In this regard, Leninism is not entirely different from other forms of communism, and many authors in fact use the words Leninism, communism, or Bolshevism interchangeably.

On the other hand, Leninism as the cult of Lenin himself – who may have opposed such a cult because of its overtly religious allusions – shows the same traits as the later cults of Stalin, Mao, or Kim Il-sung: a sort of saint-worship with its hagiographical texts, liturgical hymns ("Lenin Is With Us," "Song About Lenin," or even "The Holy Banner of Lenin"), shrines, icons, and statues, many of which not accidentally depict Lenin as a modern-day Moses showing the way to the promised land for the chosen people of the proletariat (Znamenski, 2021, p. 127).

What remains dubious is whether the ideology and the cult should be called a "new religion," a "secular religion," or just a modern phenomenon with some superficial resemblance to religious ideas and symbolism. The works on Leninism are divided on the issue, but this is not unusual in the discourse of religious/secular analogies.

See also: Bolshevism, Communism, Marxism, Socialism, Stalinism

## Sources

Gilson, É. ([1952] 2005) *The Metamorphoses of the City of God*. Translated by Colbert, J. G. Washington, DC: The Catholic University of America Press.
Keller, A. (1936) *Church and State on the European Continent: The Social Service Lecture, 1936*. London: Epworth.
Keynes, J. M. ([1925] 2010) 'A Short View of Russia', in *Essays in Persuasion*. Basingstoke: Palgrave Macmillan, pp. 253–271.
Znamenski, A. (2021) *Socialism as a Secular Creed: A Modern Global History*. New York: Lexington.

## Liberalism

When speaking of the secular religion of liberalism, one must first clarify whether the word is used in the European sense, referring to classical liberalism, or – as the American usage implies – as an equivalent of what Europeans call "social democracy" or "laborism." In the latter case, speaking of the religion of liberalism is often only an expression of contempt toward any modern, progressive, or left-wing ideology (such as feminism, evolutionism, environmentalism, animal rights activism, communism, etc., see Coulter, 2006). In such accounts, liberalism may appear not even as a secular religion but as a real, albeit false one. As Ann Coulter says in her *The Godless Church of Liberalism*:

> Of course, liberalism is a religion. It has its own cosmology, its own miracles, its own beliefs in the supernatural, its own churches, its own high

priests, its own saints, its own total worldview, and its own explanation of the existence of the universe. In other words, liberalism contains all the attributes of what is generally known as "religion."

*(ibid., p. 6)*

Although some authors realize that the medley of progressivisms has very little to do with classical liberalism, they still use words like "postmodern liberalism" or "liberal progressivism":

> "Liberalism" has evolved from a political and economic doctrine into something more totalistic. At the same time, it's disintegrating into what must be at this point hundreds of various and often contradictory sects.... Each one of them claims for itself the mantle of true "progressivism" – the chosen self-designation of liberals ever since their rather belated discovery that liberalism has a noisome reputation among the sane and healthy majority. Yet progressivism (or postmodern liberalism) passes every imaginable test to qualify as a genuine form of religion. It has developed its own peculiar dogma, sacraments, saintly and sulfurous hierarchies, relics, observances, rituals, and so forth. And that's not so surprising: the religious instinct is present in every human being. When someone becomes disillusioned with the faith of his fathers, he simply chooses another. The trouble is that, very often, he's willing to go to war on behalf of his new pseudo-religion.
>
> *(Williamson, 2019)*

How something that passes every imaginable test to qualify as a *genuine* form of religion nevertheless remains a *pseudo* is, of course, difficult to explain, and only shows the usual ambivalence of authors who ultimately balk at using the same term to a venerable, traditional religion and its latter-day competitors. In any case, the haphazard list of cosmologies, miracles, supernatural beliefs, churches, saints, worldviews, explanations of the universe, dogmas, sacraments, hierarchies, relics, observances, and rituals may better be discussed in different individual entries on the mentioned "progressive" ideologies.

Liberalism in its classical form, as a political philosophy based on freedom, pluralism, and the rights of the individual, is more interesting from a theoretical point of view. At first sight, liberalism's rejection of authority, dogma, or the liberal state's withdrawal from moral disputes seem to constitute the exact opposite of any organized and transcendental religion. At a closer look, however, it turns out that this liberalism also has (and cannot help having) its own absolute, its dogmas, and its moral commandments.

Following Juan Donoso Cortés, Carl Schmitt already recognized how "liberal constitutionalism" or the "the liberal negation of the state vis-à-vis law"

(Schmitt, [1922] 2006, p. 21) was a type of political theology reliant on a specific, deist idea of God:

> Its liberal constitutionalism attempted to paralyze the king through parliament but permitted him to remain on the throne, an inconsistency committed by deism when it excluded God from the world but held onto his existence (here Donoso Cortes adopted from Bonald the immensely fruitful parallel of metaphysics and the theory of the state). Although the liberal bourgeoisie wanted a god, its god could not become active; it wanted a monarch, but he had to be powerless.
>
> *(ibid., p. 60)*

The religion of the liberal bourgeoisie "resides in freedom of speech and of the press" (ibid., p. 62), which, however, is itself a dogmatic prescription. Later critics of liberalism either emphasize the paradoxical nature of the pluralist dogma ("the dictatorship of relativism," which does not recognize anything as definitive except its own principles, Ratzinger, 2005) or the mystical character of liberalism's true absolute, the autonomous individual. As for the latter, more sympathetic authors refer to the religious origin of this concept, the human being created in the image and likeness of God. In this respect, as John Gray wrote, "liberalism and the other political religions of our age are only the illegitimate offspring of the Judeo-Christian tradition," representing a "return of the repressed need for transcendence and the sacred" (Gray, 1993, pp. 24–25). Less sympathetic accounts speak of a simple fallacy or a case of wishful thinking. As Yuval Noah Harari's *Homo Deus* puts it: free will is an "outdated theological concept" (Harari, 2015, p. 331). "The free individual is just a fictional tale concocted by an assembly of biochemical algorithms" (ibid., p. 354). "Medieval crusaders believed that God and heaven provided their lives with meaning. Modern liberals believe that individual free choices provide life with meaning. They are all equally delusional" (ibid.). Liberalism thereby proves to be a brief transitory period between a religious past and an atheistic future, which is strangely similar to Donoso Cortés's and Schmitt's descriptions (an "interim" based on "liberal metaphysics," Schmitt, [1922] 2006, p. 62). Or, in Harari's less informed but more pretentious wording:

> Science undermines not only the liberal belief in free will, but also the belief in individualism. Liberals believe that we have a single and indivisible self . . . this liberal story is pure mythology. The single authentic self is as real as the eternal Christian soul, Santa Claus and the Easter Bunny. If you look really deep within yourself, the seeming unity that we take for granted dissolves into a cacophony of conflicting voices, none of which is "my true self." Humans aren't individuals. They are "dividuals."
>
> *(Harari, 2015, p. 338)*

This is, of course, already the sermon of another religion, that of scientism: the use of (precarious) science to make metaphysical claims.

See also: Constitutionalism, Individualism, Scientism

**Sources**

Coulter, A. (2006) *The Godless Church of Liberalism*. New York: Crown Forum.
Gray, J. (1993) *Post-Liberalism: Studies in Political Thought*. New York: Routledge.
Harari, Y. N. (2015) *Homo Deus: A Brief History of Tomorrow*. London: Vintage.
Ratzinger, J. (2005) 'Mass "Pro Eligendo Romano Pontifice:" Homily of His Eminence Card. Joseph Ratzinger, Dean of the College of Cardinals'. Available at: https://www.vatican.va/gpII/documents/homily-pro-eligendo-pontifice_20050418_en.html (Accessed: 1 December 2023).
Schmitt, C. ([1922] 2006) *Political Theology: Four Chapters on the Concept of Sovereignty*. Translated by Schwab, G. Chicago: The University of Chicago Press.
Williamson, C. (2019) 'The Wars of Religion Are Only Beginning', *Crisis Magazine*, September 25. Available at: https://crisismagazine.com/opinion/wars-of-religion-only-beginning (Accessed: 1 December 2023).

**Love**

The word "love" refers here to romantic love and not (only) to sexual attraction nor to neighborly love in the Christian sense. As Ulrich Beck's and Elisabeth Beck-Gernsheim's *The Normal Chaos of Love* states, "faith in love means you love your lover but not your neighbor" (Beck and Beck-Gernsheim, 1995, p. 180). Although romantic love was not invented in modern times, it became a form of worship – or even a "secular religion," as the same book explicitly says – more recently, something to be sought for its own sake. In the present age, the primary purpose of marriage and family is no longer political or economic; it is the fulfilment of love (ibid., p. 172). The modern types of marriage and family have in fact become a promise of "personal salvation in a domestic paradise of companionship, parenthood, and love," of which, paradoxically, the modern disintegration of the family and the rise in divorce rates are the best proofs, showing that the hopes of the faithful are so high that dissatisfaction with earthly realities is almost inevitable:

> These two poles, idealizing life as a couple and divorcing in thousands, represent two sides of a new faith quickly finding followers in a society of uprooted loners. Their hope rests in love, a powerful force obeying rules of its own and inscribing its messages into people's expectations, anxieties and behaviour patterns, leading them through marriage and divorce to remarriage.
> *(ibid., p. 173)*

Love thus appears as a truly transcendental force that is "immune to conscious or practical manipulation and cannot be reproduced on order" (ibid., p. 176). It is in fact so transcendent that one can never be certain whether its promises will be fulfilled: it requires a similar "leap of faith" as Kierkegaard's Christianity. As Francesco Alberoni puts it, falling in love means opening oneself to a new form of existence without any guarantee of achieving it. If love is returned, it is like an unmerited "gift," analogous to what Christian theologians call "grace." It is also a promise of eternity, a blissful moment in which "time ceases to exist" (Alberoni, 1983, p. 50), which also stands very close to the traditional descriptions of mystical experience.

Love's ability to give a new meaning to life or to transform/redeem the individual are also "religious" traits; the only thing that seems to be missing is an official "church." As Beck and Beck-Gernsheim put it, "We ourselves are its temples and our whishes are its prayers" (Beck and Beck-Gernsheim, 1995, p. 177). Or, in Simon May's words: it is a "religion that is all the more remarkable for being self-enforced by its votaries rather than supervised by a Church" (May, 2011, p. xiii). This does not mean that it lacks sanctuaries, symbols, or rituals, but all these are emphatically private:

> Instead of being officially sanctified and administered, this private faith is individually styled, invented and adorned: snuggling in Mickey Mouse and teddy symbols, agreeing everything yellow means love, inventing nicknames to use in our secret world, all these are efforts to counteract the nagging fear that it might end, and all could be lost and forgotten.
> *(Beck and Beck-Gernsheim, 1995, p. 181)*

The self-imposed commandments of love are also so severe that to oppose them appears to be the greatest sin. When partners no longer love each other, for instance, it becomes forbidden to maintain a relationship, regardless of any possible losses. Here, however, the lofty absolute of love becomes very difficult to distinguish from sheer egotism:

> In the critical situation of a divorce . . . the children take second place for both mother and father; their own problems take priority. While divorce proceedings are under way parents neglect their children in almost every respect; domestic order breaks down and the children are left to themselves. Parents living apart spend less time with their children and have less empathy for their needs. In the panic of the upheaval naked egotism wins.
> *(Wallerstein and Blakeslee, 1989, pp. 28–29)*

From this angle, the worship of Love as the highest God seems suspiciously similar to the worship of the self in its lowest form, the instinctive and irrational core of the human person. This is also why it remains difficult to decide whether love is a true religion, perhaps "the only generally accepted religion" of the West (May, 2011, p. 1), a "secular religion" ((Beck and Beck-Gernsheim, 1995, p. 168), a "new faith" (ibid., p. 173), an analogy of Protestant individualism (ibid., p. 174), a "quasi-religious belief," a "latter-day religion" (ibid., 175), a "non-traditional or post-traditional religion" (ibid., p. 177), or not a religion at all, because it is so thoroughly mundane: "Religion tells us there is a life after death; love says there is a life before death" (ibid., p. 176). As can be seen, sometimes the same authors are hesitant about the terminology; what most of them agree on is that love fills the vacuum left by the retreat of Christianity, so – as in many other examples in this book – the word "religion" seems to refer to the Christian analogy and not to the religious in general.

All this does not mean that everyone in today's societies follows this religion or acts according to it. But every religion has its heretics and infidels, and even "cynics often turn out to be disappointed and embittered adherents of an exaggerated faith in love" (ibid., p. 174).

See also: Individualism, Psychology, Sex

## Sources

Alberoni, F. (1983) *Falling in Love and Loving*. Available at: http://www.alberoni.it/libri-pdf/falling-in-love-and-loving.pdf (Accessed: 1 December 2023).
Beck, U., and Beck-Gernsheim, E. (1995) *The Normal Chaos of Love*. Translated by Ritter, M., and Weibel, J. Cambridge: Polity.
May, S. (2011) *Love: A History*. New Haven: Yale University Press.
Wallerstein, J. S., and Blakeslee, S. (1989) *Second Chances: Men, Women and Children a Decade after Divorce*. New York: Bantam.

# M
# MAOISM

In the literature of secular religions, Maoism is usually understood in a broad sense, meaning not just a specific brand of communist ideology developed by Mao Zedong but an entire period of Chinese history from the takeover of the Communist Party (1949) until the death of Mao (1976). As early as 1955, French sociologist Raymond Aron noted that Chinese communism contained many elements that, contrary to its Marxist-Leninist foundations, were not secular and materialistic at all: the rule of a hierarchy, a crusading fervor, and even the re-establishment of an Absolute – this time the irresistible march of history (Aron, [1955] 1962, p. 263). Other observers were more impressed by the symbols and rituals of Chinese communism: the transformation of ancient temples to shrines of "labor heroes," the public humiliation of sinners, the weekly public confessions of soldiers and citizens, or the ceremonies of self-dedication to the communist cause (Koenker, 1965, pp. 63 and 189).

During the Cultural Revolution, all these reached further heights, combined with a full-fledged personality cult of Mao. Italian writer Alberto Moravia, who visited China in 1967, described contemporary Chinese demonstrations as the equivalent of religious processions in his native country: red flags flown like the standards of religious confraternities, the picture of the leader carried around like the portrait of a patron saint, accompanied by ritual music and dance, while all participants waved a copy of the holy scripture, Mao's "little red book" (cited in Gentile, 2006, p. 123).

The analogy of the "patron saint" is perhaps even too modest. The cult of Mao used liturgical greetings like "Boundless life to Chairman Mao," metaphysical affirmations like "The thought of Mao Tse-tung must rule and transform the spirit, until the power of the spirit transforms matter," or epithets like "the sun of our heart, the root of our life, the source of our strength" and "the source of all wisdom" (Johnson, 1991, pp. 546–547). After his death, Mao was placed in a mausoleum which continues to be a site of pilgrimage ever since.

It would thus be understandable if the mentioned authors referred to Maoism as a religion per se, but the case is more complicated. Koenker's book was about "secular salvations" (including as diverse examples as those of revolutionary France, Nazi Germany, or contemporary America) but also used the words "political religion," "civil religion," "political faith," and "new mythology," not to mention the book's blurb that spoke of "covert religions, the modern counterparts to the state religions of antiquity." On the other hand, Moravia drew an analogy with a "rustic and traditional" type of Catholicism, while Gentile called it a "political religion" or the "sacralization of politics" (in his book on *Politics as Religion*, originally titled *The Religions of Politics*) and the "myth of Mao."

See also: Communism, Progress

## Sources

Aron, R. ([1955] 1962) *The Opium of the Intellectuals*. Translated by Kilmartin, T. New York: W. W. Norton and Company.
Gentile, E. (2006) *Politics as Religion*. Translated by Staunton, G. Princeton: Princeton University Press.
Johnson, P. (1991) *Modern Times: The World from the Twenties to the Nineties*. New York: HarperCollins.
Koenker, E. B. (1965) *Secular Salvations*. Philadelphia: Fortress Press.

## Marxism

It is far from obvious that Marxism is a secular religion in its own right. It is often treated together with communism, socialism, or, more recently, multiculturalism and wokeness (as "cultural" Marxism). Sometimes even Bolshevism is called a "version of Marxism, which later became known as Marxism-Leninism, as a transnational political religion with a strong millenarian zeal" (Znamenski, 2021, pp. 94–95). Or, regarding that the tradition of Marxism-Leninism was itself an invention of the Stalin era, Marxism is also sometimes conflated with Stalinism (Riegel, 2005).

Apart from such conflations, however, the original version of Marxism was called a Hegelian "belief" in the inner logic of history and the inevitable triumph of reason by Nicolai Berdyaev, who also named Engels' *Anti-Duehring* the "catechism" of Marxism (Berdyaev, 1905). His main point was that in an otherwise materialistic monism, any reference to such inner logic or inherent rationality had no other source than a "boundless faith," which was at the same time a contradiction, since it supposed "a faith in a thing-like logic, a material rationality. But a rationalistic materialism, the logic of matter is far worse than wooden iron or a black whiteness." What made this faith religion-like and not just contradictory was its dogmatic character (the *Anti-Duehring* being "the sole dogmatic part of Marxist theology") and the absolute claims of its highest entity, reason within the "thingness" of the world, "upon which it is possible to position oneself, as upon a mountain of stone."

It is true that Engels coined the term "Marxism" to express this mixture of scientific socialism and spiritual faith (Znamenski, 2021, p. 32). As former socialist, later neoconservative author Joshua Muravchik put it, Engels

> was Moses to Marx's God, Mohammed to Marx's Allah. He was the High Priest and Marx the Oracle. 'Marx stood higher, saw farther,' said Engels. Perhaps he did. But it was Engels who told the world what Marx saw, spreading the message that shaped the history of the dawning century.
> *(Muravchik, 2002, p. 99)*

The Catholic philosopher Étienne Gilson compared Marxism to a negative religion: "Marxism is the most sustained effort the world has ever known to establish the perfect coincidence of the temporal city and the Earthly City. It actively prepares the reign of the Anti-Christ" (Gilson, [1952] 2005, p. 219). He also emphasized that treating the truths of Marxism as both scientific and eternal (the essence of which lives on in Leninism and Stalinism) is not only dogmatic but paradoxical:

> The concept of religious dogma has meaning, and it is because it is religious. By being eternal, it is unchangeably imposed upon the faithful who serve it. The very concept of scientific dogma is absurd, and that is why, instead of serving it, its faithful must impose it in order to be served by it. The Party is not right because its doctrine is true. The doctrine is true because the Party is always right.
> *(ibid., p. 232)*

The party as an infallible magisterium also raises religious allusions, just as the "mysticism" of Marxism (Voegelin, 1975, p. 231) that has always been reluctant to discuss the exact features of the future communist society, which will in fact be *so* different from ours that it is impossible to describe it in the terms of present-day language.

From a very different angle, "secular religion" also appeared in books like *On Human Nature* by American ecologist Edward O. Wilson:

> Religions, like other human institutions, evolve so as to enhance the persistence and influence of their practitioners. Marxism and other secular

religions offer little more than promises of material welfare and a legislated escape from the consequences of human nature.

*(Wilson, 1978, p. 3)*

In other words, Marxism is once again accused of being down-to-earth materialistic on the one hand and metaphysically unrealistic on the other.

Libertarian economist Murray Rothbard stated (without adjectives such as "negative," "political," or "secular") that Marxism was indeed "a religious creed." He referred not only to the millenarian expectations of Marxists but also to their skill to transform the teaching to fit any situation whatsoever:

> Certainly, one obvious way in which Marxism functions as a "religion" is the lengths to which Marxists will go to preserve their system against obvious errors or fallacies. Thus, when Marxian predictions fail, even though they are allegedly derived from scientific laws of history, Marxists go to great lengths to *change* the terms of the original prediction. A notorious example is Marx's law of the impoverishment of the working class under capitalism. When it became all too clear that the standard of living of the workers under industrial capitalism was rising instead of falling, Marxists fell back on the view that what Marx "really" meant by impoverishment was not immiseration but *relative* deprivation.
>
> *(Rothbard, 1993, p. 225)*

Other examples of the religious traits of Marxism are the separation of Marx from other social scientists as a "prophet" who himself did not always understand the significance of his own words (as their truth would only later become a reality) or the insistence of some Marxists who otherwise "abandoned almost all the essential tenets of Marxism on calling themselves by the magical name 'Marxist'" (ibid., p. 226).

It is therefore a slight mistake to suggest that the "debt which Communism owed to religion has sometimes been under-emphasised by historians who are sympathetic to 'scientific' socialism and resistant to the rather separate notion that Marxism was a religiously inspired mythopoetic drama carefully camouflaged within various scientific-sounding accretions," as Michael Burleigh's *Earthly Powers* put it in 2005, also using the words "quasi-religion" and "atheistic creed" (Burleigh, 2005, p. 244).

While Burleigh's "quasi-religion" is rather a parody of Christian egalitarianism, other authors draw a more overarching analogy with religion or "spirituality" (whatever the latter means):

> Despite Marxism's atheistic stance, there are inherent in Marxism (and indeed Marxism–Leninism) many tenets that are wholly compatible with a religious and/or spiritual outlook. Marxism promises adherents a utopian future at the conclusion of linear time, in which equality, harmony and an

end to suffering await humankind. It also values asceticism, places emphasis on the inner transformation of the individual, and calls for absolute faith and self-sacrifice in order to achieve this end.

*(Pisch, 2016, pp. 57–58)*

As it has become obvious by now, some authors use the word "Marxism" to mean the set of ideas contained in Marx's works; others refer to a systemized version of Marxist thought, started by Engels and elaborated by later communist theoreticians; and still others only mean a sort of "personality cult" of Marx by mediocre epigons, who have very little to do with the authentic origins. As for the latter, Marx himself rejected early on that he or Engels should be the objects of any such worship:

> Neither of us cares a straw for popularity. Let me cite one proof of this: such was my aversion to the personality cult that at the time of the International, when plagued by numerous moves – originating from various countries – to accord me public honour, I never allowed one of these to enter the domain of publicity, nor did I ever reply to them, save with an occasional snub. When Engels and I first joined the secret communist society, we did so only on condition that anything conducive to a superstitious belief in authority be eliminated from the Rules.
> *(Marx's Letter to Wilhelm Blos in 1877, quoted by Pisch, 2016, p. 52)*

Others reject the religious comparisons of Marxism in general. As Roland Boer's *Red Theology* argues, the sources and content of Marx's "eschatology" are different from those found in truly religious (e.g., Christian communist) traditions, and its other "religious" traits are also misleading:

> Concerning the wider issue of Marxism as a secularised religion, critics may point to the rituals of socialist states, without noting that ritual is a common feature of human activity and thereby not necessarily religious. Or they may suggest that the fervour, utopianism and capacity for martyrdom are drawn from religious commitment, without realising that commitment to any cause may produce such fervour. Or they may opine that Marxism is an atheistic Gospel, a position that was first put forward by the leftleaning priest from the Russian Orthodox Church, Alexander Vvedensky (the Metropolitan of Moscow), in his debate with Anatoly Lunacharsky (Commissar for Enlightenment) in 1925 – without realising that atheism is a red herring within Marxism.
> *(Boer, 2019, p. 104)*

It is thus not at all difficult to acquit Marxism of the charge of being religious, but only at the expense of extruding some core elements from the definition of religion (ritual, enthusiasm, eschatological expectations, martyrdom, and sacred scriptures), which rather blurs the boundaries instead of making it easier to decide what is religious and what is not. After all, as Boer himself has to acknowledge: "Thus, while the very nature of the pivots is qualitatively different, it also indicates an abstract and formal analogy" (ibid., p. 116).

See also: Communism, Leninism, Socialism, Stalinism

## Sources

Berdyaev, N. (1905) 'The Catechesis of Marxism' (Катехизис Марксизма), *Вопросы жизни*, 2, pp. 369–379. Available at: https://www.berdyaev.net/1905/the-cateche sis-of-marxism/ (Accessed: 1 December 2023).
Boer, R. (2019) *Red Theology: On the Christian Communist Tradition*. Leiden: Brill.
Burleigh, M. (2005) *Earthly Powers: Religion and Politics in Europe from the Enlightenment to the Great War*. New York: Harper Perennial.
Gilson, É. ([1952] 2005) *The Metamorphoses of the City of God*. Translated by Colbert, J. G. Washington, DC: The Catholic University of America Press.
Muravchik, J. (2002) *Heaven on Earth: The Rise and Fall of Socialism*. San Francisco: Encounter Books.
Pisch, A. (2016) *The Personality Cult of Stalin in Soviet Posters, 1929–1954: Archetypes, Inventions and Fabrications*. Acton: ANU Press.
Riegel, K. G. (2005) 'Marxism-Leninism as a Political Religion', *Totalitarian Movements and Political Religions*, 6(1), pp. 97–126. https://doi.org/10.1080/ 14690760500099788
Rothbard, M. (1993) 'Karl Marx: Communist as Religious Eschatologist', in *Requiem for Marx*, edited by Maltsev, Y. N. Auburn: Ludwig Mises Institute, pp. 221–294.
Voegelin, E. (1975) *From Enlightenment to Revolution*. Edited by Hallowell, J. H. Durham: Duke University Press.
Wilson, E. O. (1978) *On Human Nature*. Cambridge: Harvard University Press.
Znamenski, A. (2021) *Socialism as a Secular Creed: A Modern Global History*. New York: Lexington.

## Medicine

Medicine is not just one scientific discipline among many. While modern physics may satisfy our curiosity about the origins of the universe or the structure of reality, medicine is a personal life-and-death matter for every human being. It is no wonder that "real religions" are also deeply concerned with health and healing. To say that the latter always connect physical well-being to spiritual recovery, making them more "transcendental" than modern medical science is also to some extent mistaken.

In 1963, Michel Foucault already observed that the French Revolution – by nationalizing the medical profession and organizing it like a clergy – did not simply take care of the individuals' bodily health but aimed to restore an "original state of health" in society, a sort of paradise where all disease (and presumably all other forms of suffering) would cease (Foucault, [1963] 2003, pp. 31–32). While Foucault spoke of the "dogmatic medicalization" of society as a "quasi-religious" conversion, more recent authors often argue that such a radical project presupposes an underlying comprehensive worldview akin to that of "real" religions, and the definition of health in official documents seems to confirm their suspicion. As Jan Domaradzki notes in his "Extra Medicinam Nulla Salus: Medicine as a Secular Religion," the WHO statement that "health is a state of complete physical, mental, and social well-being and not merely the absence of disease or infirmity" is not a true definition but a mystical formula about an ideal that goes well beyond the concrete and the measurable (Domaradzki, 2013, p. 25). Moreover, according to such a demanding definition, as Petr Skrabanek ironically adds, most of us are only healthy "fleetingly during orgasm, or when high on drugs" (Skrabanek, 1994, p. 42).

The truly transcendent character of health (or rather "super-health" to be enjoyed by "supermen" as Wendell C. Phillips, president of the American Medical Association, predicted in 1926) is also shown by the fact that its boundaries are constantly redrawn, and what once counted as a sin or perversion may at any time become a disease, or what once counted as a disease may be reformulated as a mere "condition." The lack of objective standards naturally makes it necessary to create a "theology of medicine" (Szasz, 1977) and an infallible magisterium, in this case the WHO as a "papacy" and professional associations as "bishoprics." The overarching concept of health and the magisterial pretensions of its church naturally lead to "unlimited expansion and control over endless dimensions of social life" and make it, as Domaradzki says, "truly catholic," "omnipresent," and "omnipotent" (Domaradzki, 2013, p. 25):

> It decides on one's employment, capability of getting married and having children; gives the right to abortion and child custody, decides who, when and how can die and if a person is fit to stand trial. Medical authorities influence personal decisions on feeding habits, sexual conduct and accepted stimulants. Doctors control birth, prenatal, postnatal and paediatric care; not only conception but also infertility, reproduction and sexual activity itself are also subject to their power. Medicine defines when life begins and if, at all, should begin.
>
> *(ibid., p. 26)*

Although, it might be suggested, medicine is not actually omnipotent in all of the above, its ambitions do show a tendency to control not only what is traditionally called "morals" but a much wider scope of human activities, even human life in its entirety from the cradle to the grave. If Domaradzki likened medicine to Catholicism (because of its universality) Howard Leichter compares it to Protestantism, in which good health becomes the sign of the "state of grace," "an affirmation of a life lived virtuously" (Leichter, 1997, p. 359). This also means that it separates the chosen ones from the rest, creating a community with a shared system of values, exactly what

Émile Durkheim called a "church" in the sociological sense of the word. The "rest" are those who reject any of its sacraments, like anti-vaccination movements or COVID-denialists, who are treated as heretics or witches, especially during times of crisis. Speaking of sacraments, the number one negative sacrament (or taboo) of medicine is, of course, death, which – along with the dying person – is placed outside the sphere of normality. By offering a life without suffering and death – by transplantations, gene therapy, psychiatric drugs, or in the near future nanobots inside the human body – the medical utopia (Schwartz, 1998) is not even a truly secular one, even though it promises "eternal life" with the characteristic laxity of today's language, as if "very long" was the same as "endless" and not as far from the infinite as the "very short" is.

The supposedly religious traits of medicine are in fact so many that it is difficult to see what remains secular about it. Apart from the sacred scriptures of the WHO and other medical associations, it has its less formal hagiography of prophets like Hippocrates (who may not have been a scientist in the modern sense but anticipated the advent of medical science), saints like Alexander Fleming (who invented penicillin and is not without reason buried in Saint Paul's Cathedral), or martyrs like Ignaz Semmelweis and Rosalind Franklin who sacrificed their lives for their research. As for rituals, practically all religious ceremonies have their medical counterparts: vaccinations replace baptism to introduce the newborn into the community and protect them from the evil of infection; instead of confirmation, medical examinations such as the first gynecological examination affirm one's maturity; marriage is more related to fertility clinics and family therapies than to the sacrament of matrimony; and ultimately, the dying do not meet a priest to receive the anointment of the sick, but they seek palliative treatment by a doctor (Domaradzki, 2013, p. 27). As for visible symbols, the white (or green, or blue) clothing of doctors is also more than just a technical necessity and forms an integral part of the sacred aura of the medical profession. Even in everyday language, today's people regularly use medical expressions instead of emotive or moral ones, such as "my adrenalin is high" or "it is in my genes."

It is therefore no miracle that medicine is often called not only a "cultural religion" (whatever that means) or a "secular religion" but a "truly transcendent new religion," sometimes by the same author in the same article (ibid., pp. 21 and 33). The list of attributes nevertheless suggests an analogy mostly with Catholic Christianity, which is sometimes explicitly confirmed, even at the cost of problematically equating Catholicism with religion as such (Clerc, 2004).

It should also be added that the power and self-confidence of the church of medicine have somewhat diminished recently. Some forms of alternative medicine and self-healing became powerful competitors of established (institutionalized) medical practice. Death (euthanasia) is also becoming more accepted and integrated into the normal practice of medicine. That many former diseases are redefined as special "conditions" by medical authorities shows the now wavering faith of many of the priests and adherents of medicine as a "secular religion."

See also: Biotechnology, Cloning, Genetics, Psychology, Scientism, Wellness

## Sources

Clerc, O. (2004) *Modern Medicine: The New World Religion*. Fawnskin: Personhood Press.
Domaradzki, J. (2013) 'Extra Medicinam Nulla Salus: Medicine as a Secular Religion', *Polish Sociological Review*, 181, pp. 21–38. Available at: https://www.jstor.org/stable/41969476
Foucault, M. ([1963] 2003) *The Birth of the Clinic: An Archeology of Medical Perception*. Translated by Sheridan, A. M. New York: Routledge.
Leichter, H. M. (1997) 'Lifestyle Correctness and the New Secular Morality', in *Morality and Health*, edited by Brandt, A. M., and Rozin, P. New York: Routledge, pp. 359–378.
Schwartz, W. B. (1998) *Life Without Disease: The Pursuit of Medical Utopia*. Berkeley: University of California Press.
Skrabanek, P. (1994) *The Death of Human Medicine and the Rise of Coercive Healthism*. Suffolk: The Social Affairs Unit.
Szasz, T. (1977) *The Theology of Medicine*. New York: Harper Colophon.

## Multiculturalism

When multiculturalism is called a secular or political religion, it is usually done with the same imprecision as in the case of "postmodernism," "political correctness," or "woke ideology" in contemporary conservative discourse. Canadian sociologist Mathieu Bock-Côté's *Multiculturalism as a Political Religion* in fact uses the word to denote all "New Left" ideologies that have sought to emancipate marginalized minorities since the 1960s and became a global phenomenon by the 2010s. Or even more, since this "grand narrative" (a remarkable use of a postmodern term by a conservative author) belongs to the even more overarching category of the "religion of humanity" (Bock-Côté, 2016, p. 10) and serves as a replacement of the "revolutionary faith" of Soviet communism that lost credibility in the 1950s when it turned out that "Moscow would not be the new Jerusalem" (ibid., p. 13). Multiculturalism nevertheless remains embedded in Marxism and its "revelation" that human alienation is a historical phenomenon which requires a political salvation: a "utopia" that will deliver society from all evils of the past (ibid., pp. 14–15). That is also why multiculturalism is sometimes identified as a manifestation of "Cultural Marxism" which is, however, remarkably different from its more universalistic antecedents, although no less religious: it is, as a Romanian Orthodox theologian said, "the dilution of religion into the absurd of multiple syncretic forms" (Necula, 2017, p. 131).

The specific "religious" traits of multiculturalism are its "sacralization of diversity" as an absolute value (Bock-Côté, 2016, p. 11), its creation of a "new conception of the world," in which good is represented by minorities and evil by the majority (ibid., p. 17), and its call for "repentance," a constant "ritual of negative commemoration" regarding the sins of Western civilization (ibid., p. 20). The "political" nature of this religiosity consists in the fact that it has managed to impose itself on the public sphere, offering a new source of legitimacy (ibid., p. 24) and effectively "diabolizing" or "demonizing" its enemies (ibid., p. 309).

The terminology nevertheless remains ambiguous. While words like "grand narrative," "ideology," or "totalitarian temptation" suggest that multiculturalism is, after all, a secular worldview that may be criticized in secular terms, the analogies drawn with "Islamism" (ibid., p. 309) and "fanaticism" (ibid., p. 313) suggest that it is indeed something essentially religious. After which it is no surprise that the intermediate term of "secular religion" also appears, expressing the same ambiguity (ibid., p. 314). The fact that the latter is treated synonymously not only with "political religion" but also with "totalitarianism" shows that the rhetorical strategy relies more on the negative connotations of the word "religion" (dogmatism, oppression, intolerance, etc.) than on any systematic analogy of the religious and the secular. The conclusion implicitly confirms this when it says that "Multiculturalism as a political religion writes a new chapter in the history of the subjugation of human beings and in the attempt to emaciate them in order to free them," suggesting that religion is only a byword for all manifestations of oppressive hypocrisy (ibid., p. 331).

See also: Communism, Humanism, Marxism, Postmodernism, Wokeness

### Sources

Bock-Côté, M. (2016) *Multiculturalisme comme religion politique*. Paris: Cerf.
Necula, C. (2017) 'Multiculturalism as the Religion of Politics', *Ars Liturgica*, 22(1), pp. 131–144. Available at: https://www.ceeol.com/search/article-detail?id=1007852 (Accessed: 1 December 2023).

# N
# NATIONALISM

Nationalism is one of the great topics of secular religions' literature. It is, at the same time, difficult to distinguish from other ideologies like patriotism, fascism, or Nazism (of which the latter explicitly called itself *national* socialism). According to some, it also has a close connection to democracy: "The nation is a democratic creation, the expression of the people's general will, its sovereignty" (Boia, 2002, p. 73), and during the 20th century it also became associated with communist ideologies from the Soviet Union to China and North Korea. Another problem is that nationalism often remains embedded in traditional religious frameworks. In academic literature, "religious nationalism" means more frequently a Hindu, Buddhist, or Christian type of nationalism than the creation of an entirely new, secular religion of the nation.

All this can be illustrated by the first spectacular manifestation of modern nationalism. During the French Revolution, the 1790 "Festival of the Federation" (the celebration of national unity) took place at the "Altars of the Fatherland," where a Catholic mass was celebrated by a Catholic bishop assisted by two hundred Catholic priests. Oaths were taken to the Nation, to the Law, and to the King, although the nation itself hardly existed at the time. "Everybody took the federation oath. On that day representatives of Celtic Brittany, half-Flemish Picardy, half-Spanish Roussillon, almost wholly German Alsace and Italian Corsica swore brotherhood – *fraternité* – with the French" (Hayes, 1960, p. 52).

The nation would remain an imagined community long thereafter, despite all attempts of linguistic and cultural homogenization: "imagined" in the sense that its members would "never know most of their fellow-members, meet them, or even hear of them, yet in the minds of each lives the image

DOI: 10.4324/9781003471257-15

of their communion" (Anderson, [1983] 2006, p. 6). This "image" of the nation is the representation of something that does not have any physical reality and is therefore difficult to call anything but transcendent. Let us also remember that the nation – as Jean-Jacques Rousseau's formula suggested for the revolutionaries – has always been more than a mere aggregate of its members: the "act of association produces, in place of the individual persons of every contracting party, a moral and collective body . . . endowed with its unity, its common self, its life, and its will" (Rousseau, [1762] 1999, p. 56).

It is because of its mystical nature that the idea of the nation remains inseparable from the just as mystical idea of the homeland, which is obviously not identical with the current territory of a given country: it is the "cradle" of the nation, a spiritual entity. This also means that the nation is prior to the individual, it is its creator and its ultimate goal. Loyalty to the nation overwrites all other commitments. When the French Revolution broke ties with the Catholic Church, the advocates of the new nationalist religion – like Jean-Paul Rabat, a former Protestant pastor – explicitly argued that it should take hold of the human being in its entirety:

> The secret was well known to the priests, who, with their catechisms, their processions . . . their ceremonies, sermons, hymns, missions, pilgrimages, patron saints, paintings, and all that nature placed at their disposal, infallibly led men to the goal they designated. They took hold of a man at birth, grasped him again in childhood, adolescence and adulthood, when he married and had children, in his moments of grief and remorse, in the sanctum of his conscience . . . in sickness and at death. In this way they managed to cast many far-flung nations, differing in their customs, languages, laws, color and physical makeup, into the same mold, and to give them the same opinions. O cunning lawgivers, who speak to us in the name of heaven, should we not do in the name of truth and freedom, what you so often did in the name of error and slavery?
> 
> *(Bell, 2003, p. 3)*

As the speech implies, the religion of the nation should also have its own rituals, sacred spaces, saints, and symbols. The French Revolution in fact developed so many ritual celebrations that Mona Ozouf took those as the defining elements of the whole era (Ozouf, 1988). Perhaps less spectacularly, but "National Holidays" are still celebrated today by every nation-state, most of them recalling the "birth" or the "revival" of the nation. Sacred spaces can be like the Pantheon in Paris ("the temple of the nation"), the Westminster Abbey in London, or the Yasukuni Shrine in Tokyo (while the last two also show how difficult it is to separate the "secularly" religious and the "truly" religious, at least in the case of Anglicanism or Shintoism). These are also the shrines where national heroes – the founders of the nation,

FIGURE 3  A "reliquary" of the "martyrs" (Lajos Aulich, Janos Damjanich and Karoly Vecsey) of the Hungarian war of independence 1848–1849, containing their bones and pieces of their gallows in Déri Múzeum, Debrecen, Hungary

*Source:* Déri Múzeum, VIII.75.7.1. Reproduction 6: Lukacs Tihamer, used with permission of the museum

fallen soldiers, or the martyrs of national independence – are commemorated. Martyrdom – the "ultimate sacrifice" – is of special importance as the expression of loyalty to the nation: in some cases, the cult of martyrs is fully analogous to the veneration of saints, when hearts, bones, body parts, or parts of the martyr's gallows are put on altars or in public reliquaries (Piette, 1993, pp. 14–15).

Sometimes the whole nation is seen as a "martyr," or even as a savior, "the Christ of Nations," as Poland was called after its failed national resurrections in 19th century (Nyirkos, 2023). As for symbols, the flag of the nation is often treated as a sacred object, the violation of which counts as an act of sacrilege. The raising of the flag – especially if accompanied by the singing of the national anthem – is also part of a liturgy that requires a certain posture and appropriate behavior or attire.

Despite all the similarities, however, not everyone is ready to call nationalism a religion. Benedict Anderson's *Imagined Communities* rejects the idea that nationalism "supersedes" religion or is a "religion" itself, although it adds somewhat ambiguously that it would still "make things easier if one treated it as if it belonged with 'kinship' and 'religion', rather than with 'liberalism' or 'fascism'" (Anderson, [1983] 2006, p. 5). In other words, nationalism is more than just a political ideology; although – as the present volume testifies – liberalism and fascism are perhaps also more than just political ideologies. Liah Greenfeld, who lamented that by the end of the 20th century it had "become a cliché" to call nationalism a religion, was no less ambiguous when she stated that "nationalism is an essentially secular form of consciousness" while maintaining that "it sacralizes the secular" (Greenfeld, 2006, p. 93).

To distinguish the sacralized secular from the truly secular is of course as difficult as to distinguish the truly religious from the secularly religious. As Hans Kelsen wrote:

> To consider an object as sacred *presupposes* the belief in the existence of something supernatural in the sense of *suprasensuous*. Huxley says 'that religion arose as a feeling of the sacred,' but it is just the other way around: the feeling of the sacred arose from religion as the belief in supernatural or suprasensuous beings.
> *(Kelsen, 2012, pp. 37–38)*

That is why many authors confirm – *pace* Greenfeld – that nationalism is not a secular but a real religion. The most famous example is Carlton Hayes' *Nationalism: A Religion*:

> Nationalism, like any religion, calls into play not simply the will, but the intellect, the imagination and the emotions. The intellect constructs a speculative theology or mythology of nationalism. The imagination builds an unseen world around the eternal past and the everlasting future of one's nationality. The emotions arouse a joy and an ecstasy in the contemplation of the national god who is all-good and all-protecting, a longing for his favours, a thankfulness for his benefits, a fear of offending him, and feelings of awe and reverence at the immensity of his power and wisdom; they express themselves naturally in worship, both private and public. For nationalism, again like any other religion, is social, and its chief rites are public rites performed in the name and for the salvation of a whole community.
> *(Hayes, 1960, pp. 164–165)*

Moreover, the same author realized some decades earlier that nationalism was becoming a world religion:

> The most impressive fact about the present age is the universality of the religious aspects of nationalism. Not only in the United States does the

religious sense of the whole people find expression in nationalism, but also, in slightly different form but perhaps to an even greater degree, in France, England, Italy, Germany, Belgium, Holland, Russia, the Scandinavian and Baltic countries, Poland, Hungary, Czechoslovakia, Spain, Portugal, Ireland, the Balkans, Greece, and the Latin-American republics. Nor does the religion of nationalism thrive only on traditionally Christian soil; it now flourishes in Japan, Turkey, Egypt, India, Korea, and is rearing its altars in China. Nationalism has a large number of particularly quarrelsome sects, but as a whole it is the latest and nearest approach to a world-religion.

*(Hayes, 1926, p. 117)*

In the United States, the religion of the nation is more often called a "civil religion," but this is once again difficult to call secular, since – as Robert Bellah remarked – it is "a genuine apprehension of universal and transcendent religious reality," at least "as seen in" or "revealed through" the experience of the American people (Bellah, [1966] 1991, p. 179). While the American civil religion is also a supra-denominational ("non-sectarian") phenomenon, nationalisms in the Global South are inevitably intertwined by their native religions:

For example, a common "nationalist" impulse throughout the huge and heterogenous British Empire of India has issued in the emergence of separate nations not of distinctive language, but rather of distinctive religion: Hindu India, Muslim Pakistan, Buddhist Burma, and "primitively" Buddhist Ceylon.

*(Hayes, 1960, p. 157)*

This makes the use of the concept of "secular religion" in the case of nationalism even more problematic. To add further examples, Chinese nationalism – even in its form adopted by the Communist Party, "socialism with Chinese characteristics" – has deep roots in the Confucian tradition and the imperial cult, and the same holds for Japan, where Shintoism – although it had been transformed into a national cult somewhat artificially in the late 19th century – still retained its original religious features. Arab nationalism is certainly more difficult to reconcile with the more overarching Islamic notion of the "umma" (the community of all believers, regardless of nation or ethnicity), but this seems to be a more theoretical than practical obstacle, for anti-colonialist movements in North Africa or the Middle East have always used both to justify their struggle. In Africa, the challenge of "tribalism" was also a challenge to the cult of newly emerging nation-states, but an open break with their religious underpinnings was just as impossible as in any other non-Western country. In the latter, as the Italian historian Emilio Gentile noted, new political institutions had to be legitimized in a mostly artificial (postcolonial) environment, "entirely untouched by secularization" (Gentile, 2006, p. 125). That is also why the fusion of nationalism and traditional beliefs was also mixed with the cult of charismatic leaders as the incarnations of newly created nations, as it happened in Bourguiba's Tunisia, Nasser's Egypt, Nkrumah's Ghana, Senghor's Senegal, Nyerere's Tanzania, or Sukarno's Indonesia (ibid., p. 126). So, even though many authors insist on calling nationalism a "secular religion" (Hobsbawm, 1983; Hunt, 1988; Smith, 2009), a "social religion" (Elias, 1996), a "quasi-religion" (Smith, 1994), or an "idolatry" (Cavanaugh, 2021), the separation of nationalism from genuinely religious phenomena remains just as problematic as its separation from other – allegedly secular – religions.

See also: Democracy, Fascism, Nazism, Patriotism, Revolution, Statism

## Sources

Anderson, B. ([1983] 2006) *Imagined Communities: Reflections on the Origin and Spread of Nationalism*. London: Verso.

Bell, D. A. (2003) *The Cult of the Nation in France: Inventing Nationalism, 1680–1800*. Cambridge: Harvard University Press.

Bellah, R. N. ([1966] 1991) 'Civil Religion in America', in *Beyond Belief: Essays on Religion in a Post-Traditionalist World*. Berkeley: University of California Press, pp. 168–189.

Boia, L. (2002) *Le mythe de la démocratie*. Paris: Les Belles Lettres.

Cavanaugh, W. T. (2021) 'The Splendid Idolatry of Nationalism', *Pro Publico Bono*, 9(2), pp. 4–25. https://doi.org/10.32575/ppb.2021.2.1

Elias, N. (1996) *The Germans: Power Struggles and the Development of Habitus in the Nineteenth and Twentieth Centuries*. New York: Columbia University Press.

Gentile, E. (2006) *Politics as Religion*. Translated by Staunton, G. Princeton: Princeton University Press.

Greenfeld, L. (2006) 'The Modern Religion?', in *Nationalism and the Mind: Essays on Modern Culture*. Oxford: Oneworld, pp. 93–114.

Hayes, C. J. H. (1926) 'Nationalism as a Religion', in *Essays on Nationalism*. New York: Macmillan, pp. 93–125.

Hayes, C. J. H. (1960) *Nationalism: A Religion*. New York: Macmillan.

Hobsbawm, E. (1983) 'Mass-Producing Traditions: Europe, 1870–1914', in *The Invention of Tradition*. Cambridge: Cambridge University Press, pp. 263–307.

Hunt, L. (1988) 'Foreword', in *Festivals and the French Revolution*, edited by Ozouf, M., translated by Sheridan, A. Cambridge: Harvard University Press, pp. ix–xiii.

Kelsen, H. (2012) *Secular Religion: A Polemic against the Misinterpretation of Modern Social Philosophy, Science, and Politics as "New Religions"*. Vienna: Springer.

Nyirkos, T. (2023) 'Patriotism as a Political Religion: Its History, Its Ambiguities, and the Case of Hungary', *Religions*, 14(1), p. 116. https://doi.org/10.3390/rel14010116

Ozouf, M. (1988) *Festivals and the French Revolution*. Translated by Sheridan, A. Cambridge: Harvard University Press.

Piette, A. (1993) *Les religiosités séculières*. Paris: Presses Universitaires de France.

Rousseau, J.-J. ([1762] 1999) *Discourse on Political Economy and The Social Contract*. Translated by Betts, C. Oxford: Oxford University Press.

Smith, A. D. (2009) *Ethno-symbolism and Nationalism: A Cultural Approach*. New York: Routledge.
Smith, J. E. (1994) *Quasi-Religions: Humanism, Marxism, and Nationalism*. New York: Macmillan.

## Nazism

Nazism, the German version of "national socialism" (*Nationalsozialismus*) is often subsumed under the more comprehensive category of fascism, but this is somewhat misleading and imprecise. Those who have written about Nazi ideology as a "secular" or "political" religion have been usually aware of its unique character and drafted their critique accordingly.

To begin with, the absolute of Nazism is not the traditional idea of the nation (as in the case of Italian fascism) but that of the race, even if the two are sometimes hopelessly confused in Nazi rhetoric. This confusion can never be fully eliminated, because – as the Catholic historian Christopher Dawson remarked as early as 1934 – the Nazi religion did not have a "dogmatic character," it was a "fluid and incoherent thing" that combined elements of ancient tribalism and early modern nationalism with the more recent doctrine of racism (Dawson, 1934, p. 8). It also went hand in hand with the totalization of the state, a likewise universal process in the modern age, even in democratic countries (ibid., p. 10). As Eric Voegelin's *Political Religions* (1938) emphasized, race theory was itself a modern myth (even if it was presented as science), and the vague notions of nation, people, not to mention "the spirit of the people" (*Volksgeist*) were in fact so elusive that they had to be embodied in a leader to gain any appearance of reality.

That is why dogmatics had to be replaced by propaganda and ritual (newspapers and radio, speeches and ceremonies, and rallies and parades) whose sole aim was to bring about the *unio mystica*, the emotional and spiritual communion of the people and the Führer as the people's incarnation (Voegelin, [1938] 2000, p. 64). As Rudolf Hess addressed Hitler at the 1934 *Parteitag* in Nuremberg, filmed by Leni Riefenstahl for the propaganda movie *The Triumph of the Will*: "You are Germany: when you act, the nation acts, when you judge, the people judge!" (Riefenstahl, 1935).

The omnipresence of propaganda impressed contemporary observers so much that not only Christopher Dawson saw it as a defining element of Nazism, but it also led Guy Stanton Ford to use the word "secular religion" for the first time in the English language: "the dictators of the present are not lineal descendants of the despots and tyrants of the past . . . those of today have a new and powerful technique in mass control through propaganda by radio, movie, press, education, and a secular religion of their own making" (Ford, 1935, p. vii). Propaganda was, of course, an instrument to *influence* the masses, so despite Nazism's glorification of the people and the continuous demonstrations of popular support, many authors doubted that it was a genuine mass movement. It was rather, as Raymond Aron's *The Future of Secular Religons* claimed in 1944, a well-organized worship of the leader, orchestrated by a priestly elite:

> We know now that the age of the crowd really conceals the age of the elites. It is true that without the passive or passionate support of the masses no regime is possible in our own century. But it is also true that the masses are manipulated rather than autonomous. They are maneuvered into worshiping someone they know nothing about.
> *(Aron, [1944] 2002, p. 196)*

Hitler himself acknowledged that with a church-like organization and a strong belief in its mission even a minority could accumulate in itself the majority of energies. The Nazi Party, he confirmed, was not a political party in the traditional sense of the word: "A political party is inclined to adjust its teachings with a view to meeting those of its opponents, but a *Weltanschauung* proclaims its own infallibility" (Bucher, 2010, p. 21). In *Mein Kampf*, he made it even clearer that this *Weltanschauung* – just as a religion – was not a vaguely defined ideology but something organized into a "church militant":

> Without a clearly defined belief, the religious feeling would not only be worthless for the human existence but even might contribute towards a general disintegration . . . To take abstract and general principles, derived from a *Weltanschauung* which is based on a solid foundation of truth, and transform them into a militant community whose members share the same political faith – a community which is precisely defined, rigidly organized, of one mind and one will – such a transformation is the most important task of all.
> *(ibid., pp. 22–23)*

Moreover, this church should also have its own theology of history. While many thinkers on the left labeled the Nazis conservative and retrograde, their triumph, as Raymond Aron remarked, was rather due to the aura of novelty, the fact that they remained untouched by the corruption of the old regime (Aron, [1944] 2002, p. 186). Hitler doubtless thought of his movement as a progressive one, not only in a political or social sense but also in a religious sense. As he said in one of his table talks in 1941, it would be "indescribably foolish to revive a cult of Wotan," for ancient German mythology was "outdated, was no longer viable, when Christianity appeared" (Bucher, 2010, pp. 41–42), while Christianity itself became outdated with the appearance of National Socialism. "Let the institution of the Church be overcome slowly by spiritual enlightenment," he said at the Führer's Headquarters in 1941, adding in an unmistakably prophetic tone that the coming of the "new era" might take "a few more centuries, then evolution will achieve what revolution hasn't . . . It is a shame to live at a time when you cannot yet know what the new world will look like" (ibid., p. 28).

Another, even more explicitly religious trait was Hitler's frequent recourse to divine Providence from at least 1933, as something that helped him in his struggle for power, that gave a "miraculous victory" over Poland in 1939, and that saved his life during the 1944 assassination attempt. As late as 1945, in his New Year's address, Hitler claimed that the trials and tribulations of Germany were the most certain signs that Germans were a chosen people, a unique subject of divine Providence (ibid., pp. 51–54).

Such overt references to Providence lead us back to the problems of vocabulary. Christopher Dawson's passage called Nazism a "religion," only to add a few lines later that although it had a mythology and ethic of its own, it was still "not religious in the strict sense," where the "strict sense" seems to have been reserved for Christianity, the main rival of Nazism (Dawson, 1934, p. 8). In another ambiguous passage, he nevertheless spoke of two "religious" worldviews fighting against each other, the "God-religious and the social-religious" (ibid., p. 12).

A similar ambiguity is found in Eric Voegelin, who spoke of a "political religion" which he also called "inner-worldly" (almost synonymous with "secular"), as opposed to "other-worldly" or "spiritual" religions. However, his historical examples, from the cult of Aton in Egypt to the cult of the Sun King in France, were hardly secular. Moreover, the very name *Volksgeist* (the people's spirit) made it difficult to see why belief in it might not be "spiritual" (*geistlich*).

Raymond Aron, as we have seen, mentioned "secular religions" with their "quasi-sacred" goals. These goals, however, turned out to be just as sacred as any traditionally religious ones: "if the job of religion is to set out the lofty values that give human existence its direction, how can we deny that the political doctrines of our own day are essentially religious in character" (Aron, [1944] 2002, p. 179). Nazism was also called an "ersatzreligion" (Gamm, 1962), a "political faith" (Tal, [1978] 2004) and "political theology" by the same author (Tal, [1979] 2004), while the most widespread term remains "political religion" (Bärsch, 1998; Gentile, 2006; Heer, 1968; Ley and Schoeps, 1997; Vondung, 1971). It thus remains an open issue whether Nazism should be viewed as a secular ideology, a secular or political religion, a political theology, a cult, or just a religion without an adjective.

See also: Fascism, Nationalism, Patriotism, Racism, Statism

## Sources

Aron, R. ([1944] 2002) 'The Future of Secular Religions', in *The Dawn of Universal History: Selected Essays from a Witness to the Twentieth Century*, translated by Bray, B. New York, Basic Books, pp. 177–201.

Bärsch, C.-E. (1998) *Die politische Religion des Nationalsozialismus*. München: Fink.
Bucher, R. (2010) *Hitler's Theology: A Study in Political Religion*. Translated by Pohl, R. New York: Continuum.
Dawson, C. (1934) 'Religion and the Totalitarian State', *The Criterion*, 14(54), pp. 1–16.
Ford, G. S. (ed.) (1935) *Dictatorship in the Modern World*. Minneapolis: University of Minnesota Press.
Gamm, E.-J. (1962) *Der braune Kult: das Dritte Reich und seine Ersatzreligion*. Hamburg: Rütten und Loening.
Gentile, E. (2006) *Politics as Religion*. Translated by Staunton, G. Princeton: Princeton University Press.
Heer, F. (1968) *Der Glaube des Adolf Hitler: Anatomie einer politischen Religiosität*. München: Bechtle.
Ley, M., and Schoeps, J. H (eds.) (1997) *Der Nationalsozialismus als politische Religion*. Bodenheim: Philo.
Riefenstahl, L. (1935) 'Triumph des Willens'. Available at: https://www.dailymotion.com/video/x6uajey (Accessed: 1 December 2023)
Scott, A. (2018) '(Plebiscitary) Leader Democracy: The Return of an Illusion?', *Thesis Eleven*, 148(1), pp. 3–20. https://doi.org/10.1177/0725513618800120
Tal, U. ([1978] 2004) '"Political Faith" of Nazism Prior to the Holocaust', in *Religion, Politics, and Ideology in the Third Reich: Selected Essays*. New York: Routledge, pp. 16–54.
Tal, U. ([1979] 2004) 'Structures of German "Political Theology" in the Nazi Era', in *Religion, Politics, and Ideology in the Third Reich: Selected Essays*. New York: Routledge, pp. 87–129.
Voegelin, E. ([1938] 2000) 'Political Religions', in *The Collected Work of Eric Voegelin. Volume 5: Modernity without Restraint*, translated by Schildhauer, V. A. Columbia: University of Missouri Press, pp. 19–73.
Vondung, K. (1971) *Magie und Manipulation: Ideologischer Kult und politische Religion des Nationalsozialismus*. Göttingen: Vandenhoeck & Ruprecht.

## Neoliberalism

See Capitalism.

## Nietzscheism

Although Friedrich Nietzsche is usually seen as a great atheist thinker, his philosophy (like many other forms of atheism) is also often treated as a secular – or perhaps full-grown – religion. The very idea of the Übermensch, the highest form of existence that a human being can set for itself as a goal, shows the unmistakable characteristics of a religious ideal. It is something not yet present but positioned as a promise of salvation, compared to which the "last man" of egalitarian humanism manifests the ultimate damnation of humankind (Nietzsche, [1885] 2006, p. 10). That Nietzsche himself presents this dualistic idea in the form of a religious sermon (*Thus Spoke Zarathustra*), using an Ancient Iranian prophet as his alter ego, is an ironical gesture that nevertheless reveals a deep commitment to religious symbolism and language. Nietzsche, of course, has never suggested that the Übermensch should be an object of "worship" or the center of an institutionalized "cult." For him, it was a radically individualistic ideal to be achieved by everyone's own effort. It nonetheless remains true that many of his followers – most of whom transformed the idea to serve their own ideological purposes, most notably the national socialists of Germany – did create a cult of the "superior being" or even of Nietzsche himself as its prophet.

The fact that Nietzschean philosophy is self-professedly *Beyond Good and Evil* (Nietzsche, [1886] 2002) also raises doubts about its religious character, for it shows the complete absence of any comprehensive moral code, let alone a "moral theology." Yet the very word "beyond" suggests that what we see is rather a "super-morality," a higher norm that is above all traditional ethical conceptions, which is exactly what certain "religious" authors said throughout the ages. When the ancient Greek philosopher Heraclitus said that "To god all things are fair and just, whereas humans have supposed that some things are unjust, other things just" (Heraclitus, [c. 500 BCE] 1987, p. 61) or when Saint Augustine advised Christian believers to "Love, and do what thou wilt" (Augustine, [413] 1983, p. 862), they both professed the conviction that "good and evil" were dependent on something more fundamental than the ordinary precepts of everyday morality.

This is also what Nietzsche's distinction of "superhuman" and "last man" morality implies; moreover, it follows patterns that originated in ancient Greece and were rediscovered in the Romantic era. As George Santayana said, "His religion of the Uebermensch [sic] is a fantastic romantic version of Greek aristocracy" (Santayana, [1950] 1995, p. 167).

The religious leanings of Nietzsche's philosophy – and those of his followers – are thus difficult to dismiss. As Tamsin Shaw notes, Nietzsche is still regarded as one of the founders of 20th century's "secular religions" (Shaw, 2005, p. 81). And not unjustifiably so, for Nietzsche himself often assumed the role of a prophet or even a God. To think of him as an early advocate of "critical thinking" or an heir to the "skeptic tradition" is to downplay the religious aspects of his thought. What Nietzsche and some other like-minded thinkers of the 19th century tried to create was not a secular worldview but a post-Christian synthesis, a new faith. "Nietzscheism," however – if there is such a thing – would never become an institutional "church," only a vaguely circumscribed set of beliefs in the capacities of the human being to replace God.

See also: Atheism, Humanism, Nazism

## Sources

Augustine ([413] 1983) 'Ten Homilies on the First Epistle of John', in *Nicene and Post- Nicene Fathers*, Series 1, Volume 7, translated by Browne, H. Grand Rapids: Christian Classics Ethereal Library, pp. 777–900. Available at: https://www.ccel.org/ccel/s/schaff/npnf107/cache/npnf107.pdf (Accessed: 1 December 2023).

Heraclitus ([c. 500 BCE] 1987) *Fragments*. Translated by Robinson, T. M. Toronto: University of Toronto Press.
Nietzsche, F. ([1885] 2006) *Thus Spoke Zarathustra*. Translated by Del Caro, A. Cambridge: Cambridge University Press.
Nietzsche, F. ([1886] 2002) *Beyond Good and Evil: Prelude to a Philosophy of the Future*. Translated by Norman, J. Cambridge: Cambridge University Press.
Santayana, G. ([1950] 1995) *Dominations and Powers: Reflections on Liberty, Society, and Government*. London: Transaction.
Shaw, T. (2005) 'Nietzsche and the Self-Destruction of Secular Religions', *History of European Ideas*, 32(1), pp. 80–98. https://doi.org/10.1016/j.histeuroideas.2005.05.001

# O
# OLYMPISM

See Sports.

# P
# PACIFISM

Pacifism is a strange case of secular religions: although it often appears on longer lists as a sort of "obvious" example, there has been no serious attempt to give it a more thorough analysis. In Vilfredo Pareto's *The Mind and Society*, "Socialism, Syndicalism, Radicalism, Tolstoyism, pacifism, humanitarianism, Solidarism, and so on, form a sum that may be said to belong to the democratic religion" (Pareto, [1916] 1935, p. 1294). In Carl Christian Bry's *Hidden Religions* the "world peace movement" is mentioned together with such esoteric examples as number mysticism, astrology, belief in Atlantis, theosophy, or fakir magic and also with communism, anti-alcoholism, sexual reform, or the Esperanto movement (Bry, 1925, p. 14).

More recently, in blog posts and journal articles, pacifism appears with vegetarianism as the two oldest "isms" that replace traditional religion ("often accompanied by New Ageism, followed soon by anti-capitalism, then environmentalism," Timeguide, 2013) or just mentioned in passing: "How to crack the riddle of a party that has long clung to ecopacifism as a secular religion?" (Joffe, 2022).

Although one might suspect that it is pacifism's ultimate goal, the ideal of peace as a supreme value, a state of universal salvation (and the zeal it arouses in its advocates) that incites the analogy, in the lack of more detailed discussions, this can only be conferred from the other cases of religious/secular comparisons. The only exception is the United Nations, the secular religion of which is sometimes analyzed in the context of the world peace movement.

See also: UN

## Sources

Bry, C. C. (1925) *Verkappte Religionen*. Gotha: Leopold Klotz.

Joffe, J. (2022) 'Germany's Green Pacifism Goes to War', Australian Strategic Policy Institute, 19 August. Available at: https://www.aspistrategist.org.au/germanys-green-pacifism-goes-to-war/ (Accessed: 1 December 2023).

Pareto, V. ([1916] 1935) *The Mind and Society*. Translated by Bongiorno, A., and Livingston, A. New York: Harcourt, Brace and Company.

Timeguide (2013) 'Is Secular Substitution of Religion a Threat to Western Civilization?', 22 May. Available at: https://timeguide.wordpress.com/tag/secular-religion/ (Accessed: 1 December 2023)

## Panopticism

The idea of the "Panopticon," a prison where continuous surveillance substitutes physical coercion, has often been described in religious terms. The very name of the prison, invented by the English philosopher Jeremy Bentham in 1787, raises such allusions to the "all-seeing eye of God" or the "eye of Providence," and this is not mere coincidence. Bentham consciously used theological words like "omnipresence" ("if divines will allow me the expression," Bentham, 1838–43, p. 45), and he also quoted Psalm 139 in one of his sketches on the Panopticon:

> Thou art about my path, and about my bed: and spiest out all my ways. / If I say, peradventure the darkness shall cover me, then shall my night be turned into day. / Even there also shall thy hand lead me; and thy right hand shall hold me.

As Gertrude Himmelfarb said:

> Bentham did not believe in God, but he did believe in the qualities apotheosized in God. The Panopticon was a realization of the divine ideal, spying out the ways of the transgressor by means of an ingenious architectural scheme, turning night into day with artificial light and reflectors, holding men captive by an intricate system of inspection. Its purpose was not so much to provide a maximum amount of human supervision, as to transcend the human and give the illusion of a divine omnipresence.
> *(Himmelfarb, 1968, p. 35)*

The architectural scheme involved a central observation tower within a circle of prison cells. From the tower, the prison guard could see every inmate, but the latter could not see either him or each other. In such an arrangement, the mere possibility of being watched was enough to maintain discipline, for the invisible inspector might also have been absent (Bentham, 1838–43, pp. 40–44).

"Illusion" thus refers to the fact that it is not the actual presence of the supervisor that counts, only the belief of the inmates that he is there. (Just as in the eucharist, "real presence" is a matter of belief and not experience.)

Moreover, as Bentham himself asserts, the idea of inspection is applicable not only to prisons but many other institutions: manufactories, madhouses, hospitals, schools, or, as he himself put it, practically "any institution it may be thought proper to apply it to." Omnipresence thence takes on a truly universal character:

> What would you say, if by the gradual adoption and diversified application of this single principle, you should see a new scene of things spread itself over the face of civilized society? – morals reformed, health preserved, industry invigorated, instruction diffused, public burthens lightened, economy seated as it were upon a rock, the gordian knot of the poor-laws not cut, but untied – all by a simple idea in architecture?
>
> *(ibid., p. 66)*

This seems to imply that the invisible observer is also practically omnipotent and unquestionably good. No wonder that Michel Foucault in the 20th century spoke of "panopticism" as a complete system of social control, and although he emphasized the mechanical nature of surveillance (it is "automatic," a "machine" or "machinery," a "mechanism of power," Foucault, 1995, pp. 201–205), he also made some subtle theological observations. Even if the power of panoptic surveillance stemmed from "belief" or "fiction," this alone did not diminish its effectivity: "A real subjection is born mechanically from a fictitious relation" (ibid., p. 202), replacing the more ancient, sacred forms of legitimacy. "The ceremonies, the rituals, the marks by which the sovereign's surplus power" were once manifested have now become superfluous and useless.

Rituals, however, had never been fully absent from Bentham's scheme (not even religious rituals, see Bentham, 1838–43, 4, p. 43), and it also remains dubious whether merely believing that we are viewed by an invisible viewer could be maintained without some regular, ritual corroboration. In this regard, the issue of panopticism is most closely related to the problem of "moralizing high gods" (Norenzayan et al., 2016; Whitehouse et al., 2019): the dilemma whether sociability and rule-following in complex societies were preceded by belief in a higher, omnipotent, and omnipresent moral authority, or – to the contrary – it was sociability and rule-following that gave rise to belief in such an entity. In sum, even if we accept from Foucault that our society is one "not of spectacle, but of surveillance" (Foucault, [1975] 1995, p. 217), the idea of a transcendent, omnipresent, powerful, and good-intentioned lawgiver and the social rituals connected to it (the "meticulous, concrete training of useful forces") remain more explainable in a religious framework than in a secular one, regardless of which came first.

## Sources

Bentham, J. (1838–1843) 'Panopticon; or the Inspection-House', in *The Works of Jeremy Bentham*, Volume 4, edited by Bowring, J. Edinburgh: William Tait, pp. 37–172.

Foucault, M. ([1975] 1995) *Discipline and Punish: The Birth of the Prison*. Translated by Sheridan, A. New York: Vintage Books.

Himmelfarb, G. (1968) 'The Haunted House of Jeremy Bentham', in *Victorian Minds: A Study of Intellectuals in Crisis and Ideologies in Transition*. New York: A. A. Knopf, pp. 32–81.

Norenzayan, A., Shariff, A. F., Gervais, W. M., Willard, A. K., McNamara R. A., Slingerland E., and Henrich, J. (2016) 'The Cultural Evolution of Prosocial Religions', *Behavioral and Brain Sciences*, 39, p. e1. https://doi.org/10.1017/S0140525X14001356

Whitehouse, H., Francois, P., Savage, P. E., Currie, T. E., Feeney, K. C., Cioni, E., Purcell, R., Ross, R. M., Larson, J., Baines, J., ter Haar, B., Covey, A., and Turchin P. (2019) 'Complex Societies Precede Moralizing Gods Throughout World History', *Nature*, 568, pp. 226–229. https://doi.org/10.1038/s41586-019-1043-4

## Patriotism

Patriotism is sometimes distinguished from nationalism as a less exclusive and more spontaneous form of loyalty, which preceded the emergence of modern nation-states and ethnic nationalism. This "special affection for" or "sense of personal identification with" one's homeland (Nathanson, 1993, p. 34) would nevertheless become deeply intertwined with national sentiment after the French Revolution, making it somewhat artificial to speak of a "patriotic religion" as distinguished from the "religion of nationalism." The only reason to do so is to highlight some specific elements of the former that have surfaced time and again since 1789.

During the French Revolution, the first official celebrations were organized around the Altars of the Fatherland; the song that later became the national anthem of France hailed the "sacred love of the fatherland" (*amour sacré de la patrie*); and, perhaps most importantly, the revolutionaries called themselves "patriots" as opposed to counterrevolutionaries. In the meantime, the counterrevolutionaries themselves enthusiastically copied the patriotic cult. The most striking example is Louis de Bonald's vision of a "Temple of France," in which the statues of great political and military leaders, scholars, and magistrates replaced Christian saints, while the king and his subjects were to worship the "God of France" together (Bonald, [1796] 1843, pp. 356–358); something that the Panthéon had already realized in revolutionary Paris.

The idea of the "fatherland" – a just as spiritual entity as the nation – thereby became a unifying force, the religious character of which was obvious for everyone. As the historian Jules Michelet put it in 1831: "My noble country, you must take the place of the God who escapes us, that you may fill within us the immeasurable abyss which extinct Christianity has left there.

You are for us the equivalent of the infinite" (Michelet, [1831] 1959, p. 83). Since the equivalent of the infinite is presumably another infinite, the idea is at most non-Christian but certainly not irreligious.

For Émile Durkheim, it was exactly the experience of the French Revolution that indicated how the essence of religion was not "belief in God" but practices related to something "sacred" that bound a community together. In the case of France, he even saw a continuity between the medieval and the modern ideas of the homeland: "The *patrie*, the French revolution, Jeanne d'Arc are sacred things for us that we do not allow anyone to touch" (Durkheim, 1898, p. 20). He did not speak of a "secular religion" but a real one, and in his wake authors like Marxist historian Albert Mathiez also emphasized that the French Revolution had a "veritable religion" (Mathiez, 1904, p. 12), composed of many elements (the worship of the Fatherland, the Constitution, Liberty, Nature, or Reason), among which patriotism remained central (ibid., p. 34).

In other countries, the "fatherland" (or "motherland") was an even more spiritual construction, for it did not even exist at the time of emerging patriotism. In Poland or Italy, belief in the country was a precondition for creating or – in a more mystical way – resurrecting it. The Italian unification movement was not without reason called *Risorgimento*, for the Fatherland itself was "immortal," as many monuments still testify throughout the country. "Altars of the Fatherland" were erected not only in a physical shape (the most famous being the Victor Emanuel II Monument in Rome) but also in a more "spiritual" way, as in Nazi Germany. When German field marshal Robert von Greim and his mistress, pilot Hanna Reitsch, were captured by Americans at the end of the Second World War, their interrogators did not even understand what they meant by the word:

> Greim said that Hitler had ordered him and Hanna Reitsch to leave. . . . Both kept repeating: "It was our blackest day when we were told that we could not die at our Fuehrer's side." Then they added, while tears kept running down Hanna Reitsch's cheeks: "We should all kneel down in reverence and prayer before the altar of the Fatherland." "What is the altar of the Fatherland?" I asked them, completely taken aback. "Why, the Fuehrer's bunker in Berlin."
>
> *(Dollinger, 1968, p. 234)*

This is of course an extreme case of patriotism combined with other "secular" religions (nationalism or racism), but regarding the transcendent and strikingly anthropomorphic nature of the cult of "Father" and "Mother" lands, or the extensive mythology, symbolism, and rituals that surround them, it is once again difficult to tell what is absent to speak of a "genuine" religion.

See also: Fascism, Nationalism, Nazism, Revolution

## Sources

Bonald, L.-A. ([1796] 1843) *Théorie de pouvoir politique et religieux dans la société civile*. Tome III. Paris: Adrien le cléré et c.

Dollinger, H. (1968) *The Decline and Fall of Nazi Germany and Imperial Japan: A Pictorial History of the Final Days of World War II*. Translated by Pomerans, A. New York: Crown.

Durkheim, É. (1898) 'De la définition des phénomènes religieux', *L'Année sociologique*, (2), pp. 1–28.

Mathiez, A. (1904) *Les origines des cultes révolutionnaires (1789–1792)*. Paris: Société Nouvelle de Librairie et d'Édition.

Michelet, J. ([1831] 1959) *Journal*. Volume 1 (1828–1848). Paris: Gallimard.

Nathanson, S. (1993) *Patriotism, Morality, and Peace*. Lanham: Rowman & Littlefield.

## Personality cult

See Juche, Leninism, Maoism, Populism, Stalinism.

## Political correctness

See Postmodernism, Wokeness.

## Pop culture

See Art, Entertainment, Fandom, Hip Hop, Rock.

## Populism

The religion of populism is a close relative to the religion of democracy. As Margaret Canovan observed, democracy itself can be a "redemptive vision, kin to the family of modern ideologies that promise salvation through politics," and in this form of redemptive democracy "there is a strong anti-institutional impulse" (Canovan, 1999, p. 10). The anti-institutional (and anti-elitist) impulse is represented most obviously by populism, which Canovan described as a sectarian form of religion, in distinction from the churchly one:

> Where this aspect of redemptive democracy is concerned, there may be an analogy with Weber's celebrated analysis of religious institutions. In Weber's terms, a church is an institution in which religious charisma is routinized. Its hierarchy and rituals are legitimized by divine authority, but the *Vox Dei* is mediated through them. As a result it is always vulnerable to challenge by direct appeal to divine authority. The charismatic preacher leading a grass-roots revival hears the voices of God directly, by-passing the hierarchy and rituals of the church – until his message becomes

routinized in its turn and the cycle starts again. The place of populism in democracy is in some ways similar. Populists appeal past the ossified institutions to the living people, proclaiming the vox populi unmediated.

*(ibid., p. 14)*

The basic pattern of populism, the "pure people" versus the "corrupt elite" (Mudde and Rovira Kaltwasser, 2017, p. 6), is also more radical than that of traditional democracy, as it contains two intangible absolutes, not only one, the "people," as democracy does. This dualism is in turn often described by the religious term of "Manicheism" in populism scholarship (Zúquete, 2017, p. 445). The exclusive or even "excommunicative" tendency toward those who do not belong to the community is the most clearly sectarian trait of populism, while it is also true that – unlike in churches – membership in the sect remains mostly voluntary. Other sectarian features are the monopolization of political rituals, the control of the belief system, and – if the sect is centered around a charismatic leader – the artificially created and maintained charisma of the latter (Metz and Kövesdi, 2023, p. 523).

"Charisma" itself is a word with religious overtones, as Max Weber said: "the power of charisma rests upon the belief in revelation and heroes, upon the conviction that certain manifestations – whether . . . religious, ethical, artistic, scientific, political, or other kind – are important and valuable" (Weber, [1921] 1978, p. 1117). The charisma is then sustained by myths or hagiographies that highlight the leader's fellowship with ordinary people, his extraordinary capabilities, and his consequential rise to power (Metz and Kövesdi, 2023, pp. 529–530). The mythical leader is followed with a religious zeal, maintained and reinforced by repeated rituals, such as demonstrations and popular celebrations, and saturated with symbols of the community (flags, badges, clothes), liturgical chants, and so forth (ibid., p. 537).

Institutionalization is already a step toward the establishment of a "church," which occurs in newspapers, media platforms, and party organizations. Some forms of populism are indeed much closer to totalitarian political religions and leader cults than to self-destructive religious movements (ibid., p. 541), especially when a populist movement comes to power. In such cases, populism can also become intertwined with other secular religions: "Populists in power sacralize the political arena by attributing nominally secular entities such as the nation, the state, and the leader 'religious' traits as objects of loyalty and faith" (Yabanci, 2020, p. 92).

Populism is thus difficult to separate not only from "genuine" religions but also from other "secular" ones, not to mention those cases in which the covertly and overtly religious forms of populism get mixed up. To quote Jose Pedro Zúqute: "in some radical cases (exceptions) the special relationship with a higher divine power emerges also in proclamations from the covertly religious side of religious populism" (Zúquete, 2017, p. 466). That may also explain why populism is just as frequently called "quasi-religious," "semi-religious," or "almost religious" as plainly "religious" (ibid., p. 452).

See also: Democracy, Nationalism, Statism

## Sources

Canovan, M. (1999) 'Trust the People! Populism and the Two Faces of Democracy', *Political Studies*, (47), pp. 2–16. https://doi.org/10.1111/1467-9248.00184

Metz, R., and Kövesdi, V. (2023) '"Whoever Is Not against Us Is for Us": Sectarianization of Politics in Hungary', *Politics, Religion & Ideology*, 24(4), pp. 521–542. https://doi.org/10.1080/21567689.2023.2287573

Mudde, C., and Rovira Kaltwasser, C. (2017) *Populism: A Very Short Introduction*. Oxford: Oxford University Press.

Weber, M. ([1921] 1978) *Economy and Society: An Outline of Interpretive Sociology*. Berkeley: University of California Press.

Yabanci, B. (2020) 'Fuzzy Borders between Populism and Sacralized Politics: Mission, Leader, Community and Performance in "New" Turkey', *Politics, Religion & Ideology*, 21(1), pp. 92–112. https://doi.org/10.1080/21567689.2020.1736046

Zúquete, J. P. (2017) 'Populism and Religion', in *The Oxford Handbook of Populism*, edited by Rovira Kaltwasser, C., Taggart, P., Espejo, P. O., and Ostiguy, P. Oxford: Oxford University Press, pp. 445–466. https://doi.org/10.1093/oxfordhb/9780198803560.013.22

## Positivism

See Humanism, Scientism.

## Postcolonialism

See Colonialism, Postmodernism, Wokeness.

## Posthumanism

The words "posthumanism" and "transhumanism" are sometimes used interchangeably; at other times "transhumanism" appears as a subtype of "posthumanism." It nevertheless seems better to attempt a more thorough conceptual distinction:

> The category of the human within transhumanist thought remains remarkably continuous with the human of its philosophical antecedent, Enlightenment humanism. The qualities identified as most essentially human in Enlightenment humanism – rationality, autonomy – are properties of the mind, and, conceived as such, disembodied.
>
> *(Thweatt-Bates, 2011, p. 105)*

By contrast, posthumanism is a complete break with both the concept of the human being and the tradition of humanist philosophy. In its more radical versions, such as the theories of "AI Takeover" (the replacement of humans by artificial intelligence) or "Voluntary Human Extinction" (abstaining from reproduction to save the biosphere, the ecological version of posthumanism), it not only rejects anthropocentrism but aims to eliminate – or at least acquiesces to the elimination of – the human being as such.

While posthumanism has an obvious tendency to oppose religious ways of thinking that suffer from an inherent anthropocentrism, it itself promotes an overarching worldview whose structure not accidentally resembles that of religious traditions. It has its own absolute, something that will replace humanity – be it artificial intelligence or nature – the superiority of which is affirmed with the certainty of a dogma. From this follows an eschatological doctrine (a doctrine about the "last things") that either describes the future as a catastrophe (the universal damnation of humanity) or as a salvation, although certainly not for human beings but for the universe that will be better off without the original sin meant by the very existence of humans. It has its prophets, such as Hans Moravec, who predicted in 1988 that after being engaged "for billions of years in a relentless, spiraling arms race with one another, our genes have finally outsmarted themselves," adding that the future "is best described by the words 'post-biological' or even 'supernatural.' It is a world in which the human race has been swept away by the tide of cultural change, usurped by its own artificial progeny" (Moravec, 1988, p. 1). There is, at the same time, an apparent hesitation whether Moravec himself – and others like Marvin Minsky, the father of technological posthumanism – are to be called post- or transhumanists, which once again shows how difficult it is to distinguish not only post- and transhumanism but also the "religious" and "post-religious" aspects of posthumanism itself.

Because of such difficulties, posthumanism is seldom discussed as a "secular religion"; what is more often suggested is that it blurs the boundary between the secular and the religious, just as it has destroyed the boundaries between the human and the non-human:

> Contemporary technoscientific advances have blurred the distinctions between humans and animals, humans and machines, nature from culture, artificial from organic, by which Western modernity constructed its definition of normative and exemplary humanity. The "ontological hygiene" by which the humanist subject was defined in binary opposition terms to its others (machines, animals, subaltern cultures – the "inhuman") has been breached.
> *(Graham, 2021, p. 23)*

Or maybe the distinction between ordinary human beings and "saints" is also blurred by posthumanism, as Carissa Turner Smith's *Cyborg Saints* suggests (Smith, 2020), although, once again, such an approach stands closer to the transhumanist than to the strictly speaking post-humanist idea. In any case, the word "post-humanity" (which appeared as early as C. S. Lewis's *The Abolition of Man* in the 1940s) expresses a general tendency, a movement toward a world "which, some knowingly and some unknowingly, nearly all men in all nations are at present laboring to produce" (Lewis, 1947, p. 47). Some features of posthumanism may seem utopian or truly otherworldly, as Ronald E. Osborne notes in his book on *Humanism and the Death of God*, "yet even if we do not subscribe to the most fantastic visions of cyborg (human-machine) and hybrid (human-animal) creations, we are already living in a period of critical or theoretical posthumanism" (Osborne, 2017, p. 47). Or perhaps in the era of a new religion.

See also: Artificial Intelligence, Ecology, Humanism, Scientism, Transhumanism

## Sources

Graham, E. (2021) 'Cyborg or Goddess? Religion and Posthumanism from Secular to Postsecular', *Journal of Posthumanism*, 1(1), pp. 23–31. https://doi.org/10.33182/jp.v1i1.1444

Lewis, C. S. (1947) *The Abolition of Man*. New York: Macmillan.

Moravec, H. (1988) *Mind Children: The Future of Robot and Human Intelligence*. Cambridge: Harvard University Press.

Osborne, R. E. (2017) *Humanism and the Death of God: Searching for the Good after Darwin, Marx, and Nietzsche*. Oxford: Oxford University Press.

Smith, C. T. (2020) *Cyborg Saints: Religion and Posthumanism in Middle Grade and Young Adult Fiction*. New York: Routledge.

Thweatt-Bates, J. J. (2011) 'Artificial Wombs and Cyborg Births: Postgenderism and Theology', in *Transhumanism and Transcendence: Christian Hope in an Age of Technological Enhancement*, edited by Cole-Turner, R. Washington, DC: Georgetown University Press, pp. 101–114.

## Postmodernism

Before the advent of "woke," the word "postmodern" summed up the allegedly religious traits of a variety of philosophical and socio-political movements that criticized the hegemonic narratives of the modern West. Although initially aimed to deconstruct all "grand stories," such movements – according to their critics – created their own that turned out to be just as unquestionable as those of their opponents. As Guido Giacomo Preparata wrote in his *The Ideology of Tyranny*, this was in a way logically inevitable: if the postmodern is defined as "incredulity toward metanarratives" (Lyotard, [1979] 1984, p. xxiv), it itself becomes "a special metanarrative that teaches that there are no metadiscourses" (Preparata, 2007, p. 113). Or rather, it teaches that there *should be* no metadiscourses:

> Despite its publicized pose of inebriating detachment, sardonic equanimity, and aesthetic "self-absorption," the highly regimented movement of

postmodernism is fanatical, intolerant (remember Foucault calling the Greeks "disgusting!"), ambitious, and acquisitive: it passes itself off as disaggregated and creatively unorganized, but that is far from being the case.

*(ibid., p. 112)*

The fanaticism and intolerance of this "tendentious and divisive gospel" (ibid.) is directed against a well-defined evil or rather an entire complex of evils: "the whole metaphysical, Eurocentric tradition of the 'white mythology'" (Szkudlarek, 1993. p. 108). This militant division of the world suggests the analogy of a holy war (a "paper-crusade," Preparata, 2007, p. 120), the thoughtless repetition of mantras, and even a sort of diabology: "In the postmodern book of prayer, 'Eurocentric,' 'white,' and 'metaphysical' are the customary attributes of the Devil" (ibid., p. 120). It is important to point out that all this is not about sheer moralizing: it is not the act itself that counts, but its place in the mentioned cosmic dichotomy. For instance, whether mass killing is described as a horrendous sin or a respectable custom, a massacre or a sacrifice depends on who committed it: the colonialists or the natives, the Spanish or the Aztecs, at least in postmodern historical narratives (Richardson, 1994, p. 84).

The postmodern "creed" (Preparata, 2007, p. 111) also made it to the "catechisms" of academic colleges (ibid., p. 118) or even to the "modern-day utilitarian church" of liberal capitalism (ibid., p. 119). As for the latter, not only the critics of postmodernism point out how the liberation of minorities is entangled with the logic of the market but also those who belong to the camp, like Michael Hardt and Toni Negri in their famous *Empire:*

> Marketing has perhaps the clearest relation to postmodernist theories, and one could even say that the capitalist marketing strategies have long been postmodernist, *avant la lettre* . . . Marketing itself is a practice based on differences, and the more differences that are given, the more marketing strategies can develop. Ever more hybrid and differentiated populations present a proliferating number of "target markets" that can each be addressed by specific marketing strategies – one for gay Latino males between the ages of eighteen and twenty-two, another for Chinese-American teenage girls, and so forth. Postmodern marketing recognizes the difference of each commodity and each segment of the population, fashioning its strategies accordingly. Every difference is an opportunity.
>
> *(Hardt and Negri, 2000, pp. 151–153)*

To which more hostile observers like Preparata add that the

> most absurd and indecorous of all is the above celebration of the mercantile exploitation of "otherness," of Western business's alleged attention to

and respect for other cultures, when it is known that peddling "the ethnic" is but the latest trick of corporate salesmanship.

*(Preparata, 2007, p. 129)*

The final blow to the postmodern religion is thus the allegation that it commits itself to both economic and political "orthodoxy" (ibid., p. 124).

Although Hardt and Negri maintain that we live in the "end times" of ultimate secularization, when a counterpower of diverse individuals refuses all hierarchy, transcendence, and authority, this seems to be nothing more than a play with words, since secularization in fact means immediate re-sacralization. Either by the "poor" who is the God on earth ("Today there is not even the illusion of a transcendent God. The poor has dissolved that image and recuperated its power," Hardt and Negri, 2000, p. 157) or by such mythical entities as a "life force":

> There is a strict continuity between the religious thought that accords a power above nature to God and the modern "secular" thought that accords that same power above nature to Man. The transcendence of God is simply transferred to Man. Like God before it, this Man that stands separate from and above nature has no place in a philosophy of immanence. Like God, too, this transcendent figure of Man leads quickly to the imposition of social hierarchy and domination. Antihumanism, then, conceived as a refusal of any transcendence, should in no way be confused with a negation of the *vis viva*, the creative life force that animates the revolutionary stream of the modern tradition. On the contrary, the refusal of transcendence is the condition of possibility of thinking this immanent power, an anarchic basis of philosophy: "Ni Dieu, ni *maître*, ni l'homme."
>
> *(ibid., pp. 91–92)*

This is where postmodernism is dissolved in posthumanism, just as the multitude becomes at the same time God and Devil, one and many, as Hardt and Negri's other famous work, *Multitude* claims (Hardt and Negri, 2004, p. 138). This total coalescence, or *apokatasthasis*, in which everything becomes equal to everything is, to skeptics, just another sign of postmodernism's mystical theology. Moreover, this homogeneous "kingdom of God" is already among us. For despite all talk of diversity, as historian Russell Jacoby remarks, the movement is fundamentally monolithic: "No divergent political or economic vision animates cultural diversity. From the most militant Afrocentrists to the most ardent feminists, all quarters subscribe to very similar beliefs about work, equality, and success" (Jacoby, 1999, pp. 39–40). Or, in Preparata's words: "The secret of cultural diversity is its political and economic uniformity" (Preparata, 2007, p. 134).

It should nevertheless be added that despite so many analogies and metaphors postmodernism is rarely called a "religion" without qualification. It is sometimes described as an "enigmatic enterprise, blending lyricism, political economy, and a refashioning of religion" (ibid., p. xvi); a "transliteration of religious feeling" (ibid., p. 11); or a "mythology" and "creed" (ibid., p. 214). As for its secularity, the very distinction between the religious and the secular, the sacred and the profane, or God and Devil is relativized by postmodernism itself. After all, such distinctions were only characteristic of more traditional worldviews:

> To establish themselves, traditional cults have fought long and hard against "rival divinities," which they have eventually banished as "devilish idols." When they appeared to have won the match, all "evil" disposition was subsumed under the convenient, single head of the Adversary (Satan), who was cast out of heaven and made thereby the prince of *profane* darkness.
> *(ibid., p. 12)*

The only question is whether postmodernism does not relapse into the same atavism:

> Of their "skepticism," "anticlericalism," and religion-bashing the postmodern critics have made a profession. Yet, the fanatical passion with which they have espoused Foucault's Power/Knowledge is itself the mark of religious sentiment. The Foucauldian construct is wholly metaphysical. Disbelieving the monotheistic God, while believing in life being spawned at random by the aboriginal Void, is still believing. The intangible notion of "power," Gnosticism's *dunamis*, could not be further removed from the positivist and rationalist confidence that these critics otherwise display in their daily activity.
> *(ibid., pp. 214–215)*

See also: Anarchism, Posthumanism, Wokeness

## Sources

Hardt, M., and Negri, A. (2000) *Empire*. Cambridge: Harvard University Press.
Hardt, M., and Negri, A. (2004) *Multitude: War and Democracy in the Age of Empire*. New York: Penguin.
Jacoby, R. (1999) *The End of Utopia, Politics and Culture in the Age of Apathy*. New York: Basic Books.
Lyotard, J.-F. ([1979] 1984) *The Postmodern Condition: A Report on Knowledge*. Translated by Bennington, G., and Massumi, B. Minneapolis: University of Minnesota Press.
Preparata, G. G. (2007) *The Ideology of Tyranny: Bataille, Foucault, and the Postmodern Corruption of Political Dissent*. New York: Palgrave Macmillan.

Richardson, M. (1994) *Georges Bataille*. London: Routledge.
Szkudlarek, T. (1993) *The Problem of Freedom in Postmodern Education*. Westport: Bergin and Garvey.

## Progress

Although the "religion of progress" is an oft-repeated phrase, it is typically used in connection with other belief systems (communism, socialism, humanism, scientism, and many others). What makes belief in progress "religious" is that it implies a prophetic stance, insofar as it takes not only the past but also the future for granted. As Arthur C. Danto says in his *Narration and Knowledge*:

> A prophecy is not merely a statement about the future, for a prediction is a statement about the future. It is a certain *kind* of statement about the future, and I shall say, pending a further analysis, that it is an *historical* statement about the future. The prophet is one who speaks about the future in a manner which is appropriate only to the past, or who speaks of the present in the light of a future treated as a *fait accompli*.
> (Danto, [1985] 2007, p. 9)

In this sense, all narratives that view history as a whole are essentially theological: even when they are explicitly secular or atheistic, they perceive a "plan" behind the events, even if without a God whose plan it is. In other words, those who think they know the course of history seem to occupy an external position, that of a divine observer or at least that of a mystic initiated into the higher knowledge of God. This is true of both pessimistic and optimistic theologies of history, but "secular religions" are usually more prone to optimism, a belief in progress.

As Karl Löwith's *Meaning in History* in 1949 argued, "philosophy of history originates with the Hebrew and Christian faith in a fulfilment" (Löwith, 1949, p. 2). He nevertheless spoke of a "secularization" of the eschatological pattern, although the mentioned divine perspective of all substantive philosophies of history raises doubts about the possibility of any such secularization. It is also difficult to tell when explicitly "religious" views of history were replaced by "secular" (or covertly religious) ones. For instance, if we accept what Löwith and many other authors suggest, namely that the medieval abbot Joachim of Fiore and his three ages (the age of the Father, the Son, and the Holy Spirit) constituted a turning point in thinking about history, it is not at all clear whether we speak of a fully religious (Christian) idea rooted in theological speculations or a thoroughly secular one that envisions a perfect society in this world already (ibid., pp. 149–150).

The issue does not become easier in the case of Joachim's heirs, either. Although Hegel used a similar analogy between the Trinity and world history, it is also notoriously difficult to decide whether he was a religious (Christian) thinker or someone who – despite all Christian rhetoric – radically immanentized the originally transcendent ideas of Christianity:

> God is thus recognized as *Spirit*, only when known as the Triune. This new principle is the axis on which the History of the World turns. This is *the goal* and the *starting point* of History. "When the fulness of the time was come, God sent his Son," is the statement of the Bible. This means nothing else than that *self-consciousness* had reached the phases of development, whose resultant constitutes the Idea of Spirit, and had come to feel the necessity of comprehending those phases absolutely.
> *(Hegel, [1822–1830] 2001, p. 338)*

That world history shows a triadic structure (a prehistory, the present age of transition and an imminent consummation) is such a widespread legacy of Joachim that there is practically no modern philosophy of history that has not been suspected of Joachimism (see Henri de Lubac's *The Spiritual Posterity of Joachim of Fiore*). In Hegel, the primordial unity of the spirit is followed by its alienation and its return to a higher-level unity; in Marxism, primitive communism is followed by class society and then the final stage of advanced communism; even in Nazism, the final stage of history is marked by the birth of the *Third* Reich; not to mention Francis Fukuyama's vision of the "end of history" after the premodern and the modern era, which explicitly relies on Hegel's philosophy of history.

This also shows that works of political science or history (especially the so-called big history) are not immune to the temptation of theologizing. It is in fact ironical how celebrity historians who never hesitate to mock attempts to find meaning in human activities as a quasi-religious storytelling, do exactly the same or even worse (Harari, 2015). To give a meaningful narrative of a meaningless universe is not only theology but the perhaps most foolish type thereof.

See also: Communism, Humanism, Posthumanism, Postmodernism, Revolution, Scientism, Socialism, Transhumanism

## Sources

Danto, A. C. ([1985] 2007) *Narration and Knowledge*. New York: Columbia University Press.
Fukuyama, F. (1992) *The End of History and the Last Man*. New York: The Free Press.
Harari, Y. N. (2015) *Homo Deus: A Brief History of Tomorrow*. London: Vintage.

Hegel, G. W. F. ([1822–1830] 2001) *The Philosophy of History*. Translated by Sibree, J. Kitchener: Batoche Books.
Löwith, K. (1949) *Meaning in History*. Chicago: The University of Chicago Press.
Lubac, H. (1979) *La posterité spirituelle de Joachim de Flore*. Paris: Lethielleux.

## Psychology

Psychology has been suspected of becoming a secular religion as early as 1934, when Christopher Dawson predicted that "the introduction of psychology into education" will let schools "usurp the functions that the Church exercised in the past" (Dawson, 1934, pp. 10–11). A full appreciation of psychology's importance, however, only came in the 1970s, when Paul C. Vitz published *Psychology as Religion: The Cult of Self-Worship*. This book presented modern psychology as part of a larger religious framework that included consumerism, capitalism, sex, art, and entertainment, culminating in what might be called humanistic selfism: "In short, humanistic selfism is not a science but a popular secular substitute religion, which has nourished and spread today's widespread cult of self-worship" (Vitz, [1977] 1993, p. 141).

The argument refers to the ambition of certain psychological schools to offer not just therapy but a complete worldview, an explanation of the human being's moral character, or a vision about the meaning of life. "Psychotherapy, once a restricted and specialized activity is now generalized to all of life's relations" (ibid., p. 8). One might add that since the 1970s it has become so obvious for many psychologists that their profession embraced all aspects of human life that they are always ready to answer questions in popular magazines about what it means to be human, whether there is a free will, or whether human beings are basically good or bad, all of which are at least metaphysical – if not theological – questions.

Some early theorists of modern psychology at least admitted that this was the case. As Carl Gustav Jung said, "religions are systems of healing for psychic illness," thereby blurring the boundaries between psychology and theology and giving the therapist the role of a spiritual guide: "Man is never helped in his suffering by what he thinks for himself, but only by revelations of a wisdom greater than his own. It is this which lifts him out of his distress" (Jung, 1933, pp. 240–241). In other words, "patients force the psychotherapist into the role of priest," and "that is why we psychotherapists must occupy ourselves with problems which strictly speaking belong to the theologian" (ibid., also quoted more briefly and somewhat imprecisely by Vitz, [1977] 1993, p. 2).

The fact that the healing process requires the patient's "faith" in the therapy shows that the foundations of the latter are not purely scientific (ibid., p. 41). That is also why bodies of psychologists tend to behave as a priestly magisterium, like in the case of the American Psychological Association that defines pathologies with dogmatic authority and responds to criticisms of its objectivity by stonewalling the critique, excluding other faiths from interfering in the matters of their own "secular" one (ibid., p. 143). In addition to dogmatic affirmations, rituals (e.g., theatrical confessions and testimonies in Recovery Groups, ibid., p. 24) also play a fundamental role in reinforcing faith in a chosen psychological method. Faith or spiritual experience itself may even be accepted as scientific proof:

> The "clinical evidence" of the impact of conversion or spiritual rebirth has often been used to argue the validity of such experiences. Verbal reports (whether autobiographical or by witnesses) and the great joy, wisdom, and effectiveness of the saints constitute some of the major traditional proofs of Christianity. Now we hear that such observations, in this kind of setting and relationship, are considered to constitute acceptable scientific evidence.
>
> *(ibid., p. 40)*

Speaking of saints, some psychologists like Maslow did not hesitate to speak of the heroes of self-actualization as "religious people," quoting David Levy who said that "a few centuries ago these would all have been described as men who walk the path of God or as godly men" (Maslow, 1970, p. 169). But the true absolute of the psychological religion is the Self as a Supreme Being. Vitz calls it an "idolatry" (Vitz, [1977] 1993, p. 21) showing the indecisiveness of terminology which so far used other words like "religion" without adjectives, a "secular substitute religion," and a "secular faith." In any case, the examples of self-absolutization are countless. Werner Erhard's psychological training "EST" that attracted millions of followers in the 1970s and 1980s (although Erhard himself lacked any formal psychological training) has never been shy about calling the individual a "Supreme Being," a sort of deity, that is:

> That's all life is – one big word game. Don't lie to yourself about it anymore. They even wrote it down, not long after the beginning. They said: "AND THE WORD *WAS* GOD." Of course it was. And you're IT. *You* are the Supreme Being . . . You have just re-experienced the way it is to *be* the supreme being. Everywhere . . . and nowhere. Nothing . . . and everything. No importances; no point-of-view. No time, matter, energy, mass or space. . . . So you created life/death, and *human* beings, with the intention of having them experience the human condition, and communicate with each other. The truth is that you're NOT really a human being, you're just *BE*ing human for a *time*, that's all . . . The truth is that *you're* the SOURCE of everything.
>
> *(Frederick, 1974, pp. 168–172)*

It is also remarkable how this divine "You" is beyond good and evil, since "it simply doesn't make sense to be unethical" (ibid., p. 174), or how its will is perfectly arbitrary, which makes it similar to a voluntarist conception of God: "Life is one big 'SO WHAT?'. CHOOSE" (ibid., p. 191). It may be objected that this is already light years from what any professional psychologist would subscribe to, but Vitz argues that it is only a popularization of Rogersian psychotherapy with a touch of existentialist philosophizing about a transcendent ego (Vitz, [1977] 1993, p. 28).

As for the latter, it must be added that the absolute of psychological selfism is truly transcendent in the sense that it is beyond (or behind) all empirical features of the human psyche. This transcendence may indeed be formulated in the language of existentialism: the Self first "exists" and only becomes "something" later on, or even better, it creates its own essence by the choices it makes. Although Rogers did not have any formal connection with existentialism, he used a similar language – with a touch of biblical rhetoric – when he declared that "In the beginning was I, and I was good" (Rogers and Stevens, 1967, p. 9). The biblical allusion is more than an accident, since Rogers himself spent two years at a theological seminary in his youth to prepare for religious work (Rogers, 1970, p. 8). The Self as an uncreated creator – who is, as we see, also perfectly good – is fundamentally different from anything that is determinate and therefore not authentic in the human person: age, sex, race, nationality, ethnic group, family, language, unconscious personality traits, temperament, memory, intelligence, and so on:

> Relentlessly, layer after layer of the unauthentic you is stripped away until a self results that is like a totally peeled onion, of which all that remains is the pure spiritual power of life. In practice, most of today's selfists stop long before, at some inauthentic level; but those few who follow the logic out leave science behind and end in language often indistinguishable from the traditional idea of a disembodied soul.
>
> *(Vitz, [1977] 1993, p. 53)*

Or, as a nowadays popular internet meme puts it: "As soon as you are born, you're given a name, a religion, a nationality, and a race. You spend the rest of your life defining and defending a fictional identity" (iFunny, 2023). It seems to imply in a truly mystical vein that the only thing which is *not* fictional is exactly what simpler minds would call a fiction: an imaginary center of the self which cannot be expressed by words, an ineffable mystery, or, if one thinks that it is something absolute, a genuine *Deus absconditus*.

An objection to Vitz's *Psychology as Religion* may be that it treats different schools of academic psychology and their popular representations (or misrepresentations) as if they belonged to one unitary "religion" of selfism. He himself, however, excludes experimental psychology, behaviorism, or Freudian psychoanalysis from his discussion, while other works like Ernest Gellner's

*The Psychoanalytic Movement* explicitly refer to the latter as a "secular religion," offering "a kind of secular salvation comparable in its totality to that which had previously been offered in the literal sense" (Gellner, 2003, p. xxxiii). This "soteriology," the doctrine of "individual salvation," also has its priesthood connected by a shared methodology and language, embedded in an institutional framework, a "well organized guild/church," whose task is to sustain the influence of its ideas (ibid., p. 22). Gellner nevertheless remains just as ambiguous in his terminology as most other authors. Although he sometimes distinguishes "secular religions" and "secular faiths" from "literal religions" or "religious faith proper" (ibid., pp. xxxv, 9, and 33), he also affirms that psychoanalysis believes in a "transcendent" idea, that of the Unconscious; only to add that this is, of course, a "naturalistic transcendent," which is, we might add, a just as oxymoronic term as "secular religion" (ibid., p. 169).

The "selfist" forms of psychology (for there are obviously more than one) are also closely connected to other instances of secular religions, most of all capitalism and consumerism. In many cases, it is impossible to distinguish the self-preoccupation of individualistic psychologies from the similarly individualistic approach of consumer capitalism (Vitz, [1977] 1993, p. 21). Many – if not most – self-help therapies are business enterprises (ibid., p. 26), while business and advertising use the same tools of persuasion as popular psychology does. As Philip Cushman observed, the traditional self with all its social determinations (kinship, small town communities, the church, etc.) had all but disappeared, creating an "internal vacuum" that was filled by two new social forces: psychology and advertising:

> One can see evidence of the empty self in current psychological discourse about narcissism and borderline states, the popular culture's emphasis on consuming, political advertising strategies that emphasize soothing and charisma instead of critical thought, and a nationwide difficulty in maintaining personal relationships.
>
> *(Cushman, 1990, p. 600)*

Consumer culture and advertisement, as Vitz adds, not only reinforce the psychological cult of the self. It is in fact created by them or rather by capitalism itself: "the selfist personality is in fact a creation of the material and social conditions of a late capitalist economy in which serious scarcity is, at least for most, a thing of the past" (Vitz, [1977] 1993, p. 89). It is no wonder that capitalism – and its accompanying deification of the self – is so hostile to all (other) religions that teach discipline and obedience. As Harvey Cox notes, traditional religions are about the limits of human enterprise ("How much is enough"), while capitalism teaches the exact opposite, that "There is never enough" (Cox, 2016, p. 21). This is what Cox calls the global ideology of McDonalds (ibid., p. 205) and Vitz – to change the hamburger franchise – the "religion of Burger King" (Vitz, [1977] 1993, p. 91).

The psychological and capitalist methods of self-liberation are also connected to sexual liberation, the worship of sex as a recreational activity (instead of a means of procreation) but also as a builder of identity, "Sex in the service of the ego" as Vitz says (ibid., p. 29). He goes as far as mentioning *Playboy*, *Penthouse*, and *Psychology Today* as belonging to the same corpus of sacred texts (ibid., p. 91). But this already belongs to another topic.

See also: Capitalism, Consumerism, Individualism, Selfism, Sex

## Sources

Cox, H. (2016) *The Market as God*. Cambridge: Harvard University Press.
Cushman, P. (1990) 'Why the Self Is Empty: Toward a Historically Situated Psychology', *American Psychologist*, 45(5), pp. 599–611.
Dawson, C. (1934) 'Religion and the Totalitarian State', *The Criterion*, 14(54), pp. 1–16.
Frederick, C. (1974) *EST: Playing the Game – The New Way*. New York: Delta.
Gellner, E. (2003) *The Psychoanalytic Movement: The Cunning of Unreason*. Malden, MA: Blackwell.
iFunny (2023) Available at: https://ifunny.co/picture/factswap-did-you-know-as-soon-as-you-are-born-XavLBVZN9 (Accessed: 1 December 2023).
Jung, C. G. (1933) *Modern Man in Search of a Soul*. Translated by Dell, W. S. and Baynes, C. F. New York: Harvest.
Maslow, A. H. (1970) *Motivation and Personality*. New York: Harper and Row.
Rogers, C. R. (1970) *On Becoming a Person: A Therapist's View of Psychotherapy*. Boston: Houghton Mifflin.
Rogers, C. R., and Stevens, B. (1967) *Person to Person: The Problem of Being Human: A New Trend in Psychology*. Walnut Creek: Real People Press.
Vitz, P. C. ([1977] 1993) *Psychology as Religion: The Cult of Self-Worship*. Grand Rapids: Eerdmans.

# R
## RACISM

The most obvious religion-like feature of racism is the very concept of "race." Although initially presented as a scientific concept, it has since turned out to be biologically unfounded (Yudell et al., 2016), a cultural phenomenon at best or an imaginary absolute at worst. As Julius Goldstein wrote in 1924, the leading figures of racism (Gobineau, Lapouge, Chamberlain, or Woltmann) "found in race the key to the understanding of the historical world" and in "race spirit" an ultimate "explanation of spiritual creation" (Goldstein, 1924, p. 43). Moreover, as Rudolf Rocker added in his *Nationalism and Culture* in 1937, this spiritually understood race stood beyond any visible features:

> From Chamberlain, no more than from Gobineau, do we discover what, exactly, "race" is. He is the finished mystic of the race idea, which in him condenses into a devoutly believed race mythology. External characteristics, like the shape of the skull, texture and color of the hair, the skin, the eyes, have for him only a qualified meaning; even language is not determinative. Only the instinctive feeling of cohesiveness which reveals itself through the "voice of the blood" is determinative. This "feeling of race in one's own bosom," which is subject to no control and cannot be scientifically apprehended, is all that Chamberlain has to tell us about race.
> *(Rocker, 1937, p. 308)*

That is why the sarcasm of the Soviet propaganda poster by Boris Efimov which said that "the true Aryan should be tall as Goebbels, slim as Göring, and blonde as Hitler" (Efimov, 1941) is somewhat misguided, for the race of racism has always been a transcendent idea with very loose connection to the empirical (phenotypical) characteristics of different human groups. Being "Nordic" or "Oriental" is more of an issue of character than of pure anthropology (Rocker, 1937, p. 320).

In any case, the real absolute of racism is not even race itself but that which it serves, the idea of power. As Rocker remarks,

> He who thinks that he sees in all political and social antagonisms merely blood-determined manifestations of race, denies all conciliatory influence of ideas, all community of ethical feeling, and must at every crisis take refuge in brute force. In fact, the race theory is only the cult of power.
> 
> *(ibid., p. 338)*

Racism becomes a full religion with its mandatory catechisms, its dualistic public iconography of superior and inferior races, or rituals of worshipping the former and ostracizing the latter in societies where the cult of state power is also extensively celebrated, like in Nazi Germany. Finally, it must be mentioned that sometimes supposedly anti-racist theories and practices are also accused of representing a religious idea of racism (McWhorter, 2021), but this already leads to the topic of "wokeness."

See also: Anti-racism, Nazism, Wokeness

## Sources

Efimov, B. (1941) 'A True Aryan Should Be: Tall (Goebbels), Muscular and Slim (Goering), Blonde (Hitler)', *Views and Re-Views*. Brown Digital Repository. Brown University Library. Available at: https://repository.library.brown.edu/studio/item/bdr:89315/ (Accessed: 1 December 2023).

Goldstein, J. (1924) *Rasse und Politik*. Berlin: Philo Verlag.

McWhorter, J. (2021) *Woke Racism: How a New Religion Betrayed Black America*. New York: Portfolio/Penguin.

Rocker, R. (1937) *Nationalism and Culture*. Translated by Chase, R. E. Los Angeles: Rocker Publications Committee.

Yudell, M., Roberts, D., DeSalle, R., and Tishkoff, S. (2016) 'Taking Race Out of Human Genetics', *Science*, 351(6273), pp. 564, 565. https://doi.org/10.1126/science.aac4951

## Republicanism

The parallel between religion and republicanism was discussed in an 1850 speech given by the conservative politician Juan Donoso Cortés in the Spanish parliament. The *Discourse on the General Situation of Europe* (also cited in the entries on "Anarchism" and "Constitutionalism" in the present volume) provided an overarching historical narrative in which religious and political affirmations and negations served as the interpretational framework of contemporary ideologies. While the theistic affirmations "God exists, God reigns, and God governs" were fully translatable to the political affirmations of a traditional monarchy ("the King exists, the King reigns, and the King governs"), deism and constitutional monarchy already abandoned the "God governs" and "King governs" formulas to substitute them with the idea that although God and the King existed and reigned, neither of them had an actual influence on human affairs. The next step in the process was to replace God with nature and the political ruler with the people, thereby eliminating the very idea of "rule" or "governance," for it is a contradiction to say that the ruler and the ruled or the governor and the governed are one and the same. (Donoso Cortés, [1850] 2007, pp. 74–75. For a similar view in earlier French counterrevolutionary thought, see Joseph de Maistre's *On the Origins of Sovereignty*: "The people is sovereign, they say; and over whom? Over itself apparently. The people is therefore subject. There is surely something equivocal here, if not an error, for the people that *commands* is not the people that *obeys*," Maistre, [1794] 1996, p. 46).

Donoso Cortés explicitly spoke of a "pantheistic" theology and a "republican" politics. It must be observed, however, that the term "republic" referred not to a political form distinguished from "democracy" (as in the works of Immanuel Kant or the American Federalists) but to the rule of the people unbridled by any other authority. That is why Carl Schmitt could later change Donoso Cortés' wording from republican to "democratic" without transforming its original meaning:

> in democratic thought the people hover above the entire political life of the state, just as God does above the world, as the cause and the end of all things, as the point from which everything emanates and to which everything returns.
> *(Schmitt, [1922] 2006, p. 49)*

That is also why people who were less influenced by either Donoso Cortés or Schmitt would also equate a sort of pantheism or naturalism not with republicanism but with democracy. As C. S. Lewis – whom most people today know as the author of the *Narnia Chronicles* – said:

> At this point a suspicion may occur that Supernaturalism arose from reading into the universe the structure of monarchical societies. But then of course it may with equal reason be suspected that Naturalism has arisen from reading into it the structure of modern democracies. The two suspicions thus cancel out and give us no help in deciding which theory is more likely to be true. They do indeed remind us that Supernaturalism is the characteristic philosophy of a monarchical age and Naturalism of a democratic, in the sense that Supernaturalism, even if false, would have been believed by the great mass of unthinking people four hundred years

ago, just as Naturalism, even if false, will be believed by the great mass of unthinking people today.

*(Lewis, 1947, p. 18)*

It should be noted, however, that Donoso Cortés' republicanism – unlike modern democracy – was in no way a self-sufficient political form, only a transitory stage between deistic constitutionalism and overtly atheistic socialism or anarchism. It is also of some importance that he never spoke of republicanism as a full-fledged "cult" with its established churches or rituals, so it would be more apt to say that for him it was a political theology and not a political or secular religion.

See also: Anarchism, Constitutionalism, Democracy, Socialism

## Sources

Donoso Cortés, J. ([1850] 2007) 'Discourse on the General Situation of Europe', in *Readings in Political Theory*, translated by McNamara, V., and Schwartz, M. Ave Maria: Sapientia Press, pp. 67–82.

Lewis, C. S. (1947) *Miracles: A Preliminary Study*. London: Geoffrey Bles.

Maistre, J. ([1794] 1996) *Against Rousseau*. Translated by Lebrun, R. A. Montreal: McGill-Queen's University Press.

Schmitt, C. ([1922] 2006) *Political Theology: Four Chapters on the Concept of Sovereignty*. Translated by Schwab, G. Chicago: The University of Chicago Press.

## Revolution

That revolution may become a religious concept was most obvious in the case of the French Revolution of 1789. As mentioned in other entries of this book (Constitutionalism, Human Rights, Nationalism, and Patriotism), the revolutionary cult was a mixture of many different sub-cults, while the Revolution itself would also be held sacred by its participants and later enthusiasts.

During the Revolution not only dogmatic manifestations declared the holiness of the Constitution, Human Rights, the Fatherland, or the Nation, but new ceremonies were invented, such as civic baptism and civic marriage (of which the latter has remained a parody of church wedding ever since). The Revolution created many festivals on the model of Christian holy days (Ozouf, 1988). The "Feast of the Federation" was introduced in 1790, the "Feast of Freedom" and the "Feast of Law" were celebrated in 1792, and from 1793, an entirely new revolutionary calendar was introduced that made the proclamation of the republic the beginning of a new era, very much like Christ's birth in Christianity or the Hijra in Islam.

The revolutionary religion had its liturgical spaces as well. After the Champ de Mars and the Altars of the Fatherland, the Church of Saint Genevieve was transformed in 1791 into a "Temple of the Nation" or

"Pantheon." Since Pantheon literally means a temple of "all gods," it seems an understatement that the heroes of the Enlightenment and the Revolution buried here were treated as "saints" only. In rhetoric at least, they were more like deities, which is why the French sociologist Albert Piette could speak of both "canonization" (in the case of revolutionaries killed by the rebels of Vendée) and "divinization" (in the case of Jean-Paul Marat). Marat was in fact likened to Jesus Christ, called a Messiah, and his embalmed heart was put on an altar as the "remains of a god" (Piette, 1993, pp. 14–15).

The example of saints or gods or the feast days of civic virtues (also introduced by the revolutionary calendar) naturally suggests that the revolution had a comprehensive moral doctrine, even though the latter is absent even from many "real" religions. Moreover, in 1793, overtly religious "cults" were invented, such as the Cult of Reason celebrated in the Notre Dame or the Cult of the Supreme Being (that replaced the former with an even more explicitly religious ceremony in 1794).

The moral efficiency of such cult(s) was especially spectacular in France's wars that began in 1792. Advocates and adversaries of the war both used the same religious (or rather Christian) language. The Girondine orator Jacques Pierre Brissot spoke of a "crusade of millions" (Beik, 1970, p. 203), Robespierre of "armed missionaries" (Mason and Rizzo, 1999, p. 161), and even enemies of the Revolution like Joseph de Maistre acknowledged that it was Robespierre's "infernal genius," a negative but still transcendent force, that was the guarantee of the miraculous military successes of France: "Even now it is still Robespierre who is winning the battles" (Maistre, [1797] 1994, p. 60).

Similar features have also been present in other countries. The story of the revolution has served as a foundation myth in such diverse cases as that of the Soviet Union, communist China, or Fidel Castro's Cuba. (Note that the word "myth" does not necessarily mean a "false" narrative; it only refers to the fact that such narratives serve as general explanations and justifications, for instance, portraying the new regime as a leap from the world of necessity to the world of freedom, a redemptive moment in history.)

In some cases, for instance in Ernesto "Che" Guevara's book *Guerilla Warfare*, the use of religious – again, mostly Christian – language is truly striking. "Sacrifice" is an instrument for steeling revolutionary character; the revolution has its "martyrs" like Camilo Cienfuegos who "practiced loyalty like a religion"; moreover, these martyrs are immortal: "Who killed him? We should ask instead: Who destroyed his body? Because men like him live on in the people as long as the people will it to be so." They "fought with faith," whereby they became symbols of "continual and immortal renewal"

(Guevara, [1961] 2006, pp. 7–9). In more ironic wording, the guerilla fighter is like a member of a religious order:

> There is a pejorative saying: "The guerrilla fighter is the Jesuit of warfare." This suggests qualities of treachery, of surprise, of secretiveness, that are obviously essential elements of guerrilla warfare. Naturally, it is a special kind of Jesuitism, promoted by circumstances, which necessitate acting at certain moments in ways different from the romantic and sporting conceptions with which we are taught to believe war is fought.
> *(ibid., p. 19)*

The "small nucleus" of the revolutionary vanguard is indeed capable of working "miracles" (ibid., p. 20), and the "guerrilla fighter, as the conscious element of the vanguard of the people, must display the moral conduct of a true priest of the desired reform." As a monk or priest, the guerilla soldier should also be an "ascetic" (ibid., p. 49), and here one is reminded of the similar behavioral codes of crusaders, known from Bernard of Clairvaux's *In Praise of the New Knighthood*, which likewise prohibited excess in clothing, frequent bathing, combing one's hair, or playing dice and chess (Bernard [c. 1120] 2000). Or, as Guevara advised:

> A change of clothing can be carried, but this usually shows inexperience. The usual practice is to carry no more than an extra pair of pants, eliminating underwear and other articles, such as towels. The guerrilla fighter learns through experience to conserve their energy in carrying a backpack from one place to another, and will, little by little, get rid of everything that has no essential value. . . . It is worthwhile also to bring a book, which can be exchanged for others among members of the guerrilla band. These books can be good biographies of past heroes, histories, or economic geographies, preferably of the country, and works of general character that can raise the cultural level of the soldiers and discourage the tendency toward gambling or other undesirable pastimes.
> *(Guevara, [1961] 2006, pp. 64–65)*

Crusaders as members of a religious order also practiced "chastity," just as their modern-day followers should be aware of the danger of having sexual liaisons:

> The temptation women present to young men living away from their usual lifestyle in a special psychological situation is well known. As dictators are well aware of this weakness, they will try to use it for infiltrating spies. Occasionally, the relationship of these women with their superiors is clear

and even notorious; at other times, it is extremely difficult to prove even the slightest evidence of contact; therefore, it is necessary also to prohibit relations with women.

*(ibid., p. 135)*

In addition to poverty and chastity, the revolutionary warrior should also exercise the third monastic virtue of obedience:

The revolutionary in a clandestine situation preparing for war should be a complete ascetic; this is also a test of one of the qualities that will later be the basis of their authority: discipline. If an individual repeatedly disobeys the orders of his superiors and makes contact with women, develops friendships that are not permitted, etc., he should be separated immediately, not merely because of the potential danger in the contacts, but simply because of the violation of revolutionary discipline.

*(ibid.)*

All this, of course, is an ironic overstretching of the analogy but shows at least so much that revolutionary thinking and practice show a remarkable similarity to more traditional, "religious" ideas. The worship of something sacred with its corresponding liturgies, liturgical calendars, and liturgical spaces; a comprehensive moral doctrine; an esoteric language; myths of origin and salvation; sacrifice; the veneration of martyrs and saints; a belief in immortality; and the existence of a priesthood or even a religious order exercising asceticism, all inspired by a transformative vision of humanity. In this sense, the Revolution will always remain an eschatological concept, the expression of something that has already started, should be fought for today, but will only become a reality tomorrow. As Daniel Cohn-Bendit said after the apparently failed 1968 revolts in France:

Reader, you have come to the end of this book, a book that wants to say only one thing: between us we can change this rotten society. Now, put on your coat and make for the nearest cinema. Look at their deadly lovemaking on the screen. Isn't it better in real life? Make up your mind to learn to love. Then, during the interval, when the first advertisements come on, pick up your tomatoes or, if you prefer, your eggs, and chuck them. Then get out into the street, and peel off all the latest government proclamations until underneath you discover the message of the days of May and June. Stay awhile in the street. Look at the passers-by and remind yourself: the last word has not yet been said.

*(Cohn-Bendit and Cohn-Bendit, 1968, p. 256)*

See also: Constitutionalism, Human Rights, Nationalism, Patriotism, Progress

## Sources

Beik, P. H. (ed.) (1970) *The French Revolution: Selected Documents*. New York: Palgrave Macmillan.
Bernard of Clairvaux ([c. 1120] 2000) *In Praise of the New Knighthood: A Treatise on the Knights Templar and the Holy Places of Jerusalem*. Translated by Greenia, C. Kalamazoo: Cistercian Publications.
Cohn-Bendit, D., and Cohn-Bendit G. (1968) *Obsolete Communism: The Left-Wing Alternative*. Translated by Pomerans, A. London: Penguin.
Guevara, E. (1961 [2006]) *Guerilla Warfare*. Melbourne: Ocean Press.
Maistre, Joseph de ([1797] 1994) *Considerations on France*. Translated by Lebrun, R. A. Cambridge: Cambridge University Press.
Mason, L., and Rizzo, T. (ed.) (1999) *The French Revolution: A Document Collection*. Boston: Houghton Mifflin.
Ozouf, M. (1988) *Festivals and the French Revolution*. Translated by Sheridan, A. Cambridge: Harvard University Press.
Piette, A. (1993) *Les religiosités séculières*. Paris: Presses Universitaires de France.

## Rock

Art and entertainment, including the cult of artists and entertainers, are discussed in separate entries of this book. Rock music, however, as one of the most powerful movements of cultural change in the 20th century has its own literature, some of which realized early on its parallels with religious movements. Or rather, these had been already discovered by the musicians themselves: Jimi Hendrix said several times that rock music was like a "church," a "new kind of Bible," the only thing he "believed in"; the Grateful Dead admitted that "they looked upon their music as something like a religion," just as Brian Jones of the Rolling Stones said that music was his "religion," and the examples could be cited endlessly (Cloud, 2013).

In journalism, it was also in the late 1960s that Albert Goldman first wrote of the "almost mystical union" offered by rock music or Benjamin DeMott of "Rock as Salvation" in an eponymous *New York Times* article: "Rock can possess quasi-religious force. It leads me past myself, beyond my separateness and difference into a world of continuous blinding sameness – and, for a bit, it stoneth me out of my mind" (cited by Cohen, 2016, p. 48). In academic literature, sociologist William Shepherd called rock music a "new religiosity" in which rituals and experience superseded the dogmatic side of traditional religions (Shepherd, 1972), while Bernice Martin spoke of the "Sacralization of Disorder," the paradoxical potential of rock music to create a Durkheimian community of the faithful by dress, behavior, music, and lyrics that were otherwise expressively individualistic, anarchic, or "anti-structure" (Martin, 1979).

As Martin also noticed, however, the ambiguously rebellious impulse of rock music – including its latest manifestation in punk music – was all too often domesticated and commercialized, which was in turn "inherent in the nature of symbols of anti-structure themselves" (ibid., p. 119). In this regard, as Hungarian sociologist János Kőbányai wrote in 1982, the history of rock music showed significant analogies with the dynamics of institutionalization in Christianity. In the 1950s and early 1960s, in the apocalyptic mood of the Cold War, the fear of nuclear destruction suddenly swinged to the opposite extreme, an impatient and irrational optimism, which was, however, more of an act of compensation.

Although the new movement was incapable of changing the actual structure of society and only offered an escape route, it did in fact transform everyday life, the forms of communication, and moral habits, just like Christianity did in the early centuries (Kőbányai, 1982, p. 69). Listening to music was like a ritual or ceremony, and in the beginning, it involved mainly the marginalized groups of society, giving them a sense of community or even creating real communities, in which there was still no great difference between "priests" and "lay people," musicians and their audience (ibid., p. 70). For a short happy time, going to a concert was not to "watch a spectacle" but to express belonging to a community, the sacred spaces of which were also more often small shrines (clubs) than large stadiums and open-air festivals.

Although the latter offered the illusion of an exodus or pilgrimage, it also meant that the congregation was gradually transformed into a faceless crowd, while the musician (either as a priest or a saint) became accessible only from afar or through his or her image: a poster, an LP cover, or the pull-out of a pop magazine. By this time the liturgy also involved its altar boys (roads and security guards), professional leaders of prayer (MCs), and a complete choreography of descendance from heaven, a procession of carrying around the star as a living icon, surrounded by a blaze of glory, and wearing a ceremonial dress that could not even be worn on a weekday (ibid., p. 74).

The "churchification" of rock music was, of course, always accompanied by the emergence of new sects that did not give in to the logic of business. But all these were only different forms of the same phenomenon that some authors call "quasi-religious" (see DeMott), an experience with "religious dimensions" (Sylvan, 2002), a "cult" (Till, 2010), or a "secular religion" (Farber, 2015). It is once again remarkable how most accounts that give comprehensive lists of analogies or assert that the youth culture dominated by music provides "almost everything for its adherents that a traditional religion would" (Sylvan, 2002, p. 4) finally refrain from speaking of a religion proper. The exact reasons for the distinction remain unclear, even though the literature on the topic is extensive. With some malice one can also say that "The idea of rock music as a secular religion is a familiar topic that has been beaten to death by now" (Wagner, 2008).

See also: Art, Entertainment, Fandom

## Sources

Cohen, J. D. (2016) '"Can Music Save Your Mortal Soul?": A Bibliographic Survey of Rock as Religion', *Intermountain West Journal of Religious Studies*, 7(1), pp. 47–86. Available at: https://digitalcommons.usu.edu/imwjournal/vol7/iss1/3 (Accessed: 1 December 2023).

Cloud, D. (2013) 'Rock Music as Religion', *Way of Life Literature*, 30 October. Available at: https://www.wayoflife.org/reports/rock_music_as_religion.html (Accessed: 1 December 2023).

Farber, J. (2015) 'Fifty Years Ago, Rock and Roll became "Rock," and Music Started to Have More Social Comment, Powered by Bob Dylan, the Rolling Stones and The Who', *New York Daily News*, 14 June. Available at: https://www.nydailynews.com/2015/06/14/fifty-years-ago-rock-and-roll-became-rock-and-music-started-to-have-more-social-comment-powered-by-bob-dylan-the-rolling-stones-and-the-who/ (Accessed: 1 December 2023).

Kőbányai, J. (1982) *Beat-ünnep*, in *Rock évkönyv 1981*. Edited by Sebők, J. Budapest: Zeneműkiadó, pp. 68–77.

Martin, B. (1979) 'The Sacralization of Disorder: Symbolism in Rock Music', *Sociological Analysis*, 40(2), pp. 87–124. https://doi.org/10.2307/3709782

Shepherd, W. C. (1972) 'Religion and the Counter-Culture – A New Religiosity', *Sociological Inquiry*, 42(1), pp. 3–9.

Sylvan, R. (2002) *Traces of the Spirit: The Religious Dimensions of Popular Music*. New York: New York University Press.

Till, R. (2010) *Pop Cult: Religion and Popular Music*. New York: Continuum.

Wagner, N. (2008) 'The Beatles: Life After Death – Resurrection or Resuscitation?', *Bezalal Journal of Visual and Material Culture*, 10. Available at: https://journal.bezalel.ac.il/en/protocol/article/2927 (Accessed: 1 December 2023).

# S

# SCIENTISM

To say that science is like a religion is the greatest insult, at least for those who see science as the realm of pure rationality or a tool to liberate humanity from religious superstitions. The fact, however, that science is part of so many secular religions' narrative (humanism, Marxism, different types of atheism, economy, or ecology) raises the suspicion that belief in science itself might be a (perhaps even more comprehensive) secular religion.

It is, of course, crucial to distinguish science as an instrument for investigating the physical world from science as the key to the meaning of life as such. The question is not whether science can ever become the latter (as Wittgenstein realized, "We feel that even when all possible scientific questions have been answered, the problems of life remain completely untouched," Wittgenstein, [1922] 2001, p. 88), but whether in trying to do so, it does not become similar to the metaphysical or religious systems it wishes to replace. If science is indeed a tool to liberate humanity from religion, it has to be at least partially (functionally) analogous with it. To avoid the "religionization" of science, its experts should exercise thoughtful and tenacious self-control, unless, of course, they think that religions themselves are nothing but primitive forms of science, in which case the problem disappears. Although the latter view – represented by James George Frazer's *The Golden Bough* at the end of the 19th century – has since received devastating criticism (as Wittgenstein wrote, it is "nonsense" that religious rituals spring from "erroneous notions about the physics of things," Wittgenstein, [1931] 2018, p. 42), its more recent versions remain a favored tool of popular science literature.

Scientism – the belief that science can solve the exact same problems that philosophical and religious systems could not – is not only a transcendent belief but a necessarily eschatological one. Celebrations of science as the savior of humanity, the harbinger of universal peace, and a new era of perfection became journalistic clichés already during the 19th century. At the opening of the Great Exhibition in 1851, the *Illustrated London News* wrote that Science (with a capital S) took "the first steps toward drawing into closer and more indissoluble union the long-estranged brethren of the great human family," while technological achievements like railroads led to a "practical annihilation of space and time," which in turn

> softened the lingering asperities of traditional hatreds, and convinced the people of Europe . . . that, if they had known as much of each other fifty or sixty years ago as they do now, there would, in all likelihood, have been no battles of the Nile, the Baltic, or Trafalgar.
> *(Illustrated London News, 1851, p. 343)*

In 1857, the *New York Evening* declared that telegraphy would "make the great heart of humanity beat with a single pulse," while another newspaper account predicted that "the kingdom of peace" will thereby be set up (Mosco, 2004, p. 120). Looking back from the era of global warming, it is tragicomical how even coal mining and the use of steam engines were celebrated as saviors or "demiurges," "the mediating spirit whom the Lord entrusted to carry out the great ideas of creation" (Jókai, 1869, p. 21).

In addition to the optimistic faith in the creative and redemptive force of science, a blind veneration of certain scientific traditions also caught the eye of observers. Orthodox Darwinism, for instance, as Gilbert Keith Chesterton noticed, had become such an object of veneration, at least in popular science which served the masses' desire for comforting, final explanations, which was, however, a falsification of true science: "Unfortunately, science is only splendid when it is science. When science becomes religion, it becomes superstition" (Chesterton, 1922, p. 496).

Moreover, the artificially construed tradition of science also falsified history, neglecting those antecedents that did not fit in the secularization-as-enlightenment narrative. Medieval science is still often omitted from popular histories, and the religious ideas of early modern thinkers are just as frequently ignored, although, as science historian Lawrence Principe notes in a 2015 volume titled *Scientism: The New Orthodoxy*, "Virtually every contributor to scientific knowledge before the nineteenth century was also a believing Christian, many very deeply religious, and many of them clergy" (Principe, 2015, p. 49). At the same time, a just as problematic line of secular saints and heroes emerges:

> They created a litany of martyrs – most notably Bruno and Galileo, but also Roger Bacon, Michael Servetus, and others – and a hagiography of sinless and oppressed reformers and visionaries that populated the

scientists' camp. They implicitly recast scientists as prophets and priests, the recipients of special favor and enlightenment, who brought forth truth and struggled to spread a gospel of science and progress against the darkness and ignorance of the pagans (i.e., the old priesthood of religion).

*(ibid., p. 50)*

Although the martyrdom of some on the list (like Bruno or Servetus) had nothing to do with their scientific views (it is dubious whether they had any such views at all), and Galileo's or Bacon's imprisonment is also a later myth, the narrative remains powerful, mainly because those who still spread it are just as uneducated in history as in philosophy or theology. As psychologist Richard N. Williams notes: "Of concern to many in various intellectual traditions is the fact that the metaphysics of scientism is being enforced in cultural and intellectual discourse by purveyors often lacking adequate training in metaphysics or even in the philosophy of science" (Williams, 2015, p. 8). A striking example is when a leading contemporary scientist does not even understand the meaning of simple words as "nothing" and when he is reminded of the fact that "quantum nothingness" (something with measurable qualities) is not nothing, only calls such an argument "moronic" (Andersen, 2012).

According to the critics of scientism, the same ignorance has characterized the crusades led by the preachers of scientism since John William Draper's *History of the Conflict between Religion and Science* (1874) which famously stated that "Roman Catholicism and Science are recognized by their respective adherents as being absolutely incompatible; they cannot exist together . . . mankind must make its choice – it cannot have both" (Draper, 1874, p. 363). More recent popularizers of science – like Richard Dawkins – are downright proud of their ignorance:

Dawkins, for example, when challenged about his ignorance of theology, responded that this "presupposes . . . that there is something in Christian theology to be ignorant about. The entire thrust of my position is that Christian theology is a non-subject. It is empty. Vacuous. Devoid of coherence or content."

*(Giberson and Artigas, 2007, p. 11)*

Such an attitude (a blind faith in one's conviction that is resistant to any conflicting view) is not even simply religious but something worse. As Principe puts it: "the strong scientism of the modern day is not merely a religion but is in fact a kind of *fundamentalism*" (Principe, 2015, p. 51). Fortunately, the real everyday practice of science has very little to do with what the *Oracles of Science*, as a 2007 volume calls Richard Dawkins, Stephen J. Gould, Stephen Hawking, Carl Sagan, Steve Weinberg, and Edward O. Wilson, offer for the general audience. It is not about "origins" or other problems on a cosmic scale; many scientists are not atheists or agnostics; and most of their research does not aim to compete with religion (Giberson and Artigas, 2007, pp. 7–9). It should not be forgotten, though, that even the normal, everyday practice of science presupposes a conviction that is not based on facts but is the very precondition of gaining facts:

> The limits of human knowledge that should ensure the existence of doubt pertain equally to both science and theology. Can we determine true and complete causes of phenomena or only the apparent ones? Are what we conclude to be causes always true causes or only correlations? Do our senses give us reliably true knowledge of the external world? Is the universe regular and uniform? None of these questions that stand at the heart of scientific investigation can be answered with certainty; each requires an act of affirmative faith that allows the scientific enterprise to function.
>
> *(Principe, 2015, pp. 56–57)*

A "faith" is certainly not enough to define a religion, but at least it shows so much that even without the excesses of scientism, science is not hermetically separated from other human endeavors. This is especially important to remember when speaking of social sciences, in which "facts" are even less tangible and more theory-dependent than in natural sciences, and the replication of results is sometimes very difficult (French, 2016). At the same time, social sciences have a closer connection to political decision-making, which makes them more prone to becoming part of a political religion, but this already belongs to other topics (from democracy to economics and postmodernism).

See also: Evolutionism, Humanism, Progress, Technology

## Sources

Andersen, R. (2012) 'Has Physics Made Philosophy and Religion Obsolete?', *The Atlantic*, 23 April. Available at: https://www.theatlantic.com/technology/archive/2012/04/has-physics-made-philosophy-and-religion-obsolete/256203/ (Accessed: 1 December 2023).

Chesterton, G. K. (1922) 'Our Notebook', *The Illustrated London News*, 8 April, p. 496.

Draper, J. W. (1874) *History of the Conflict between Religion and Science*. New York: D. Appleton and Co.

French, D. (2016) 'Is Social Science Just a Modern False God?', *New York Post*, 7 October. Available at: https://nypost.com/2016/10/07/is-social-science-just-a-modern-false-god/ (Accessed: 1 December 2023).

Giberson, K., and Artigas, M. (2007) *Oracles of Science: Celebrity Scientists versus God and Religion*. Oxford: Oxford University Press.

Illustrated London News (1851) 'The Great Exhibition', *The Illustrated London News*, 3 May, pp. 343–344.

Jókai, M. (1869) 'Fekete gyémántok'. Available at: https://mek.oszk.hu/00600/00691/00691.pdf (Accessed: 1 December 2023).
Mosco, V. (2004) *The Digital Sublime: Myth, Power, and Cyberspace*. Cambridge: The MIT Press.
Principe, L. M. (2015) 'Scientism and the Religion of Science', in *Scientism: The New Orthodoxy*, edited by Williams, R. N., and Robinson, D. N. London: Bloomsbury, pp. 41–61.
Williams, R. N. (2015) 'Introduction', in *Scientism: The New Orthodoxy*, edited by Williams, R. N., and Robinson, D. N. London: Bloomsbury, pp. 1–21.
Wittgenstein, L. ([1922] 2001) *Tractatus Logico-Philosophicus*. Translated by Pears, D. F., and McGuinness, B. F. New York: Routledge.
Wittgenstein, L. ([1931] 2018) 'Remarks on Frazer's The Golden Bough', in *The Mythology in Our Language*, translated by Palmié, S. Chicago: HAU Books, pp. 29–75.

## Selfies

Taking and sharing selfies, especially "bragging selfies" on social media, is often described as a way of creating an ideal self, a "new us" (Mirzoeff, 2015, p. 21), or "humanity 2.0" (Godart, 2016, p. 175). Some authors even speak of this new self as an "idol," a transcendent manifestation of "hyper-individualism" (ibid., pp. 168 and 174), or a secular form of "deification" (Nygaard, 2019, p. 2). Although calling selfie culture a full-fledged "secular religion" sounds like an overstatement, it does have some traits that may justify such a radical claim.

In the most general sense, as Mathias Ephraim Nygaard notes, if the word "religion" is used as a description of human activities "having to do with ultimate concerns and the creation of meaning and community," there is no reason to deny selfie culture the status of religion (ibid., p. 4). After all, the selfie "transcends the object" (ibid., p. 5); it is a symbol of something and not the thing itself. Its transcendence means that it is beyond the empirical: it is endowed with a life of its own that makes the representation more important than what it represents: "The bragging selfie displays the possession of some desired entity or experience, portraying the person in a situation of consuming or embodying it" (ibid., p. 6). It also means that the symbolic self is presented as a higher form of existence, something above the ordinary, "possessing something others do not have to the same extent." Thereby the bragging selfie functions in the same manner as "hagiographic representations" in traditional religions, portraying a given person as someone who has attained an ideal that is yet to be pursued by others. To expand the analogy, one may even say that the uploading of selfies to Instagram or Facebook and the gathering of "likes" is something like a ritual and that its "temples" are the social media platforms themselves.

Where the analogy falls short is, of course, the lack of any official dogma or sacred scripture, let alone any institutionalized "church" or "priesthood." But these are also absent from many, allegedly "genuine" religions, and even in the most institutionalized forms of the latter, we always find "loose vernacular religious practices . . . outside the reach of religious professionals" (ibid., p. 4). In this sense, sharing selfies may be treated as an analogy of these vernacular practices but certainly not as a "half secular, half religious" phenomenon.

> This process of creating a self can be thought of as religious on several accounts. The most basic argument . . . is that it is religious in creating a level of transcendence beyond the physical. That which gives the selfie-life its meaning is not the physical as such. The physical rather serves as a steppingstone for moving in the direction of ideals. These ideals are religious in being fetishes, that is objects with a magical power in social relations. Moreover, the social relations implied are performed on a platform that is perceived by some users as more real than physical life. In so far as the selfie-practitioner identifies with the image and its setting in a net of similar images this ideal reality takes precedence over every day physical life. They exist in a reality set apart from every-day life, a common definition of the religious. They are non-corporeal and non-temporal realities. The concluding argument is that the whole process in the end results in a self-creating subject, which by many definitions is a marker of divinity.
> *(ibid., p. 13)*

In sum, it remains dubious whether selfie culture is in fact a "secular" religion, a "secular" form of deification or apotheosis, something "religion-like," "quasi-religious," "para-religious," or "pseudo-religious," or just a religion plain and simple. Supposing, of course, that the latter has any definite meaning.

See also: Entertainment, Individualism

## Sources

Godart, E. (2016) *Je selfie donc je suis: Les metamorphoses du moi à l'ère du virtuel.* Paris: Albin Michel.

Mirzoeff, N. (2015) *How to See the World.* New York: Penguin Random House.

Nygaard, M. E. (2019) 'Selfies as Secular Religion: Transcending the Self', *Journal of Religion and Society*, 21, pp. 1–21. Available at: http://hdl.handle.net/10504/124381 (Accessed: 1 December 2023).

## Selfism

See Psychology.

## Sex

Speaking of sex as a religious idea began much earlier than the current culture wars, in which sex and religion often appear as each other's antipodes.

The French philosopher Georges Bataille wrote as early as 1944 that "desire for a woman's body, for a tender, erotically naked woman" was a substitute for religion for him, a truly otherworldly experience: "I escape the illusion of any solid connection between me and the world," culminating in the claim that "My true church is a whorehouse" (Bataille, [1944] 1988, p. 12).

While Bataille – and many later authors – viewed sexual "ecstasy" as something antithetical but also deeply similar to a mystical experience, Michel Foucault's *The History of Sexuality* spoke of sexual propaganda as a sort of preaching, including its theology, theologians, and not least its moral and social code:

> But it appears to me that the essential thing is . . . the existence in our era of a discourse in which sex, the revelation of truth, the overturning of global laws, the proclamation of a new day to come, and the promise of a certain felicity are linked together. Today it is sex that serves as a support for the ancient form – so familiar and important in the West – of preaching. A great sexual sermon – which has had its subtle theologians and its popular voices – has swept through our societies over the last decades; it has chastised the old order, denounced hypocrisy, and praised the rights of the immediate and the real; it has made people dream of a New City. The Franciscans are called to mind. And we might wonder how it is possible that the lyricism and religiosity that long accompanied the revolutionary project have, in Western industrial societies, been largely carried over to sex.
>
> *(Foucault, 1978, pp. 7–8)*

Conservative authors like Roger Scruton in his *Sexual Desire* also emphasized both the emotional and moral character of the analogy:

> At many points in what follows, my discussion will make contact with religion, not only because – as has been frequently observed – erotic and religious sentiments show a peculiar isomorphism, but also because religious experience provides the securest everyday background to sexual morality.
>
> *(Scruton, 1994, p. 14)*

The Anglican priest Charles Pickstone's *The Divinity of Sex*, on the other hand, found in sexuality a surrogate religious path to "mystery":

> In this book, I am going to suggest that there is an underlying common thread: namely that sex has taken on many of the functions once performed by religion. In particular, sex has become a path to an encounter with primordial mystery. . . . But more than this, in our present

condition sex is not only one possible route to the encounter with mystery, it is also the most popular. This is the primary reason why sex is so important and why it is invested with such extraordinary power: it is one of the main modes of access, for those of us who are not nuclear scientists, astrophysicists or cell biologists, to the mystery of life itself; access that can be found almost nowhere else in our world, given the general lack of interest in religion, the traditional path to the mystery of life.

*(Pickstone, 1996, p. 3)*

Although it is not at all clear how nuclear scientists and lovers have access to the same "mystery of life," so much seems certain that sex is analogous to religion because it is omnipresent in society and has an overwhelming spiritual force to shape it. It is also transcendent in the sense of being "beyond" ordinary experience (ibid., p. 6). Yet, although the cover of the book itself shows Bernini's "Ecstasy of Saint Teresa" to underline the mystical analogy, sex remains a weak substitute for religion:

On the sunny beaches of a society bathed in a warm, shallow tide of spirituality – a society that has, of course, immensely strong dikes in place to keep out the ocean swell – sex has become a rather strange religion substitute. Where once religion could be seen as the sublimation of people's natural but repressed sexual impulses, today it is clear that our investment in the copious mythology of sex is, in fact, the result of our natural religious instincts being diverted, rechanneled.

*(ibid., p. 11)*

The most detailed comparison between sex and religion, however, is not found in a book but in a journal article written by conservative cultural critic Mary Eberstadt in 2016. In it, sex appears as the essence of the "church of secularism," which has:

- a "new body of belief" or "secular catechism," a "fundamental faith" in the sexual revolution as a boon to all humanity
- a "first commandment," which says that no sexual act between consenting adults is wrong; therefore whatever contributes to consenting sexual acts is an "absolute" good, and anything interfering with them is wrong
- a main evil in the form of traditional restrictions and attitudes
- "secular saints," the victims of these restrictions and attitudes (women and sexual minorities)
- "religious rituals" such as abortion, which is in fact not a mere choice but a "sacrosanct," communal "rite" through which some people enter the "secularist-progressive" community

- a "neo-puritanical" intolerance toward competitors
- a "hagiography" of "proselytizers" for abortion and contraception (Margaret Sanger, Helen Gurley Brown, Gloria Steinem) or "crypto-scholastics" whose work is off-limits for intellectual revisionism (Alfred Kinsey and Margaret Mead)
- "quasi-monastic ascetics" of the National Abortion Rights Action League and Planned Parenthood
- foreign "missionaries" who carry the "secularist sacraments" of contraception and abortion to women in poorer countries around the world
- a "demonology" of this "substitute faith," which includes the Roman Catholic hierarchy, the major spokesmen for evangelical Protestantism, legal groups involved in religious-liberty cases, conservatives, or any apostate who deviates from the "secularist code."

It is therefore a little surprise that this "bedrock of contemporary progressivism can only be described as quasi-religious," while the final word is once again that it is a "faith," even if a "secularist" one, which is nevertheless a "church":

> The so-called culture war, in other words, has not been conducted by people of religious faith on one side and people of no faith on the other. It is instead a contest of *competing* faiths: one in the Good Book, and the other in the more newly written figurative book of secularist orthodoxy about the sexual revolution. In sum, secularist progressivism today is less a political movement than a church.
>
> *(Eberstadt, 2016)*

The connection between the sexual revolution and the more broadly understood progressive project is less inimically pointed out by Tara Isabella Burton's *Strange Rites: New Religions for a Godless World*. Tracing back the origins of sexual utopias to the 19th century, she confirms that the religion of sex belongs to a broader vision of "human transcendence," which is in turn connected to the cult of "inalienable, constitutional, and natural rights to love whom I may" (Burton, 2020, pp. 142–143). The focus on "individualism, personal choice, and the authenticity of the self" creates an "ethos of autonomy" (ibid., p. 145) or even a "theological system" (ibid., p. 146) with its corresponding "institutions, vocabulary, and rituals" (ibid., p. 150). The emancipation of different, formerly marginalized forms of sexual behavior – also supported by the entertainment industry and the "consumer-capitalist model of sexuality" (ibid., p. 164) – in turn creates a new social and political environment. "The establishment of these new sexual-social relationships – and, with them, the wider community bonds fostered in their respective scenes – is as political as it is personal" (ibid., p. 146). This is also part of the body-soul dualism of the sexual religion. As Burton asserts,

> Sexual utopianism is, at core, the systemized creation of idealistic churches that preach the doctrine of human perfectibility and transcendence and that envision the fulfillment of the body and the soul as one and the same ... Our sexual utopianism and spiritual self-care, ultimately, are two sides of the same coin.
> 
> *(ibid., pp. 163–164)*

As in the case of ecstasy or mysticism, sex becomes "religion" when it is not simply a corporeal but a spiritual adventure.

See also: Consumerism, Entertainment, Love, Psychology

## Sources

Bataille, G. ([1944] 1988) *Guilty*. Translated by Boone, B. Venice: The Lapis Press.
Burton, T. I. (2020) *Strange Rites: New Religions for a Godless World*. New York: Public Affairs.
Eberstadt, M. (2016) 'The First Church of Secularism and Its Sexual Sacraments', *National Review*, 15 June. Available at: https://www.nationalreview.com/2016/06/its-dangerous-believe-religious-freedom-sexual-revolution/ (Accessed: 1 December 2023).
Foucault, M. (1978) *The History of Sexuality*. Volume 1. Translated by Hurley, R. New York: Pantheon Books.
Pickstone, C. (1996) *The Divinity of Sex: The Search for Ecstasy in a Secular Age*. New York: St. Martin's Press.
Scruton, R. (1994) *Sexual Desire: A Philosophical Investigation*. London: Phoenix.

## Singularity

See Artificial Intelligence.

## Skateboarding

At first sight it seems an exaggeration to write a whole book on skateboarding as a secular religion. Or rather a "lifestyle religion," another category invented to distinguish new, "to some extent religious" ideas and practices from more traditional (and, supposedly, more genuine) ones. In the final analysis, however, the distinction turns out to be just as illusory as in most other cases, since skateboarding shares enough elements with the latter to call it a religion without adjectives.

It has its "origin myth" with its corresponding "holy land," California as a sort of garden of Eden; an "esoteric" sacred language that separates its adepts from outsiders; and a system of values that provides not only a general ethical framework but also a "meaning" of life (O'Connor, 2020, pp. 49–50).

In addition, skateboarding has what O'Connor explicitly calls "gods" of a "polytheistic universe" (Andrew Reynolds, Jamie Thomas, Tony Hawk, Christian Hosoi, or Salman Agah, ibid., p. 68). More moderate authors speak only of "saints" (like "Saint Hawk," Senrud, 2018, p. 217), but this does not substantially affect the religious analogy. Although this analogy often seems superficial or ironical, it might be argued that there is a "superhuman" element of worship, in a similar way as in the case of comic superheroes (Morrison, 2011, p. xvii) who are in turn also often likened to religious personalities (like Superman to Christ, Kozlovic, 2002). Because of the extraordinary powers attributed to great skateboarders, O'Connor himself thinks that "the notion that skateboarders can be considered gods holds some merit" (O'Connor, 2020, p. 71). The worship also has its iconography:

> The cross insignia of independent trucks treads a line between Nazi insignia and Papal sacrality. The countless logos of skateboard companies, void of religious connections, end up invoking devotion and even worship. Many skateboarders have tattooed their bodies with the logos of the favourite skateboard brands mirroring Geertz's claim that religion is a system of symbols that elicit "long-lasting moods and motivations."
> 
> *(ibid., p. 92)*

Moreover, this symbolism is often explicitly religious, combing elements of Christianity (or devil-worship as its contrary), Hinduism, Daoism, or Rastafarism, making it somewhat confused but certainly not "secular" (ibid., p. 95).

All these elements (and many others from pilgrimages to the rituals of play) help to create a shared identity, a spiritual community that resembles a church; the only remaining difference being the lack of institutionalization, for individual freedom is such an important value that it excludes the possibility of having anything like a formal hierarchy. Yet with skateboarding becoming an Olympic sport that is required to create its national and international organizations, even this last distinctive mark seems to evaporate (ibid., p. 292).

The only reason, therefore, to reject the idea of skateboarding as a religion seems to be the bad reputation of the word "religion" in contemporary discourse.

See also: Sport, Entertainment

## Sources

Kozlovic, A. K. (2002) 'Superman as Christ-Figure: The American Pop Culture Movie Messiah', *Journal of Religion & Film*, 6(1), pp. 1–25. Available at: https://digitalcommons.unomaha.edu/jrf/vol6/iss1/5/ (Accessed: 1 December 2023).

Morrison, G. (2011) *Supergods: Our World in the Age of the Superhero*. London: Jonathan Cape.
O'Connor, P. (2020) *Skateboarding and Religion*. Cham: Palgrave Macmillan.
Senrud, C. (2018) 'The Patron Saints of Skate', in *Jenkem Vol. 2: More Skateboarding, Smut, Shenanigans*, edited by Michna, I. Brooklyn: Jenkem Magazine in association with WINS, pp. 214–219.

## Social Justice Culture (SJC)

Since "wokeness" has become a mostly negative word by the early 2020s, more sympathetic authors – like Tara Isabella Burton – go back to the terminology of "social justice culture" and "social justice movements" to describe the utopian tendencies of the anti-establishment, anti-racist, and anti-sexist features of the latter (Burton, 2020, p. 166). She nevertheless confirms that this "civil religion" is not substantially different from its authoritarian or reactionary counterparts, which pose a just as dangerous – or perhaps even more dangerous – threat to traditional religion (ibid., p. 199).

See also: Wokeness

### Sources

Burton, T. I. (2020) *Strange Rites: New Religions for a Godless World*. New York: Public Affairs.

## Social media

See Selfies.

## Socialism

The religious traits of socialism were detected as early as the mid-19th century. As Juan Donoso Cortés put in his *Discourse on the General Situation of Europe* in 1850: socialism is an "economic sect," a negation – or rather the exact opposite – of Catholicism. To fight it on purely economic grounds would thus be a mistake, for as a "sect" (that has its "pontiffs" in Germany, its "disciples" in France, and its "fanatics" in Italy, Donoso Cortés, [1850] 2007, pp. 71–72), it is also a religious idea that denies both divine authority in religion and coercive power in politics. It is also important that Donoso Cortés made no distinction between socialism and anarchism, which his reference to Proudhon expressed most clearly: "Proudhon then comes forth, gentlemen, and declares: 'There's no government'" (ibid., p. 75).

That socialism is the negation of religion, yet in some sense a religion itself is of course a problematic statement. Similar ambiguities appear in other early references to socialism like that of Henri-Frédéric Amiel, a Swiss moral philosopher who wrote about the Paris commune in 1871:

> The international socialism of the *ouvriers*, ineffectually put down in Paris, is beginning to celebrate its approaching victory. For it there is neither country, nor memories, nor property, nor religion. There is nothing and nobody but itself. Its dogma is equality, its prophet is Mably, and Baboeuf is its god.
>
> *(Amiel, [1871] 1887, p. 121)*

Socialism thus has no "religion" but nevertheless has a "dogma," a "prophet," and even a "god," which may be understood as a mere figure of speech, unless it is suggested that the principle of equality is indeed something that can neither be proved nor questioned, or that the French forerunners of modern socialism are venerated as superhuman figures and infallible authorities.

As Nikolai Berdyaev noted in 1906, socialism (in its most perfect form, social democracy) was not simply about the organization of economic life or the satisfaction of the economic needs of humanity. It is a "whole creed," a doctrine about the "meaning of life, about the purpose of history," a totalizing worldview that also encompassed "socialist morality, socialist philosophy, socialist science, and socialist art" (Berdyaev, 1906). By 1917, however, he had changed his mind, admitting that social democracy was no longer such a radical vision, at least in most parts of Europe. "Only within the consciousness of the Russian Bolsheviks does the revolutionary socialism remain a religion" (Berdyaev, 1917). In contrast, Carl Schmitt's *Political Theology* repeated Donoso Cortés' verdict that all forms of socialism were essentially anarchistic, a negation of both political and religious authority, thereby constituting a (however negative, or even "diabolical") political theology (Schmitt, [1922] 2006, p. 63).

The same vacillation – whether socialism was a religion or an antireligion – kept haunting later authors, most notably the French sociologist Raymond Aron, who finally decided that it was both:

> And yet, insofar as socialism is an antireligion, it is also a religion. It denies the existence of an afterlife, but it brings back to earth certain hopes that, in the past, were inspired by transcendental beliefs alone. I propose to use the term *secular religions* to designate doctrines that, in the souls of our contemporaries, take the place of the faith that is no more, placing the salvation of mankind in this world, in the more or less distant future, and in the form of a social order yet to be invented.
>
> *(Aron, [1944] 2002, p. 178)*

The word "secular," however, refers rather to a this-worldly version of Christianity ("the secularization of the Christian vision," a "socialist eschatology," ibid., p. 179) and not of religion in general. The other parallels (the conflict of "rival sects" within the movement, the definition of "heresy" by "councils" defining "dogmas," ibid., p. 180) again point to an analogy with Christianity or, more precisely, with Catholicism. The same holds for mass rituals and their symbolism (icons, hymns, flags, ibid., p. 184).

Although conservative critics such as Irving Kristol later suggested that by the mid-1970s, socialism had lost most of its great theologians ("In the case of contemporary socialism, there are no Church Fathers, only heretics, outside the reach of established orthodoxies," Kristol, 1976, p. 5), as well as its powerful millennial vision, it remained true that the countries of the so-called actually existing socialism preserved most of the ritual and symbolic elements of their more radical past. All children in the pioneer movement were taught catechisms based on the model of the Ten Commandments; official liturgies were held on feast days like May 1 or November 7; the pictures of communist leaders were still carried around in demonstrations; the statues of Lenin stood in every large city in the Eastern Bloc; and the Mausoleum of Lenin still attracted crowds of pilgrims in Moscow.

All this shows, at the same time, that the use of the word "socialism" is hopelessly confused in the literature of secular religions. Donoso Cortés and Carl Schmitt treated socialism and anarchism as two essentially identical concepts, Berdyaev called social democracy and Bolshevism two different forms of socialism; while Amiel, Aron, or Kristol tended to equate socialism with communism. Moreover, Donoso Cortés called socialism a religious and political "negation," Schmitt called it a "political theology," Berdyaev a genuine "religion," Aron a "secular religion" (meaning that it was both a "religion" and an "antireligion"), while Kristol used words like "secular religion," "pseudo-religion," and "post-Christian religion" interchangeably.

All this shows the deeply problematic nature of such comparisons. If something has pontiffs, disciples, fanatics, dogmas, prophets or even gods, a creed about the meaning of life and history, an overarching moral teaching, a (however diabolical) absolute, an eschatological vision, heresies and excommunications, symbols, rituals, and catechisms, it remains difficult to tell why it is not a religion, only something "secular" or "pseudo."

On the other hand, attempts that deny any substantial similarity are no less problematic. What distinguishes a secular hierarchy from a religious one? What makes its followers' fanaticism a secular one and its infallible teachings ideological and not religious? How is a secular belief in the end of history (something that is by definition not an empirical reality but an ideal to be achieved) different from an eschatological belief in the "things unseen"? One may, of course, say that secular ideologies envision a paradise on earth, but that is not alien to some "real" religions, either, at least in their millenarian versions. The distinction of secular and religious orthodoxy and heresy is just as problematic, for they both rely on the assumption that even eternal truths are to be defended by this-worldly, political means, if necessary. And again, if secular rituals and symbols are to be distinguished from religious ones, it remains to be asked how the very concepts of "ritual" and "symbol" can be understood in ways that remain completely free of religious or metaphysical connotations.

Apart from such problems, an important question concerns the extension of the concept of socialism. As seen before, socialism is sometimes discussed together with anarchism, communism, and Bolshevism. More rarely, it is also put in the same bag as Nazism (a form of national *socialism*; see Kuehnelt-Leddihn, 1974; Znamenski, 2021). Religious traits of socialism are also discovered in such different forms as the Swedish model of social democracy, Kibbutz socialism, Tanzanian "village socialism," the ethno-racial state of Zimbabwe, or the postmodern "cultural left" (Znamenski, 2021).

In Sweden, the defining elements are faith in the power of social engineering, the creation of a new "family" of the nation, attempts to transform traditional lifestyle, or excessive state propaganda led by a priesthood of enlightened experts (ibid., pp. 201–202). In Israel, socialism is (or rather was) a tool of ethnic mobilization and self-defense in the 1920s–1950s. As a Kibbutz resident said,

> I value Marxism very highly. In times like ours when there is no faith and there is no God, Marxism does provide you with a weltanschauung; it does fit every theory and every science into a scheme and, thus, it brings order out of chaos.
>
> *(ibid., pp. 227–228)*

In Africa, the national applications of "the political religion of socialism, which was tied to aggressive social engineering and collective mobilization," was amended by the cult of charismatic dictators (ibid., pp. 269–270). As for the postmodern "cultural left," it is usually denounced because of its mythical idealization of the oppressed:

> In a religious-like manner, New Left activist Casey Hayden, described her feelings about the American people of "color" as the newly found classes of the "chosen ones": "We believed that the last should be the first, and not only should be the first, but in fact were first in our value system. They were first because they were redeemed already, purified by their suffering, and they could therefore take the lead in the redemption of us all." Another New Left writer characteristically titled his book about "unspoiled" and "authentic" rural blacks in Mississippi *A Prophetic Minority*.
>
> *(ibid., p. 361)*

Prophecies of the future, statements about sin and redemption, or moral commandments issued by a priesthood of intellectuals thus prove to be common elements of socialist thinking, this time combined with the apocalyptic language of ecologism:

> Since the apocalyptical notion of decline is an enduring part of the Western tradition, the failure of the *Limits of Growth* and *Population Bomb* prophecies did not affect new doomsday scenarios. Neither did it prevent arrogant attempts to predict future development of the world on the basis of computer models. In contrast to premodern prophecies about the end of the world that had worn a religious garb, modern and postmodern apocalyptic scenarios have been dressed into the language of science, yet still carrying a strong ahistorical religious tone.
>
> *(ibid., p. 374)*

But this is perhaps the concept of socialist religion stretched to its widest possible limits.

See also: Bolshevism, Communism, Ecology, Nationalism, Nazism, Postmodernism, Statism, Wokeness

## Sources

Amiel, H.-F. ([1871] 1887) *Amiel's Journal: The Journal Intime of Henri-Frédéric Amiel*. Translated by Ward, H. London: Macmillan.

Aron, R. ([1944] 2002) 'The Future of Secular Religions', in *The Dawn of Universal History: Selected Essays from a Witness to the Twentieth Century*, translated by Bray, B. New York: Basic Books, pp. 177–201.

Berdyaev, N. (1906) 'Социализм как религия', *Вопросы философии и психологии*, 17(5), pp. 508–545. Available at: http://relig-library.pstu.ru/catalog/35/book-35.pdf (Accessed: 1 December 2023).

Berdyaev, N. (1917) 'The Religious Foundations of Bolshevism' (Религиозные основы большевизма), *Русская свобода*, 8 August. Available at: https://www.1260.org/Mary/Text/Text_Berdyaev_The_Religious_Foundations_of_Bolshevism_en.htm (Accessed: 1 December 2023).

Donoso Cortés, J. ([1850] 2007) 'Discourse on the General Situation of Europe', in *Readings in Political Theory*, translated by McNamara, V., and Schwartz, M. Ave Maria: Sapientia Press, pp. 67–82.

Kristol, I. (1976) 'Socialism: An Obituary for an Idea', *The Alternative: An American Spectator*, 10(1), pp. 5–8.

Kuehnelt-Leddihn, E. R. (1974) *Leftism from de Sade and Marx to Hitler and Marcuse*. New Rochelle: Arlington.

Schmitt, C. ([1922] 2006) *Political Theology: Four Chapters on the Concept of Sovereignty*. Translated by Schwab, G. Chicago: The University of Chicago Press.

Znamenski, A. (2021) *Socialism as a Secular Creed: A Modern Global History*. New York: Lexington.

## Sports

It is important to note that sports are called secular religions not because some sports enthusiasts use phrases like "golf is my religion" or "football is like a religion to me." In most cases, such phrases only express a strong sense of commitment without any intention to draw a systematic analogy. In a few but non-negligible instances, however, sports are treated as much more, the manifestation of a higher, spiritual aim, the "ideal of superior life and aspiration to perfection," as already the Olympic movement's foundational texts confirmed in the late 19th century (Piette, 1993, p. 47). Or, as Gilbert Keith Chesterton remarked as early as 1920:

> The whole modern way of making the world better, which is so scientifically designed to make it worse, can be clearly and compactly realized in the single case of sports, or games. It is a fashionable and familiar example; it ought to be a frivolous and amusing example; but it is not. Sport is not so much a modern relaxation as a new religion; and is more serious and unsmiling even than most new religions.
> *(Chesterton, [1920] 2020, p. 9)*

According to Chesterton, points of identity include the "monastic" rules of sport groups ("the shaving of the head, the starving of the body, the heroic and inhuman devotion to the brotherhood" or "the intoning of strange and unearthly litanies that seem to belong to another world") but also the universalistic aspirations of modern sports.

That sport is indeed a "new" religion is also confirmed by authors like Michael Novak who insist that "A sport is not a religion in the same way that Methodism, Presbyterianism, or Catholicism is a religion. But these are not the only kinds of religion" (Novak, 1976, p. 18). Although he still prefers the word "civil religion," this is not to mean that "civil" is merely "secular" or that the word "religion" should be taken in a metaphorical way:

> I am arguing a considerably stronger point. I am saying that sports flow outward into action from a deep natural impulse that is radically religious: an impulse of freedom, respect for ritual limits, a zest for symbolic meaning, and a longing for perfection. The athlete may of course be pagan, but sports are, as it were, natural religions. There are many ways to express this radical impulse: by the asceticism and dedication of preparation; by a sense of respect for the mysteries of one's own body and soul, and for powers not in one's own control; by a sense of awe for the place and time of competition; by a sense of fate; by a felt sense of comradeship and destiny; by a sense of participation in the rhythms and tides of nature itself.
> *(ibid., p. 19)*

There are many other examples which argue that sport not only resembles religion but – depending on the definition we use – may in fact be called as such: "the state of being grasped by an ultimate concern, a concern which qualifies all other concerns as preliminary and which itself contains the answer to the question of meaning and of our life" (Hoffman, 1992, p. 3).

Although defining religion as a matter of ultimate concern is always problematic, it remains true that such broad definitions may always be amended by morphological and functional analogies, of which a complete list may be assembled:

- belief in an "absolute" that is beyond the realm of everyday experience
- an idea of "perfectibility" that raises human beings above their present status in an imperfect world
- an overarching moral code that regulates people's lives in all their relevant aspects
- the devotion or even "asceticism" with which this moral code is followed
- the presence of "monastic" communities which serve as the prime example of such devotion
- or "rituals" that are performed regularly, uniting the faithful in one community and offering a common source of identity.

To which one might add that such rituals are performed under sacred symbols (the five rings of the Olympic flag, the Olympic flame, national symbols, or those of a given sports team). Stadiums and sports halls are sacred places, sites of pilgrimage (Ritchie and Adair, 2004, p. 13) or saint-worship, and "the sacralization of (super) human athletes' performances" (Amara, 2011, p. 44). Moreover, any sport that is more than just a personal pastime is regulated by magisterial offices like national and international associations, and "the same could be said about the religious-like institutional role of the IOC as the sole guardian of Olympism 'orthodoxy'" (ibid.). Although the word "religious-like" and the quotation mark around "orthodoxy" once again suggest that sport is not a "real" but a "secular" religion, the very status of Olympism as a universal philosophy beyond religious divides (and its efforts to suppress all other explicit religious symbolism by competing athletes, groups, or nations) shows the exact opposite. It rather acts as a "super-religion" creating tensions between the Olympic Movement and traditional religions, which is most clearly visible in the case of Muslim participants, who are routinely denied the possibility of wearing their own cloths or religious symbols (ibid., p. 45).

Yet whether we call Olympism (and sports in general) a "new religion," a "civil religion," a "secular religion," or a "pseudo-religion" (Adair, 2004, p. 60), it remains obvious that such tensions can only be explained by the structural analogy between these and other, rival forms of religiosity. One might of course say that "it would be misleading to propose sport as a new form of religion," but even then, we must acknowledge at least so much that it "lies somewhere between the religious and the secular – betwixt the sacred and the profane" (Gammon, 2004, p. 41). The only problem is that the boundaries of the religious and the secular, or the sacred and the profane can never be precisely drawn, of which sports are an excellent example.

See also: Boxing, Football, Kung Fu, Skateboarding

### Sources

Adair, D. (2004) 'Where the Games Never Cease: The Olympic Museum in Lausanne, Switzerland', in *Sport Tourism: Interrelationships, Impacts and Issues*, edited by Ritchie, B. W., and Adair, D. Clevedon: Channel View Publications, pp. 46–76.
Amara, M. (2011) 'Olympic Sport and Internationalism Debates in the Arab-Muslim World: Between "Modernity" and "Authenticity", "Globalisation" and "Localisation"', in *Internationalism in the Olympic Movement: Idea and Reality between Nations, Cultures, and People*, edited by Preuss, H., and Liese, K. Wiesbaden: VS / Springer, pp. 37–52.
Chesterton, G. K. ([1920] 2020) *The New Renascence: Thoughts on the Structure of the Future*. Berkeley: Omo Press.
Gammon, S. (2004) 'Secular Pilgrimage and Sport Tourism', in *Sport Tourism: Interrelationships, Impacts and Issues*, edited by Ritchie, B. W., and Adair, D. Clevedon: Channel View Publications, pp. 30–45.
Hoffman, S. J. (ed.) (1992) *Sport and Religion*. Champaign: Human Kinetics.
Novak, M. (1976) *The Joy of Sports*. New York: Basic Books.
Piette, A. (1993) *Les religiosités séculières*. Paris: Presses Universitaires de France.
Ritchie, B. W., and Adair, D. (ed.) (2004) *Sport Tourism: Interrelationships, Impacts and Issues*. Clevedon: Channel View Publications.

## Stalinism

"Stalinism" may refer to a form of government in the Soviet Union from the 1920s to 1953, the ideology of this era, or more specifically, to the personality cult of Joseph Stalin himself. As an ideology, Stalinism represents a radical version of communist dogmatics and eschatology, with all its corresponding symbolism, rituals, and emotional excesses. As for the cult of Stalin, it remains a matter of debate whether the word "cult" refers to truly religious worship or should be seen as just a metaphor. Although the external manifestations of the cult were spectacular (icons of the leader present everywhere from homes to workplaces or carried around in public ceremonies; his birthday celebrated as a public feast; his teachings cited as infallible directives; songs and poems dedicated to him; etc.), some still maintain that, in essence, all this remained a "heroic" and not a "religious" cult (van Ree, 2016).

The main argument is that it lacked any true "deification" of the leader: people did not pray to him or attribute explicitly superhuman, miraculous powers to him. On the other hand, as many observers note, the cult of heroes is itself a religious phenomenon: "At its root, after all, the word 'hero' conveys an interweaving of man with God. From classical antiquity onward, the hero was invested with powers that were expressly *super*human" (Lambert and Mallett, 2007, p. 454). In other words, Stalin may not have been treated the same way by Stalinists as Jesus Christ by Christians, but belief in his absolute goodness and infallibility, coupled with his virtual omnipresence and multi- if not omnipotence ("Nothing was too small not to be attributable to his leadership, guidance and solicitude," Gill, 2021, p. 4) did create a transcendent aura that is hard to describe in secular terms. Ironically, communists themselves were less eager to distance themselves from religious language than some modern scholars:

> The first official biography of the "Red pope" was produced by French communist writer Henri Barbusse in 1935. The writer depicted Stalin as a superman who was endowed with magic powers and godlike characteristics: "If Stalin has faith in the masses, it is reciprocated. It is veritable religion that the New Russia holds for Stalin. He has saved. He will save." Stalin, who was born of "thunder and lightning," lived a life of a monk for the Marxist cause: "He had neither home, no family; he lived and thought exclusively for the Revolution." That biography became the foundational text that triggered Stalin's cult both in the Soviet Union and beyond. In fact, for Barbusse this project was a culmination of his "liberation" trilogy, where the first two volumes narrated the biography of Jesus Christ.
> *(Znamenski, 2021, p. 128)*

Although it is often claimed that Stalin himself was opposed to the excesses of his cult, he was in fact aware of the transcendent nature of his divine image and its difference from the actual person:

> Yuri Zhdanov is quoted as reporting a family argument in which Vasilii, Stalin's younger son, stated that he is a Stalin too! According to Zhdanov, Stalin replied: "No you're not . . . you're not Stalin and I'm not Stalin. Stalin is Soviet power. Stalin is what he is in the newspapers and portraits, not you, no not even me."
> *(Pisch, 2016, p. 42)*

Or when the writer Mikhail Sholokhov criticized the adulation directed at Stalin, Stalin replied smiling, "What can I do? The people need a god" (ibid.). Even if all such talk could be dismissed as ironical or metaphorical, it remains an unsettling question why there was so much of it, and why it fit so well with all the other "religious" (dogmatic, symbolic, and ritual) elements of Stalinism. As a final note, it should be mentioned that Stalinism also fit well with the other secular religions of the era:

> In many respects, socialism grew out of the nineteenth-century belief in the miracles of industrial revolution and science and a simultaneous fear of the industrial order they were unleashing. Hence, obsessive attempts to

place power into the hands of benevolent government experts that were expected to know better how to construct from above better material and social life. Out of this science, technology, and state's worship, there emerged collectivist projects of social and biological engineering. Stalin's socialism, Hitler's national socialism, and Chinese Maoism are the most grotesque manifestations of that mindset.

*(Znamenski, 2021, p. xiv)*

In one way, Stalinism itself became a sort of national or patriotic socialism, with one chosen nation leading the way to the communist heaven; as Andrei Znamenski wrote, "a hybrid of traditional class-based Marxism and patriotic Soviet mythology peppered with traits of Russian nationalism" (ibid., p. 112).

See also: Communism, Leninism, Nationalism, Statism

### Sources

Gill, G. (2021) 'The Stalin Cult as Political Religion', *Religions* 12(12), p. 1112. https://doi.org/10.3390/rel12121112

Lambert, P., and Mallett, R. (2007) 'Introduction: The Heroisation–Demonisation Phenomenon in Mass Dictatorships', *Totalitarian Movements and Political Religions*, 8(3–4), pp. 453–463. https://doi.org/10.1080/14690760701571106

Pisch, A. (2016) *The Personality Cult of Stalin in Soviet Posters, 1929–1953: Archetypes, Inventions, and Fabrications.* Acton: Australian National University Press.

van Ree, E. (2006) 'Stalinist Ritual and Belief System: Reflections on "Political Religion"', *Politics, Religion & Ideology*, 17(2–3), pp. 143–161. https://doi.org/10.1080/21567689.2016.1187600

Znamenski, A. (2021) *Socialism as a Secular Creed: A Modern Global History.* Lanham: Lexington Books.

## Statism

As British socialist author and politician Harold Laski once said, "What the Absolute is to metaphysics, that is the state to political theory" (Laski, [1915] 1997, p. 6). By this, he referred to the Hegelian view of the state as a unity, in which all social groups "are to be but the ministrants to its life; their reality is the outcome of its sovereignty, since without it they could have no existence" (ibid., p. 1). He also added that the absolutization of the state was only a reversal of the medieval idea of the church absorbing the state; it was moved by a similar sort of "mystic monism" (ibid., p. 3). The early modern state incorporated the church and society just as much as the latter had tried to incorporate in itself the state and society in the Middle Ages.

Which already raises the question of whether we should speak of a "secular" religion of the state or rather a "new" religion, one that is characterized not by the secularization of religious ideas but by the "migration of the holy" from the church to the state as John Bossy and William Cavanaugh suggest (Bossy, 1985; Cavanaugh, 2011). Moreover, the state is not necessarily an impersonal absolute or an abstract locus of the sacred but perhaps a personal deity. As Laski realized, "We talk of England, Greece, Rome, as single personal forces, transcending the men and women who compose them" (Laski, [1915] 1997, p. 3). The same is confirmed by more recent authors who ironically say that "States are people, too," in the sense that we attribute intentions and actions to them without any reasonable evidence:

> [I]t is crucially important to here indicate and ever so closely observe the fact . . . that the states are not, properly speaking, *real*. This is an ontological claim, one that demands a definition of real. What states do not possess as entities is a physical essence that exists independently outside the human mind . . . there are people acting in their name, we have them demarcated on maps, identified by flags, worn them on sleeves and mobilized them in green metal. But: the state is no-one in particular, not a picture, a flag, or a tank – all of these are symbols for something which cannot be seen, but we either believe is there, or are just ready to play along.
> *(Luoma-aho, 2012, pp. 55–56)*

On the other hand, there are those who maintain that all this is metaphorical talk, and the rise of the state was indeed "a process of secularization" like the German jurist Ernst-Wolfgang Böckenförde did in 1967:

> The emergence of the state . . . has to do with the detachment of the political order as such from its spiritual and religious origin and evolution; with its "becoming secular" in the sense of exiting a world in which religion and politics formed a unity to find a purpose and identity of its own, conceived in secular (political) terms; and, finally, with the separation of the political order from the Christian religion and from any specific religion as its foundation and leaven.
> *(Böckenförde, [1967] 2020, p. 153)*

The problem of "religious origin" nevertheless raises the possibility that the emergence of the state (by which most authors mean the emergence of the *modern* state in the European, Christian context) might still produce at least "secular" religion. Yet the distinction of secular and genuine religions in this case turns out to be just as problematic as in many other cases.

First, we must observe that premodern societies – and especially non-European ones – did not separate "secular" and "religious" spheres; the only division was a sort of "division of labor" between what we today would call "political" or "administrative" powers and the tasks of "religious" experts or priests. Political leaders were nevertheless sacred persons, just as priests served as agents of the political community; rituals and buildings have had both political and religious significance, at least if we cling to such an anachronistic terminology that was itself created much later, during the rise of the modern state. The Eurocentrism of this terminology was clearly indicated by such authors as Eric Voegelin:

> When one speaks of religion, one thinks of the institution of the Church, and when one speaks of politics, one thinks of the state. These organizations confront one another as clear-cut, firm entities, and the spirit with which these two bodies are imbued is not one and the same. The state and secular spirit conquered their spheres of power in the fierce battle against the Holy Empire of the Middle Ages, and in the course of this struggle linguistic symbols developed, which do not reflect reality as such but seek to capture and defend the opposite positions of the struggle.
> *(Voegelin, [1938] 2000, p. 27)*

In other words, "secular spirit" can only be defined in contrast to Christian spirit and not to religious spirit in general, and even in this case, it will be a linguistic construction and not the representation of things as they are. To separate the ideology of the state from Christian theology has indeed been impossible throughout the Middle Ages, as the complex story of state/church relations aptly shows.

Although the division of powers is thought to have been declared by Jesus Christ's "Render unto Caesar the things that are Caesar's, and unto God the things that are God's" (Matthew 22:21) and several medieval documents reasserted this division (from Pope Gelasius' *Duo sunt* letter to Bernard of Clairvaux's *De consideratione*), the fact is that kingship never lost its sacred character. The coronation and anointment of medieval emperors and kings was treated as a sacrament from the early Middle Ages to the Council of Trent in the 16th century, which finally fixed the number of sacraments at seven, excluding coronation. The emperor ruled "in God's place" (*in vice Dei*, Kantorowicz, 1957, p. 77) or as a "surrogate of God on earth" (Coleman, 2000, p. 19). Emperor Charles II was called "savior of the world" by none other than Pope John VIII in the 9th century (Kantorowicz, 1957, p. 83).

It was only after the successful efforts of the medieval papacy to monopolize "the spiritual strata and turn them into a sacerdotal domain" (ibid., p. 60) that kings started to seek other – but just as sacred – justifications for themselves. Law – especially Roman Law – became such a source of justification with its own sacred scripture, the *Corpus Iuris*, its *Templum Iustitiae* envisioned by Placentinus at the end of the 12th century, its "priests of Law," explicitly called as such, and its pontifex in the person of the king. As King Roger II of Sicily declared: "The royal office presumes for itself a certain privilege of priesthood" (ibid., pp. 107–118). Even if the word "secular religion" was not used, something astonishingly similar appeared when legal texts like the *De sacris et sacratis* mentioned laws as a form of "human holiness":

> There is one thing holy which is human, such as laws; and there is another thing holy which is divine, such as things pertaining to the Church. And among the priests, some are divine priests, such as presbyters; others are human priests, such as magistrates, who are called priests because they dispense things holy, that is, laws.
>
> *(ibid., p. 121)*

The religion of laws (a forerunner of the cult of modern constitutions that Condorcet would first call a "political religion" in the late 18th century) was but one example of the sacralization of political power. To call the community of the emerging state a "mystical body" was also a borrowing from the church, which defined itself as such (at least since the 12th century, after the original meaning of the mystical body was transferred from the eucharist to the church; see Lubac, [1944] 2007). The rituals of power also openly relied on Christian sources:

> the successful conclusion of the Hundred Years War had stimulated a political cult which, by borrowing a good deal of the ritual of the feast of Corpus Christi, annexed to the profit of monarchy the most powerful sacred symbol in Christianity.
>
> *(Bossy, 1985, pp. 154–155)*

As William Cavanaugh remarked, not only the king of France "applied Eucharistic imagery to his royal presence and made reference to the mystical body of France," but also Queen Elizabeth of England "created public rituals based on the Corpus Christi procession in which she occupied the place formerly reserved for the host" (Cavanaugh, 2014).

At the same time, as the references to the unity of the ruler and the community in a "mystical body" foreshadowed, the emerging nation-state would soon attribute similar divine qualities for itself. When the king or queen was no longer conceived as the personification of the state and civil society took its place, the latter was often described "as it were, the only divinity that [the philosopher] can acknowledge on earth" (Gentile, 2006, p. 17).

From this time on, the religion of the state became inseparable from the religion of the nation or the homeland but also from other ideologies. As Luigi Sturzo, Catholic priest and founder of the Italian People's Party, remarked at the end of the First World War, it was not only German nationalism that revealed the "absurd practice of the pantheistic conception of the state that subjects everything to its power," the same spirit penetrated the "liberal and democratic" nations of Europe, creating "a new lay religion" of the "sovereign, absolute state" (Sturzo, [1918] 1915, p. 388). Or, as Christopher Dawson said in 1934, "the movement towards state control in every department of life" (including education, birth control, or economic regulation) is "a universal one," "not to be confused with the political tenets of a party, whether Communist or Fascist" (Dawson, 1934, pp. 2–3).

In sum, the rise of the modern state – as distinguished from earlier forms of political authority that never had the same all-embracing character – was a "process of secularization," only if by secularization one means a growing independence from the already existing religious institutions. In any other sense, it was a "process of sacralization," the creation of a new absolute, endowing it with personal attributes of a transcendent deity, or excluding the very possibility of not belonging to it. "Not having a nationality is an exception in our world, and a risky one, because we live our lives in a world inhabited by states" (Luoma-aho, 2012, p. 55). This is a dogmatic requirement, just as the compulsory worship of its symbols (flags or coats of arms) or the prescribed behavior when its rituals are performed (the singing of anthems or the inauguration of leaders). Let us also add that the worship of the state and its coercive power still does not have any feasible alternatives: even supranational institutions like the United Nations confirm that they are a community of "sovereign nation-states." The word "sovereign," however, is also of religious origins: something "higher than the highest," an attribute of God in medieval literature that was only later transferred to political leaders and entities like the state (Quaritsch, 1986).

See also: Constitutionalism, Democracy, Nationalism, Patriotism, UN

## Sources

Böckenförde, E.-W. ([1967] 2020) 'The Rise of the State as a Process of Secularization', in *Religion, Law, and Society: Selected Writings*, edited by Künkler, M., and Stein, T. Oxford: Oxford University Press, pp. 152–167.

Boia, L. (2002) *Le mythe de la démocratie*. Paris: Belles Lettres.

Bossy, J. (1985) *Christianity in the West 1400–1700*. Oxford: Oxford University Press.

Cavanaugh, W. T. (2011) *Migrations of the Holy: God, State, and the Political Meaning of the Church*. Grand Rapids: Eerdmans.

Cavanaugh, W. T. (2014) 'The Church in the Streets: Eucharist and Politics', *Modern Theology* 30(2), pp. 384–402. https://doi.org/10.1111/moth.12103

Coleman, J. (2000) *A History of Political Thought: From the Middle Ages to the Renaissance*. Malden: Blackwell.

Dawson, C. (1934) 'Religion and the Totalitarian State', *The Criterion*, 14(54), pp. 1–16.

Gentile, E. (2006) *Politics as Religion*. Translated by Staunton, G. Princeton: Princeton University Press.

Kantorowicz, E. (1957) *The King's Two Bodies: A Study in Mediaeval Political Theology*. Princeton: Princeton University Press.
Laski, H. ([1915] 1997) *Studies in the Problem of Sovereignty*. London: Routledge.
Lubac, H. ([1944] 2007) *Corpus Mysticum: The Eucharist and the Church in the Middle Ages*. Translated by Simmonds, G. Notre Dame: University of Notre Dame Press.
Luoma-aho, M. (2012) *God and International Relations: Christian Theology and World Politics*. New York: Continuum.
Quaritsch, H. (1986) *Souveränität: Entstehung und Entwicklung des Begriffs in Frankreich und Deutschland vom 13. Jahrhundert bis 1806*. Berlin: Duncker und Humblot.
Sturzo, L. ([1918] 1915) 'Stato moderno e libertà', in *I discorsi politici*. Roma: Istituto Luigi Sturzo, pp. 388–390.
Voegelin, E. ([1938] 2000) 'Political Religions', in *The Collected Work of Eric Voegelin. Volume 5: Modernity without Restraint*, translated by Schildhauer, V. A. Columbia: University of Missouri Press, pp. 19–73.

## Superintelligence

See Artificial Intelligence, Transhumanism.

# T
# TECHNOLOGY

The religion of technology appears in many entries of this book from economics and entertainment to artificial intelligence and transhumanism. Technology or rather technologies are therefore better described as denominations of a common church, or manifestations of an overall religious mysticism in which humans are elevated above nature and become masters of their own fate.

The technological sphere is one – higher – level of a dualistic universe, the opposite of the lower, natural sphere. One is tempted to call it a technological "heaven" which – as all other heavens – has its preachers or prophets, its churches, its vision of history, and its corresponding moral commandments:

> From the beginning, the institutions of modern engineering education founded in the 19th century have been surrounded by a kind of quasi-religious aura, a very strong tendency for the modern engineer to appear as the anointed priest of science – both in the public image and in the self-interpretation of the role. The vision of progress – which from the 19th century increasingly means technological progress – is itself very definitely associated with religious expectations and associations.
>
> *(Kovács, 2021, p. 122)*

As David Noble observed in his *The Religion of Technology*, the very beginnings of technological progress were inspired by millenarian visions (Noble, 1998), so a sort of religious utopianism is a remaining birthmark of the whole project. Regardless of whether the Kingdom of God is described in terms of material welfare, amusement and pleasure, or human enhancement, technology offers a perfect achievement of any or all of those. In this sense, technology (and science, of which it is an application) is anything but the manifestation of pure rationality. As Jason A. Josephson-Storm's *The Myth of Disenchantment* suggests, they are not even secular *religions* but stand closer to magic, and therefore the thesis of "demythologization" in the modern era is in fact the central myth of the latter (Josephson-Storm, 2017).

Finally, in addition to the dualistic cosmology of technology, its priests, churches, prophecies, and myths, it also has a very powerful moral message, which commands – in almost all instances, from cloning to computer development – that technological progress cannot and should not be stopped or reversed. For those who fear the dangers of unbridled progress, there is a reassuring message, in which, of course, one must believe, for it can never be sufficiently proven. "The basic article of faith for our civilization – which is at least as strong as the dogma of the Holy Trinity for medieval people – is that there is a technical-technological solution for everything" (Kovács, 2021, p. 134).

See also: Artificial Intelligence, Biotechnology, Cloning, Ecologism, Entertainment, Fascism, Humanism, Posthumanism, Scientism, Transhumanism

### Sources

Josephson-Storm, J. Ā. (2017) *The Myth of Disenchantment: Magic, Modernity and the Birth of the Human Sciences*. Chicago: The University of Chicago Press.
Kovács, G. (2021) *A kiborg és az emberi állapot*. Budapest: Liget Műhely.
Noble, D. (1998) *The Religion of Technology: The Divinity of Man and the Spirit of Invention*. New York: Alfred A. Knopf.

## Thinness

The *Religion of Thinness* is not just a piece of superficial witticism but the topic of several articles and a whole book by American religious scholar Michelle Lelwica that discusses obsession with the "ideal" female body as a functional and substantive analogy of traditional religions.

> First, . . . for many women in the US today, the quest for a slender body serves what has historically been a "religious" *function*: providing a sense of purpose that orients and gives meaning to their lives, especially in times of suffering and uncertainty. Second, this quest has many *features* in common with traditional religions, including beliefs, myths, rituals, moral codes, and sacred images – all of which encourage women to find "salvation" (i.e., happiness and well-being) through the pursuit of a "better" (i.e., thinner) body.
> *(Lelwica, 2011, p. 257)*

The purpose of the analogy is not only to criticize this quest but to raise suspicions about any clear-cut divisions between "religion," "culture," and "the body" (ibid., p. 258). Thus, in contrast to many other secular-religious analogies, the aim is not to prove that the religion of thinness is something "transcendent" but the exact opposite "that the seemingly transcendent truths of religion are, in the end, *human constructs*, variously created and developed through somatic, psychic, and social processes in response to the mystery, the suffering, the transience, and the beauty of life" (ibid.). After which it is somewhat curious that the distinction of "real" and "not-so-real" religions is smuggled back into the argument, when the author concedes that "the 'Religion of Thinness' isn't exactly a religion," only a "secular devotion," a "cultural religion," or a "quasi-religious quest." (Or sometimes a "religious quest," which once again confirms the "fuzziness" of the categories, ibid., p. 260).

In any case, the more detailed list of features suggests a full-fledged religion (whatever that is) and not just a quasi or cultural one:

- thinness as an "ultimate concern" (in Paul Tillich's theological sense of the word)
- "myths" spread by the media about the happy lives thin people lead
- images of flawless female bodies to inspire followers (akin to "religious iconography")
- "rituals" that organize the faithful's daily life (counting calories, checking one's weight on the scale, exercising, starving, purging, etc.)
- a set of moral values and vocabulary (like "good food" and "bad food," which suggest that the person who eats them is also good or bad)
- a community of women who share the same commitment
- a promise of salvation: "We are told that by achieving the perfect body we will achieve the health, happiness, and well-being we've been looking for. And we believe that our problems will fall away with the pounds we shed."

*(Lelwica, 2009, pp. 37–38)*

That is perhaps why other authors such as Sharlene Hesse-Biber who write of the "Cult of Thinness" also fall back on terms like "religious cult," "religious asceticism," or just "religion" (Hesse-Biber, 1996, pp. 9, 45, 69), emphasizing that the moral virtues associated with thinness (restraint, moderation, and self-control) are of an explicitly religious, more precisely, Puritan origin. The distinction of the "secular" or "quasi" religion of thinness from "genuine" religions may thus be even more difficult than it first seemed.

See also: Beauty, Food, Wellness

## Sources

Hesse-Biber, S. (1996) *Am I Thin Enough Yet? The Cult of Thinness and the Commercialization of Identity*. Oxford: Oxford University Press.

Lelwica, M. M. (2009) *The Religion of Thinness: Satisfying the Spiritual Hungers behind Women's Obsession with Food and Weight.* Carlsbad: Gürze.

Lelwica M. M. (2011) 'The Religion of Thinness', *Scripta Instituti Donneriani Aboensis*, 23, pp. 257–285. https://doi.org/10.30674/scripta.67400

## Transhumanism

The very definition of transhumanism – advocacy of the use of technology to transcend the limitations of the human being – contains some elements usually associated with religions. It suggests that the present human condition is flawed, that it needs redemption, and that the future state of humanity will be so much different from everything that preceded it that it is practically unimaginable from our current point of view.

Most transhumanists will nevertheless deny that transhumanism is a religion, relying on the rhetoric used by many other schools of thought suspected of the same: namely, that it is a scientific undertaking, and even when it fulfills the expectations of traditional religions, it should be understood not as a continuation but as a replacement of the latter. Nick Bostrom's "History of Transhumanist Thought," for example, starts with the Sumerian epic of Gilgamesh and the quest for the elixir of life in the Middle Ages but describes these as "natural" ambitions to gain "physical" immortality in an age when "the boundary between mythos and science, between magic and technology, was blurry" anyway. The following narrative then reiterates the dilettantish history of enlightenment from the "otherworldliness and stale scholastic philosophy" of the Middle Ages to the birth of science and liberty in the modern era, supplemented by a "Transhumanist Declaration" that, despite all scientific blather, very much resembles a religious credo. It "envisions" a future without aging, cognitive shortcomings, and suffering; it "believes" in humanity's unrealized potential; it drafts out social, political, and moral principles (a "moral vision"); and all this in a profoundly transcendent way, extending its scope to those who do not even exist: "humans, non-human animals, and any future artificial intellects, modified life forms, or other intelligences to which technological and scientific advance may give rise (Bostrom, 2005).

There are, of course, transhumanists who know their own religious motives better. Historically, Julian Huxley described himself as a "midwife" of a "religion without revelation" that he sometimes also called "transhumanism." In a similar vein, William Sims Bainbridge spoke of creating a "Religion for a Galactic Civilization 2.0," while others variously called transhumanism a "functional analogy of religion," a "religion without dogma," or "religion 2.0" (Damour, 2019).

Regarding the fact that there are also traditional religions that embrace transhumanism (see the Mormon Transhumanist Association), it is ultimately impossible to decide whether it is a secular, a secular-religious, or a religious phenomenon. As in many other cases, the number of parallels with traditional religions is striking. In addition to the eschatological, transcendent, and universalistic elements listed so far, one might also point to more superficial similarities: the prophets and priests of transhumanism from J. B. S. Haldane, J. D. Bernal, and Julian Huxley to FM-2030, Max More, or Ray Kurzweil; its sacred scriptures which remain valid regardless of how many of their predictions have proved to be false (see the case of FM-2030, who, as his chosen name suggests, expected to live until 2030 but died 30 years earlier, or the ever-changing timelines of when AGI or immortality can be achieved); or its churches like Humanity+ which take on the task of education (preaching) and mission.

What nevertheless lends transhumanism a distinctively religious character is its ambiguous anthropo-theology. On the one hand, present human beings are conceived as mentally and physically limited, while on the other they are capable of creating the instruments of their own salvation, transforming the universe and (almost) giving birth to a new God:

> Our civilization will then expand outward, turning all the dumb matter and energy we encounter into sublimely intelligent – transcendent – matter and energy. So in a sense, we can say that the Singularity will ultimately infuse the universe with spirit. Evolution moves toward greater complexity, greater elegance, greater knowledge, greater intelligence, greater beauty, greater creativity, and greater levels of subtle attributes such as love. In every monotheistic tradition God is likewise described as all of these qualities, only without any limitation: infinite knowledge, infinite intelligence, infinite beauty, infinite creativity, infinite love, and so on. Of course, even the accelerating growth of evolution never achieves an infinite level, but as it explodes exponentially it certainly moves rapidly in that direction. So evolution moves inexorably toward this conception of God, although never quite reaching this ideal. We can regard, therefore, the freeing of our thinking from the severe limitations of its biological form to be an essentially spiritual undertaking.
>
> *(Kurzweil, 2005. p. 389)*

How we know that transhuman evolution will create not only a more intelligent but also a more beautiful and more loving universe is not clear, however. After all, "love" is not something that can be mastered the same way as mathematical skills (Peters, 2022), and as of 2023, there are also signs that artificial intelligence – with which the future human being should have a symbiotic relationship – is in many ways only a magnified copy of its creator. As John Gray's *Seven Types of Atheism* commented on Kurzweil's prophecy, it is utterly improbable that anything like the emergence of a new God will ever happen:

> Not because the technologies will not work. Humans may well use science to turn themselves into something like gods as they have imagined them to be. But no Supreme Being will appear on the scene. Instead there will be many different gods, each of them a parody of human beings that once existed.
> *(Gray, 2018, p. 70)*

## Sources

Bostrom, N. (2005) 'A History of Transhumanist Thought', *Journal of Evolution and Technology*, 14(1), pp. 1–25. Available at: https://nickbostrom.com/papers/history.pdf (Accessed: 1 December 2023).

Damour, F. (2019) 'Can Transhumanism Be Explained by or Reduced to Religion?', *Revue d'Éthique et de Théologie Morale*, 302(2), pp. 11–27. https://doi.org/10.3917/retm.303.0011

Gray, J. (2018) *Seven Types of Atheism*. New York: Farrar, Straus and Giroux.

Kurzweil, R. (2005) *The Singularity Is Near: When Humans Transcend Biology*. London: Penguin.

Peters, T. (2022) 'Will Superintelligence Lead to Spiritual Enhancement?', *Religions*, 13(5), p. 399. https://doi.org/10.3390/rel13050399

# U
# UFOs

In the case of UFOs, the main question is not whether their sightings are real or not but how one interprets them. The common "religious" thread of interpretations is that UFOnauts or aliens represent a higher intelligence, either in an inimical (satanic) form or, more frequently, in a benign (angelic, or even divine) one. Sometimes the belief in UFOs explicitly replaces religious narratives, when it suggests that the ancient myths of gods were in fact descriptions of extraterrestrial visitors whose traces are still everywhere from the Egyptian pyramids to the Nazca Lines (see Erich von Däniken's books, at least half of which mention "gods" in their titles: *Chariots of the Gods, Gods from Outer Space, Miracles of the Gods, Signs of the Gods, The Return of the Gods, The Gods Were Astronauts*, etc.). The narrative nevertheless remains strikingly similar to the myths it tries to supersede. As early as 1959, famous Swiss psychiatrist Carl Gustav Jung wrote about "flying saucers" as a "modern myth," noting that the round shape of UFOs (as described by most witnesses) was itself an ancient archetype:

> There is an old saying that "God is a circle whose center is everywhere and the circumference nowhere." God in his omniscience, omnipotence, and omnipresence is a totality symbol par excellence, something round, complete, and perfect. Epiphanies of this sort are, in the tradition, often associated with fire and light. On the antique level, therefore, the UFOs could easily be conceived as "gods."
> 
> *(Jung, [1959] 1978, p. 21)*

The very fact that UFOs are unidentified *flying* objects inevitably raises religious allusions. As American theologian Ted Peters remarked, "The symbolic quality of transcendence native to UFOs is due to their obvious association with the sky, with heaven, with the mathematical infinity of outer space. Infinity fills us with a sense of awe and holiness" (Peters, 1977, p. 271). In addition to transcendence, as Jung also mentioned, UFOnauts possess a sort of omniscience, through electronic surveillance and mental telepathy. "Augustine is famous for saying, 'God is closer to me than I am to myself, hence he knows me better than I do.' The super-savior theology seems to assign this quality of omniscience to the celestial messengers" (ibid., p. 273). Jung himself described such a testimony by a contactee, Orfeo Angelucci:

> We see the individuals of earth as each one really is, Orfeo, and not as perceived by the limited senses of man. The people of your planet have been under observation for centuries but have only recently been re-surveyed. Every point of progress in your society is registered with us. We know you as you do not know yourselves. Every man, woman and child is recorded in vital statistics by means of our crystal disks. Each of you is infinitely more important to us than to fellow Earthlings because you are not aware of the true mystery of your being.
>
> *(Jung, [1959] 1978, p. 113)*

"Mystery" is another key element that makes belief in UFOs – according to American religious scholar Diana Walsh Pasulka – truly religious. Alien artifacts are just as unexplainable as the origin of the Shroud of Turin (the burial cloth of Jesus) or the existence of angels: "One cannot put an angel under a microscope. It is this aspect, the mysterious sacred, that distinguishes religion from other organized practices like sports or fandoms. In religions, one finds the inexplicable, sacred event, or a mysterious artifact" (Pasulka, 2019, p. 242).

Other mysterious features of UFOnauts or aliens are their perfection and longevity (in some accounts true immortality, Peters, 1977, p. 275), which may also be taken as a sign of moral superiority. After all,

> The Western biblical tradition to which we are heirs understands both the shortening of life (Genesis 6:3) and its termination in death (Romans 5:12) as the result of sin. It follows that if these extraterrestrials have great longevity or even immortality, then they either never had sin or are gradually outgrowing it.
>
> *(ibid.)*

This is also what makes them suitable for the role of saviors. Jung already explained the emergence of UFO belief by the "situation of collective distress or danger" (Jung, [1959] 1978, p. 13) in an atmosphere of unpredictability and in the shadow of nuclear catastrophe during the Cold War. "The present situation is calculated as never before to arouse expectations of a redeeming, supernatural event" (ibid., p. 22). The old-fashioned word "redemption" is of course replaced by something like "ultimate transformation," perhaps on this earth but more preferably on another planet:

> The transportation to the new planet will include a transformation of the very nature of human living. Psychic tension will be relieved in a world of such harmony. The vale of tears known here on earth will be replaced with the bliss of a new heaven created by technology.
>
> *(Peters, 1977, p. 275)*

Technology and science are indeed so important for UFO believers that most of them will reject the comparison to religion exactly on this ground. This, however, as Jung already observed, is only a case of religious sublimation:

> This attitude on the part of the overwhelming majority provides the most favorable basis for a projection, that is, for a manifestation of the unconscious background. Undeterred by rationalistic criticism, it thrusts itself to the forefront in the form of a symbolic rumor, accompanied and reinforced by the appropriate visions, and thus activates an archetype that has always expressed order, deliverance, salvation, and wholeness. It is characteristic of our time that the archetype, in contrast to its previous manifestations, should now take the form of an object, a technological construction, in order to avoid the odiousness of mythological personification. Anything that looks technological goes down without difficulty with modern man. The possibility of space travel has made the unpopular idea of a metaphysical intervention much more acceptable.
>
> *(Jung, [1959] 1978, pp. 22–23)*

Or, as Ted Peters said, the UFO phenomenon is a "scientized myth":

> It is myth because it seeks to create an organized world of meaning anchored in a reality transcendent to the ordinary mundane existence of earth. It is scientized because our deeper inner religious intentions are frustrated by the lack of contemporary language capable of communicating transcendence. Because of this, today's religious concern for the infinite and eternal is compressed into the naturalistic and scientific framework of the finite and temporal.
>
> *(Peters, 1977, pp. 261–262)*

All this, however, does not rule out the existence of overtly religious – or at least "spiritual" – communities of UFO belief, of which Peters already gave examples (Understanding Inc., the Cult of The Two, or the Aetherius

Society), and there are also more recent lists in sources such as the *Encyclopedic Sourcebook of UFO Religions* (Lewis, 2003) or the *UFO Religions* (Partridge, 2003). The "secular religions" of UFOs nevertheless remain those that distance themselves from overtly religious traditions and present themselves as scientific, which at the same time means that they must also distinguish themselves from mainstream science that usually condemns their views as pseudo-scientific. The fact that the prophets and the witnesses are often "persecuted" by the establishment yet they remain firm in their faith is only another point of identity with the so-called genuine religions.

See also: Scientism, Technology

## Sources

Jung, C. G. ([1959] 1978) *Flying Saucers: A Modern Myth of Things Seen in the Skies*. Translated by Hull, R. F. C. Princeton: Princeton University Press.
Lewis, J. R. (ed.) (2003) *Encyclopedic Sourcebook of UFO Religions*. Amherst: Prometheus.
Partridge, C. (ed.) (2003) *UFO Religions*. New York: Routledge.
Pasulka, D. W. (2019) *American Cosmic: UFOs, Religion, Technology*. Oxford: Oxford University Press.
Peters, T. (1977) 'UFOs: The Religious Dimension', *Cross Currents*, 27(3), pp. 261–297. Available at: http://www.jstor.org/stable/24458392

## UN

The United Nations is a church of many interrelated faiths: for example, the faith in human rights, democracy, the rule of law, and progress. These cannot be separated, thus forming a coherent, overarching worldview and normative framework for human conduct (asserted by various documents by the UN and the Office of the High Commissioner for Human Rights, OHCHR). The very foundation of the United Nations (after two world wars in the 20th century) was, according to Mika Luoma-aho, a politico-theological act:

> The Charter is not a testament of the nearly hundred million of dead over the World Wars – I see little point in looking for meaning behind such an idea. But when we read the Charter as a secularized form of a biblical covenant things begin to lock into place, the whole make sense. This covenant is inaugurated in the shadow of the untold sorrow of the World Wars and the threat of a third looming, like the sword of Damocles, above mankind. The leaders did not want to write off the dead bodies of the World Wars as a meaningless loss of human life. What they did instead was that they wrote of it a new beginning: made it into a meaningful sacrifice that commits – no: *must* commit – the succeeding generations to one another.
>
> *(Luoma-aho, 2012, p. 104)*

The idea of meaningful sacrifice is part and parcel of belief in providential history, while the very universality of principles (as confirmed by the UN Millennium Declaration in 2000) lends them a transcendent flavor: "We reaffirm our commitment to the purposes and principles of the Charter of the United Nations, which have proved timeless and universal" (UN, 2000). Let us recall that timeless means eternal in the more powerful sense of the word: not only endless in time but standing above or beyond time itself, a truly divine attribute, while universal could just as well be translated into Greek as "Catholic." It is even more curious how anything can "prove" to be so. Timelessness and universality cannot be proven by any number of facts in any time span.

However, since those principles are still often violated by some of the UN's own member states, the community remains a thoroughly eschatological one whose real essence will only become manifest in an unspecified future state. (The City of God, as St. Augustine might say, will be mixed with the Earthly City until the Judgment Day.) Until then, we have the ritual confirmations of principles (anniversaries, summits, and declarations) or symbols like the map of the world surrounded by olive branches (another image of religious origin) which all refer to something that is yet to come, if ever: in this case, the earthly paradise of world peace.

See also: Democracy, Human Rights, Progress

## Sources

Luoma-aho, M. (2012) *God and International Relations: Christian Theology and World Politics*. New York: Continuum.

OHCHR 'Administration of Justice and Law Enforcement'. Available at: https://www.ohchr.org/en/topic/administration-justice-and-law-enforcement (Accessed: 1 January 2023).

OHCHR 'OHCHR and Democracy'. Available at: https://www.ohchr.org/en/democracy (Accessed: 1 December 2023).

UN 'Global Issues: Democracy'. Available at: https://www.un.org/en/global-issues/democracy (Accessed: 1 December 2023).

UN (2000) 'United Nations Millennium Declaration'. Available at: https://www.ohchr.org/en/instruments-mechanisms/instruments/united-nations-millennium-declaration (Accessed: 1 December 2023).

## Übermensch

See Nietzscheism.

# V
# VEGANISM

The main reason why veganism is sometimes labeled a "secular" or "new" religion is its asceticism, which many outsiders associate – rightly or wrongly, probably both – with a crusading zeal and intolerance. Christian authors are especially sensitive to this attitude. As Anglican priest Angela Tilby writes in an article called "The Secular Religion of Veganism," it is not the vegan principle of non-violence against animals that she finds revolting but the "moral puritanism" with which vegans preach that "we can become pure in body and mind by an exercise of will" and try to impose this rule on others. Moreover, such methods are also incompatible with the peacefulness of the original message: "Some vegans, while campaigning against animal cruelty, have resorted to threats against people in the food industry which I have found disturbing, even hypocritical." (The actual case Tilby refers to is the resignation of the editor of Waitrose's *Food* magazine after complaints about his anti-vegan remarks in a private message, Tilby, 2018).

It may sound surprising that a religious author names intolerance and hypocrisy as the defining elements of religion, but at a closer look, there is also a deeper, theological message, which creates a tension between the biblical notion of the human being as the crown of creation and veganism's insistence on the essential similarity of human and non-human animals. Although ethical veganism – the moral opposition to all forms of animal exploitation, including food, clothing, hobbies, etc. – does not necessarily imply that all animals should have the same moral and legal status, only that the amount of suffering should be kept at the lowest possible level, this latter principle is indeed treated as an absolute.

When vegans answer to their critics (such as Jordan Peterson, who repeatedly called veganism a secular religion) that veganism is not religion but

DOI: 10.4324/9781003471257-22

science ("Science, not faith, is what drives us vegans to commit to an ethical lifestyle," Hartley, Favata, and Anderson, 2018), they tend to forget that ethics, which is about what we should do, can never be a part of science, which is about how things are. A scientific proposition can at most be an element of a hypothetical imperative: *if* you want A, then do B. Moreover, vegans themselves acknowledge that their categorical imperative is an overarching one, encompassing the whole person: "Ethical veganism is a moral viewpoint that affects every aspect of a person's life" (Farrell, 2022).

A 2020 court ruling in the UK in fact confirmed that ethical veganism was a "protected class akin to religion under law designed to shield people from discrimination in the workplace and beyond." Although it did not mean that veganism was a "religion," only that it belonged to the broad category of "philosophical and religious beliefs," the very name of the category shows how the law itself is unable to properly distinguish between the two. As the UK Equality Act says, a belief should be

> genuinely held; be a belief and not an opinion or viewpoint based on the present state of information available; be a belief as to a weighty and substantial aspect of human life and behavior; attain a certain level of cogency, seriousness, cohesion and importance.
>
> *(Heil, 2020)*

If these criteria are met, then the separation of secular and religious beliefs is either impossible or without significance.

Ethical vegans may thus reject the label (which many of them do because of the same reason they are called religious: the contemporary disgust with the word "religion," especially if it is an "organized" one), but it does not alter the fact that they have an ultimate principle, a complete worldview with its corresponding moral commandments and a firm belief in the cause. An even more religion-like element of this belief is the idea of sin (causing unnecessary suffering to animals) and redemption (through asceticism, which is, after all, the heart of veganism).

All these are pedantically listed in the many catechisms issued for simple believers (Hartley, Favata, and Anderson, 2018), which contain further interesting advice and consolations that are amazingly familiar from religious guidebooks (e.g., how to deal with a hostile, unenlightened outside world or how to remind ourselves that we belong to the community of "early awakened").

See also: Animal Rights, Ecology, Science, Vegetarianism

### Sources

Farrell, C. (2022) 'What Is Ethical Veganism?', *Paris Smith*, 31 January. Available at: https://parissmith.co.uk/blog/what-is-ethical-veganism/ (Accessed: 1 December 2023).

Hartley, S., Favata, M., and Anderson, E. (2018) 'FAQs about Veganism', *The Reasoned Vegan*. Available at: https://thereasonedvegan.com/faqs-about-veganism/ (Accessed: 1 December 2023).

Heil, E. (2020) '"Ethical Veganism" Is a Protected Class Akin to Religion in the UK after a Landmark Ruling', *The Washington Post*, 3 January. Available at: https://www.washingtonpost.com/news/voraciously/wp/2020/01/03/ethical-veganism-is-a-protected-class-akin-to-religion-in-the-u-k-after-a-landmark-ruling/ (Accessed: 1 December 2023).

Tilby, A. (2018) 'The Secular Religion of Veganism', *Church Times*, 9 November. Available at: https://www.churchtimes.co.uk/articles/2018/9-november/comment/columnists/angela-tilby-the-secular-religion-of-veganism (Accessed: 1 December 2023).

## Vegetarianism

While vegetarianism has been practiced by many traditional religions, and – according to some accounts – it has also become a "secular religion" of the West by the 18th century (Rothstein, 2007), it was between the two world wars that vegetarianism was most often labeled a "hidden" or "surrogate" religion.

In Carl Christian Bry's *Verkappte Religionen*, it is placed among an amazing number of other examples: abstinence, number mysticism, astrology, Zionism, antisemitism, yoga, belief in Atlantis, the Esperanto movement, sexual reform, rhythmic gymnastics, the cult of the Übermensch, Faust-exegesis, communism, psychoanalysis, the world peace movement, anti-alcoholism, theosophy, expressionism, admiration of the genius, fakir magic, the hatred of freemasons and Jesuits, and occultism, "and these are just a few movements that are called hidden religions" (Bry, 1925, p. 14).

The German author, of course, refers to the apocalyptic intellectual atmosphere of the interwar period, when a variety of strange ideas circulated all over Europe. In this atmosphere vegetarianism also often looked like a mystical fashion on par with magic and occultism. In turn, by the word "hidden" Bry meant something that was both "related and opposed to" traditional religion, a not "other-worldly" but "behind-worldly" belief system:

> Hidden religion, in contrast, says: behind your ordinary life and behind the ordinary world lies something so far hidden, something that has been suspected for a long time but was never given to us, a possibility that has never been realized before, but which we can and now want to get, and are in the process of getting it.
>
> *(ibid., 16)*

Within this scheme, vegetarianism is presented just as an intolerant and dualistic faith as any other. "For example, vegetarianism claims that plant food creates flowering health just as meat eating undermines health," which implies that it must hate its enemies at least as much as it cherishes its own ideas (or more). With a characteristic slippery-slope argument, Bry adds that it might also become "tyrannical" if it evolves into a political movement:

> What if one day the government discovers that eating meat undermines health and it is a form of the crudest cannibalism, like the vegetarians claim? What if the government discovers that subjects, instead of spending their money on fashion and finery, should rather spend it for the common good in the form of higher taxes? What if the ban on stimulant alcohol is followed by the ban on stimulant tobacco? Where is the limit of tyranny?
> *(ibid., p. 127)*

Less cartoonish but just as broad-brush pictures of vegetarianism also took it for granted that vegetarianism was just one of the second- or third-grade surrogates of genuine religions. As Hungarian Catholic theologian Antal Schütz said:

> Further down the religious ladder are those . . . who seek the cure for all problems and the purpose of their lives in a cultural program or a cultural phenomenon, e.g. the transformation of the economic order (socialists), the solution of the Jewish question, vegetarianism, spiritualism, etc. (*surrogate religions*).
> *(Schütz, 1937, p. 16)*

That extreme political ideologies like Nazism were so often associated with vegetarianism may be unfair but not unexplainable. As Tristram Stuart's *The Bloodless Revolution*, the fullest history of vegetarianism in the modern age acknowledges, it was not Hitler's individual hobby to be a vegetarian but a complete worldview shared by many other Nazi leaders (like Rudolf Hess) that permeated various parts of state life, leading – among others – to the strictest animal protection laws in Germany introduced by Hermann Göring and supported by Heinrich Himmler (Stuart, 2008, pp. 437–444). This is not to mean that vegetarianism was a Nazi "political religion,"

> But the disturbing fact remains that sentimental relations to animals are by no means incompatible with cruelty toward humans; indeed, they are frequently seen to coincide in misanthropic individuals who fail to incorporate satisfactorily into human society and turn to animals for more compliant social interactions. Recent scholars have pointed out that the Nazis' animal protection laws reveal a distinctly xenophobic emphasis, for example in banning kosher and halal methods of slaughter.
> *(ibid., p. 442)*

Interestingly, a similar charge was brought up against modern Western vegetarianism by Australian ecofeminist Val Plumwood, who complained about the "crusading versions" of rights-based vegetarianism which are aggressively ethnocentric and reject indigenous customs, viewing meat eating as a new "original sin" (Plumwood, 2000, p. 286). More recent descriptions also routinely emphasize the alleged aggressivity and intolerance of the vegetarian "religion" as if those were the core features of religion in general. As a modern blogger states:

> I don't mind vegetarians unless they start getting sanctimonious about it. . . . It is only when they become a religion substitute that they become problematic, but unfortunately that happens far too often. When something is internalised like a religious faith, it becomes almost immune to outside challenge, a faith unaffected by exposure to hard reality. But like religious faith, it remains a powerful driver of behaviour, and if the person involved is in power, potentially a powerful driver of policy. It can drive similar oppression of those with other world views, in much the same way as the Spanish Inquisition, but with a somewhat updated means of punishing the heretics. In short, the religion substitutes show many of the same problems we used to associate with the extremes of religion.
>
> *(Timeguide, 2013)*

If we understand well, the most religious-like feature of vegetarianism is that people have faith in it, which is – once again – a seedbed of intolerance, even if, as the author with some resignation has to admit, in an "updated" (presumably not *as* violently intolerant) form as in the case of religious persecutions. When religion becomes synonymous with the Inquisition, however, we might rightly suspect that the author does not have a very sophisticated idea of religious history, and in lack of concrete examples of the vegetarian inquisition, it might also be raised whether he knows vegetarianism any better.

See also: Animal Rights, Science, Veganism

## Sources

Bry, C. C. (1925) *Verkappte Religionen*. Gotha: Leopold Klotz.

Plumwood, V. (2000) 'Integrating Ethical Frameworks for Animals, Humans, and Nature: A Critical Feminist Eco-Socialist Analysis', *Ethics and the Environment*, 5(2), pp. 285–322. Available at: http://www.jstor.org/stable/40338997

Rothstein, E. (2007) 'Review: The Bloodless Revolution', *The New York Times*, 23 February. Available at: https://www.nytimes.com/2007/02/23/arts/23iht-idbriefs24A.4700379.html (Accessed: 1 December 2023).

Schütz, A. (1937) *Dogmatika: a katholikus hitigazságok rendszere*. Budapest: Szent István Társulat.

Stuart, T. (2008) *The Bloodless Revolution: A Cultural History of Vegetarianism from 1600 to Modern Times*. New Yok: W. W. Norton and Company.

Timeguide (2013) 'Is Secular Substitution of Religion a Threat to Western Civilization?', 22 May. Available at: https://timeguide.wordpress.com/tag/secular-religion/ (Accessed: 1 December 2023).

# W

## WAR

The concept of "holy war" has always existed in different traditions, but the worship of war in the so-called secular societies is a basically modern phenomenon. As Emilio Gentile remarks in his *The Sacralization of Politics in Fascist Italy*, the First World War was seen by many as a redemption ("the myth of war-as-regeneration"), a tragic "hierophany": "Everyone acts as though seized by a holy terror. On the battlefield, he feels close to God," as the Italian writer Scipio Slataper noted in his diary in 1915, a few weeks before his death (Gentile, 1996, p. 16). Fascists also used phrases like the "Holy Eucharist of war" that transformed a whole generation "molded of sacrificial metal" (ibid., p. 23). In books and movies, war does have this transcendent quality:

> To interpret war as religion, it must be imbued with mystical qualities and heroic – if not superhuman – characters. Indeed, Soviet war films of the 1940s through 1960s did just this. Self-sacrifice and fevered patriotism ennobled its participants and legitimized the Soviet experiment.
> *(Steve Huggins, cited by Donaldson, 2022)*

The cult of war, however, is not merely part of the larger secular religions of fascism, nationalism, patriotism, or communism. Its own distinctive – and most divine – features, as Joseph de Maistre already observed in the 19th century, are its omnipresence, its indeterminacy and unpredictability, and its irreducibility to a science or a doctrine (Rosenberg, 2019, p. 35). As he wrote in the *St Petersburg Dialogues:*

> War is therefore divine in itself, since it is a law of the world. War is divine through its consequences of a supernatural nature . . . War is divine in the

DOI: 10.4324/9781003471257-23

mysterious glory that surrounds it, and in the no less inexplicable attraction that draws us to it. War is divine in the protection granted to its great leaders, even the most venturesome, who are rarely struck down in battle, and then only when their reputation can no longer be increased and when their mission has been fulfilled. War is divine by the way in which it breaks out. I do not want to excuse anyone too easily, but how many of those regarded as the immediate authors of war are themselves carried along by circumstances! At the precise moment caused by men and prescribed by justice, God himself comes forward to avenge the iniquity committed against him by the inhabitants of the world. War is divine in its results, which absolutely escape the speculations of human reason, since they can be totally different for two different nations, even though the war appears to have affected them both equally. . . . War is divine by the indefinable force that determines success in it.

*(Maistre, [1821] 1993, pp. 218–219)*

Maistre was, of course, a Catholic believer himself, so he did not speak of war as a "deity," only as a manifestation of the divine. The attributes of war nevertheless remained transcendent, which left open the possibility of making war an object of independent worship. Today, when the mysticism, the rituals, and the symbols of war (from uniforms to flags) are still everywhere but reverence to them has obviously declined, it becomes even more ambiguous whether war might be an act of God, a deity itself, or the center of a secular religion. Ironical manifestations like the cult of Saint Javelin that developed during the war in Ukraine clearly show this ambiguity. The origin of Saint Javelin's picture goes back to Chris Shaw's "Kalashnikov Madonna" that depicted the Virgin Mary with an AK-47 assault rifle, which was later changed to an FGM-148 Javelin anti-tank weapon (St. Javelin, 2023). It became an internet meme after the Russian invasion of Ukraine in 2022, boosting morale and used to merchandise products. It is at the same time difficult to decide whether it has anything to do with secular or political religions or should be viewed simply as a parody of Christian iconography. It may in fact be viewed as both, a thoroughly postmodern phenomenon that raises grotesque – but ultimately positive – connotations, showing the ongoing force of religious imagery in an allegedly secular age.

See also: Nationalism, Patriotism, Revolution

## Sources

Donaldson, M. (2022) 'Come and See', *8Sided Blog*, 27 February. Available at: https://8sided.blog/come-and-see/ (Accessed: 1 December 2023).

Gentile, E. (1996) *The Sacralization of Politics in Fascist Italy*. Translated by Botsford, K. Cambridge: Harvard University Press.

Maistre, J. ([1821] 1993) *St Petersburg Dialogues or Conversations on the Temporal Government of Providence*. Translated by Lebrun, R. A. Montreal: McGill-Queen's University Press.

Rosenberg, D. (2019) 'Joseph de Maistre on War and Peace: Ritual and Realism', *The Philosophical Journal of Conflict and Violence*, 3(2), pp. 35–51. https://doi.org/10.22618/TP.PJCV.20204.1.201003

St. Javelin (2023) 'Know Your Meme'. Available at: https://knowyourmeme.com/memes/st-javelin-saint-javelin (Accessed: 1 December 2023).

## Warmism

"Warmism" is a derogatory term for the "ideology" of climate change. It is sometimes called a secular religion (or something similar), in a characteristically vague language:

> [A]s people move away from traditional religion, the powerful inner drive remains to feel "holy," that you are a good person, doing the right thing, on some moral high ground. It is a powerful force built into human nature, similar to the desire to feel social approval and status. When it is no longer satisfied by holding to religious rules, it may crystallise around other behaviours, that can mostly be summarised by "isms." Vegetarianism and pacifism were the oldest ones to be conspicuous, often accompanied by New Ageism, followed soon by anti-capitalism, then environmentalism, now evolved into the even more religious warmism.
> *(Timeguide, 2013)*

Books that discuss "warmism" as a totalitarian ideology also use a plethora of religious terms: the "myth" of climate change, its "catechism" written for "proselytes" and "believers," the guardians of its "temple," its "prophets," and their "apocalyptic" predictions. The latter literally go back to the Book of Genesis in the Bible: "one can find in the Flood the key ingredients of warmism: the mischiefs of mankind, climatic catastrophe, the point of no return, and the elimination of life on earth" (Prud'homme, 2015).

Nevertheless, since "warmism" ultimately proves to be an ideology (and not even a great ideology but a "caricature" thereof), the religious terminology once again seems to be nothing more than a rhetorical tool to make fun of someone's enemy. For more sophisticated discussions of the religious traits of climate activism and environmentalism, see the entry on ecology in the present volume.

See also: Ecology

## Sources

Prud'homme, R. (2015) *Warmism as an Ideology: Soft Science, Hard Doctrine*. Paris: Toucan.

Timeguide (2013) 'Is Secular Substitution of Religion a Threat to Western Civilization?', 22 May. Available at: https://timeguide.wordpress.com/tag/secular-religion/ (Accessed: 1 December 2023)

## Wellness

As Tara Isabella Burton writes in her book on "remixed" or "intuitional" religions, it would be a mistake to think that wellness culture is only about corporeal perfection. It is also about "the body as the locus of personal spiritual growth" (Burton, 2020, p. 157). Or, as Michelle Lelwica says in her book about religion and the "culture of physical improvement," in commercial culture's view, bodies are not just "objects we can work on and work out, monitor and manipulate, defy, compel, transfigure, and fix" but "advertisements for who we are as a person. Paradoxically, the improvable body is both *subject to* the will of the self and a *visible manifestation* of that self" (Lelwica, 2017, p. 34).

Wellness – in contrast to "fitness" which emphasizes physical improvement – thus refers to a "holistic approach to healthy living, characterized by physical, mental, and social well-being," as Clementine Prendergast claims in her "How Wellness Became a Secular New Age Religion" (Prendergast, 2018). The paradox – which in turn links wellness culture to more traditional religious phenomena like monasticism – is that it offers spiritual growth through conscious self-limitation and self-discipline, a sort of "ethereal asceticism" (Burton, 2020, p. 92). This asceticism means not only workout but also diets, strict rules of eating and drinking, and a kind of "self-mortification" (Prendergast, 2018).

All this, as Michelle Lelwica notes, presupposes a metaphysical view of the "soul," albeit not in the medieval Christian sense of the word which always supposed an intimate connection between the soul and the body, but in the early modern, Cartesian sense that views the soul as a "sovereign" over the body (Lelwica, 2017, p. 33). The message "your soul can control your body" is also brought home by wellness companies like SoulCycle that are "selling a double ideal of purification: one simultaneously characterized by material improvement (you'll look like Michelle Obama or Lady Gaga, two notable SoulCycle alums) and by spiritual transcendence" (Burton, 2020, p. 91). The iconography of idols is remarkably similar (albeit not identical) to that of medieval saints:

> Despite their obvious differences, the educational and inspirational *functions* of these images are similar. Just as historical Christians were inspired by saintly role models (i.e. holy women and men depicted in stained glass windows, sculptures, icons, and paintings), so people today look to the paragons of commercial culture (i.e. rock stars, athletes, models, and

movie stars on TV and in films, advertisements, the internet, and magazines) to guide their self-definition.

*(Lelwica, 2017, p. 34)*

As Lelwica adds, there is a whole "pantheon of iconic figures and dramas" that capture our imaginations perhaps more effectively than Christian saints and their life stories ever did, for the latter were to be followed by a conscious decision, while the modern examples of perfection rather act on our subconscious, whether we are aware of it or not. The importance of rituals is also obvious, and here the religious analogy is truly helpful because it explains why rituals are not mere "externalities":

> Just as a culture's visual images of somatic perfection remind us of its body norms, so its recommended rituals enable us to internalize these norms, absorbing, assimilating, incorporating them into our flesh to the point where they become second nature, beyond the level of conscious awareness . . . Aspects of both medieval and modern ritual activity – prescribed disciplined conduct with a moral aim, and symbolic behavior with a practical end – can be seen in the contemporary culture of physical improvement: bodies are regulated, trained, and corrected according to a "pre-defined model of excellence" (the ideal body), with the twofold goal of cultivating the virtue of self-mastery and pursuing/communicating a privileged status within society.
>
> *(ibid., pp. 37–38)*

Rituals are also essential in creating communities of the faithful. The gym is not just a place to exercise but something like a monastery, a space where like-minded people get together, empowering each other. Not just as a community of equals, however, but under the guidance of charismatic, if not divine, spiritual leaders, "The high priests of wellness watch over us all the time," as Prendergast says, "As you enter the central London studio 'Barry wants you' is written above the door; hailing in totalitarian spirit with an omnipotent force" (Prendergast, 2018).

Sacred scriptures and official manifestos (the "Soul Etiquette" or "Your Soul Matters," Burton, 2020, p. 92) are also part of the religion of wellness, and these are already becoming a political (or biopolitical) message in the Foucauldian sense:

> Whereas in premodern Western societies, social order was preserved through the threat of public torture or execution (e.g. crucifixion, hanging, beheading, burning), today such order is maintained through individual self-surveillance: we police our bodies and strive to comply with prevailing medical, aesthetic, and moral standards in exchange for others' approval.

By ritually monitoring, regulating, and normalizing our flesh according to the normative ideal, we not only avoid public derision; we help sustain the dominant culture's social/symbolic hierarchy of bodies.

(Lelwica, 2017, p. 40)

This hierarchy also means – inevitably – that people with physical disabilities, too much belly fat or who are simply old, will look "sinful." Like in the Christian drama, the human being is supposed to have been born good, it was only "by big Pharma, by processed food, by civilization itself" that we fell short of our best of life. "Our sins, if they exist at all, lie in insufficient self-attention or self-care . . . We have to listen to ourselves, to behave authentically, in tune with what our intuition dictates. Others, after all, are potential enemies" (Burton, 2020, p. 94).

All this, of course, will not convince everyone (and certainly not anyone in the business) that wellness, beauty, or physical enhancement is a "religion" and not a perfectly rational, let alone scientific, this-worldly enterprise.

I seriously doubt that most readers see these images and the prescriptions surrounding them as in any way related to the symbols and rituals of traditional religion. But this may be because they assume an overly narrow and disembodied view of "religion." In Western societies today, religion is often seen as operating in a separate sphere – apart from "secular" society. Moreover, religion is often assumed to be primarily a matter of *belief* (narrowly defined as cognitive agreement with certain doctrines or faith statements), while flesh-and-blood experiences are thought to be either antithetical or peripheral to "spiritual" concerns. But both the history of Christianity and the contemporary pursuit of physical improvement suggest that through ritual activities, bodies participate in the construction of metaphysical meanings, and that the line dividing sacred/secular truths is far from clear.

(Lelwica, 2017, p. 39)

See also: Capitalism, Consumerism, Entertainment, Medicine, Psychology, Sex, Thinness

## Sources

Burton, T. I. (2020) *Strange Rites: New Religions for a Godless World*. New York: Public Affairs.
Lelwica, M. (2017) *Shameful Bodies: Religion and the Culture of Physical Improvement*. London: Bloomsbury.
Prendergast, C. (2018) 'How Wellness Became a Secular New Age Religion', *Dazed*, 13 December. Available at: https://www.dazeddigital.com/beauty/article/42563/1/wellness-secular-new-age-religion (Accessed: 1 December 2023).

## Wokeness

In the beginning, "woke" was a positive word, applied mostly to persons and movements fighting racial prejudice and discrimination. From the mid-2010s, its meaning started to include other forms of social justice politics (LGBTQ rights, climate activism, etc.) and began to become a pejorative, first in the vocabulary of its conservative opponents, then to a large extent in general discourse as well.

It is remarkable how becoming a pejorative was also connected to calling it a new or quasi-religion by its critics (Romano, 2020). As early as 2020, the year when George Floyd's murder put the word in the forefront, James Lindsay wrote about a "Woke Religion," using Émile Durkheim's functionalist definition (cited in so many other entries in the present volume): "religions are . . . phenomena that organize a community around a shared sense of morality and, relatedly, purpose in life" that also "have something inseparable to do with a recognition of the *sacred* and its being set apart from the profane" (Lindsay, 2020).

In this case, it is the "cosmic battle for liberation" which makes the individual part of the community and gives purpose and meaning to their life. The sacred may not be a transcendent "god" but still something of infinite moral value which cannot be questioned in any circumstance, and loyalty to which may be represented in many different forms:

> Maybe it is pronouncing declarations of faith and sinfulness; maybe it is believing all victims of certain kinds of systemic oppression about their interpretations of their own experiences in life, taking a picture of your middle finger pointed toward Trump Tower and sharing it on social media, knowing everyone's pronouns and announcing yours, avoiding problematic words, or finding ways to disrupt "white comfort," even as a spiritual act of making oneself, if white, "uncomfortable." These displays of virtue, at least when organized, define the liturgical forms of a practice of faith.
> *(ibid.)*

Lindsay nevertheless confirms that wokeness is a "postmodern faith," in which God is replaced by other, more mysterious deities ("systems of social power") and formalized liturgical modes with "something decentralized, chaotic, and even ironic." It does not change the fact that in wokeness there is an element of transcendent belief in something invisible that only becomes accessible by a spiritual conversion. As James M. Patterson puts it in his "Wokeness and the New Religious Establishment," using transgender identity as an example:

> Transgender identity – in which one's inward gender identity is said to differ from one's bodily sex – offers a useful snapshot of woke metaphysics.

> Wokeness is grounded in a Gnostic understanding of the world, which distinguishes between appearances accessible to everyone and the reality perceptible only to a certain few. To join the community of those who recognize this ultimate reality, one must undergo a kind of "awakening" – or, in identity-politics parlance, "become woke."
>
> *(Patterson, 2021)*

In 2021, the book-length study of linguist John McWhorter (who previously wrote on "anti-racism" and "electism" in a similar way) called "woke racism" a "new religion," thereby returning to the more traditional use of the word in racial justice movements. The religious features of his description were less novel: he used such, by now well-known clichés as "superstition" (belief in factually unverifiable claims); "clergy" (a select elite with a monopoly on teaching); "original sin" (something beyond personal faults that accompanies a person from birth); "evangelical" mentality (a zeal to convert those who are yet lost in the darkness of sin); "apocalyptic" thinking (waiting for a redemptive moment that will dispel the darkness of the present); or a ban on the "heretic" (silencing dissent instead of rational discussion). McWhorter therefore does not speak of a "secular" or "quasi" religion but a real one:

> I do not mean that these people's ideology is "like" a religion. I seek no rhetorical snap in the comparison. I mean that it actually is a religion. An anthropologist would see no difference in type between Pentecostalism and this new form of antiracism. Language is always imprecise, and thus we have traditionally restricted the word religion to certain ideologies founded in creation myths, guided by ancient texts, and requiring that one subscribe to certain beliefs beyond the reach of empirical experience. This, however, is an accident, just as it is that we call tomatoes vegetables rather than fruits. If we rolled the tape again, the word religion could easily apply as well to more recently emerged ways of thinking within which there is no explicit requirement to subscribe to unempirical beliefs, even if the school of thought does reveal itself to entail such beliefs upon analysis.
>
> *(McWhorter, 2021, p. 23)*

The reference to Pentecostalism betrays that McWhorter's woke religion is rather a parody of a certain type of American religiosity than an actual case of religion as such. Also in 2021, Michael Shellenberger and Peter Boghossian came up with a detailed picture of what they considered to be the different forms of woke religion. Returning to the broad sense of wokeness (or even further broadening its scope) they put issues such as "racism, climate change, trans, crime, mental illness, drugs, homelessness" on the left margin, and religious concepts such as "original sin, guilty devils, myths, sacred victims, the elect, supernatural beliefs, taboo speech, purifying rituals, purifying speech" on the top, suggesting that all of the former have all characteristics of the latter (Shellenberger and Boghossian, 2021).

In 2022, two books were published with almost the same title: Andrew Doyle's *The New Puritans* and Noah Rothman's *The Rise of the New Puritans*, this time comparing social justice movements or wokeness not to religion in general but to a fanatically moralizing subtype thereof. The bases of comparison served with little novelty: in Doyle, these were witch-hunting, an obligatory creed, an apocalyptic struggle, sectarianism, language policing, sacred scriptures, infallible revelations, unquestionable dogmas, persecution of heretics, and, ultimately, a withdrawal from rational discourse into a transcendental world of fantasies (Doyle, 2022). Rothman also emphasized the irrational and intolerant features of wokeness ("an unflappable faith in their own righteousness," a new class of activists saying, "you're not eating right," "you're not consuming the right media," and "you're not thinking the things you should"), ultimately defining it as "pseudo-religious" (Rothman, 2022, pp. x–xi).

It is not surprising that new atheists like Richard Dawkins also criticize wokeness as an example of religious intolerance and irrationality, although he himself draws an analogy with Catholicism only (comparing the concept of whiteness and transgender identity to the dogmas of original sin and transubstantiation) in a YouTube video (Dawkins, 2023). It is more surprising when someone does something similar in a Catholic newspaper, as Toby Young did, writing about "wokeism":

> It would now be more accurate to describe it as a religion. That's hardly an original observation, but it's worth reiterating. The beliefs outlined above are not based on science or reason, but on dogma. It has its own religious symbols – the rainbow flag – as well as a liturgy, including Black History Month and Transgender Day of Remembrance. It even has its own rites – taking the knee, "doing the work," engaging in public bouts of racial self-flagellation. And it acquired its first martyr in George Floyd.
> *(Young, 2023)*

Others naturally realized that comparing wokeness to Christianity was in fact an "insult to the Church," regarding the substantive differences in their conceptions of sacrifice, sin, or salvation (Rowley, 2023), while others took notice of the weaknesses of the formal analogy. As Patrick J. Casey remarked,

> Since the dividing line between anti-intellectual and dogmatic versus not doesn't map onto whether the group is a religion or not, calling such groups a religion obscures rather than reveals the real issue. Anti-intellectualism and dogmatism are not distinctively *religious* problems; they are *human*

problems. . . . As for religion, it has been too readily available as a scapegoat for things that go wrong in society. . . . We need to stop calling whatever we don't like a "religion."

*(Casey, 2023)*

As we have seen, most descriptions of the religion of wokeness or social justice culture do not rely on the two criteria of anti-intellectualism and dogmatism only. But the functionalist definition of religion that appears in them (and many other examples in this book) again and again is no less problematic:

With a functionalist definition of religion, virtually anything that binds people together into a community can be properly considered a religion. This makes the concept of religion so amorphous that it becomes essentially useless as an analytic category.

*(ibid.)*

Which may very well be the case, and that is what this whole book was all about.

See also: Anti-Racism, Electism, Postmodernism.

## Sources

Casey, P. J. (2021) 'Stop Calling "Wokeness" a Religion: Introducing the Taxonomy of Woke Religion', *Heterodox Academy*, 20 October. Available at: https://heterodoxacademy.org/blog/stop-calling-wokeness-a-religion/ (Accessed: 1 December 2023).

Dawkins, R. (2023) 'Does Woke Count as a Religion?', *YouTube*, 10 October. Available at: https://youtu.be/cubkdBuvJAQ (Accessed: 1 December 2023).

Doyle, A. (2022) *New Puritans – How the Religion of Social Justice Captured the Western World*. London: Constable.

Lindsay, J. (2020) 'A First-Amendment Case for Freedom from the Woke Religion', *New Discourses*, 9 September. Available at: https://newdiscourses.com/2020/09/first-amendment-case-freedom-from-woke-religion/#SupremeB (Accessed: 1 December 2023).

McWhorter, J. (2021) *Woke Racism: How a New Religion Has Betrayed Black America*. New York: Portfolio/Penguin.

Patterson, J. M. (2021) 'Wokeness and the New Religious Establishment', *National Affairs*, Summer. Available at: https://www.nationalaffairs.com/publications/detail/wokeness-and-the-new-religious-establishment (Accessed: 1 December 2023).

Romano, A. (2020) 'A History of "Wokeness." Stay Woke: How a Black Activist Watchword Got Co-opted in the Culture War', *Vox*, 9 October. Available at: https://www.vox.com/culture/21437879/stay-woke-wokeness-history-origin-evolution-controversy (Accessed: 1 December 2023).

Rothman, N. (2022) *The Rise of the New Puritans: Fighting Back Against Progressives' War on Fun*. New York: Broadside Books.

Rowley, M. (2023) 'Comparing Wokeness to Christianity Is an Insult to the Church', *Quillette*, 20 February. Available at: https://quillette.com/blog/2023/02/20/com

paring-wokeness-to-christianity-is-an-insult-to-the-church/ (Accessed: 1 December 2023).

Shellenberger, M., and Boghossian, P. (2021) 'Woke Religion: A Taxonomy', *Substack*, 11 November. Available at: https://boghossian.substack.com/p/woke-religion-a-taxonomy (Accessed: 1 December 2023).

Young, T. (2023) 'Woke: The New Religion?', *Catholic Herald*, 25 May. Available at: https://catholicherald.co.uk/woke-the-new-religion/ (Accessed: 1 December 2023).

Printed in the United States
by Baker & Taylor Publisher Services